Without MERCY

Obsession and Murder Under the Influence

GARY PROVOST

POCKET BOOKS
New York London Toronto Sydney Tokyo Singapore

POCKET BOOKS, a division of Simon & Schuster
1230 Avenue of the Americas, New York, NY 10020

ISBN: 0-671-66997-4

First Pocket Books paperback printing December 1990

10 9 8 7 6 5 4 3 2 1

Cover photo by Tim Chapman / *The Miami Herald*

Printed in the U.S.A.

For early-morning cuddles and late suppers, for reading pages and writing letters, for staying at home and coming along, for taking notes, for magic spells, for coffee in bed, and for long, perfectly arced shots that usually go in, this book is lovingly dedicated to my honey, Gail.

Acknowledgments

This book could not exist if I did not have the cooperation of a number of people who took the time to remember moments from their own lives and answer my questions.

For generously giving me their time in interviews I want to thank Vivian Andre, Kenny Baldwin, James Allen Bryant, James Campbell, Dee Casteel, Bob Davis, Robert Edward, Steve Fitzgerald, George Freitas, Hal Henry, Sally Hicks, Richard Higgins, Donna Hobson, Ona Hostutler, Cynthia Kaiser, Art Koch, Sandra Lochard, Calie Maitland, Susan Mayo, Frank Natale, Jay Novick, Jenny O'Neil, John Parmenter, Bill Rhodes, Joanne Rivera, Pat Swanson, Wayne Tidwell, Dr. Jethro Toomer, Sally Weintraub, Reid Welch, Todd White, and Warren Woods.

Also, there are several other people who spoke to me but have asked me not to mention their names. My thanks to them.

I want to thank Rob MacGregor, for background material on Santeria; Philip Needleman for the use of his house during part of the research; Allan Provost, for bringing the story to my attention; Gail Provost, for reading and commenting on the manuscript in progress; Paula Tulley of the Florida Department of Corrections for arranging my prison visits; Marta Villacorta, Superintendent of the Broward County Correctional Institution, for allowing me as much visiting time as I needed; and Lee Weissenborn for providing me with a copy of the trial transcript.

I also want to thank various staff members of the Boston Public Library, the Miami Public Library, and the records room at the Dade County Courthouse.

Thanks, too, to my agent, Russ Galen, for taking the book on in midstream and pulling it safely to the other side.

And a special thanks to my editor at Pocket Books, Claire Zion, for having faith in the book to begin with and for her wise and valuable editing when it was almost done.

Without MERCY

Preface

On the day I arrived in Miami to look into the Venecia-Fischer murders, there was a heartbreaking story in the *Miami Herald*. A young German woman had been murdered while visiting the city. Kersten Kischniok and her boyfriend, Dieter Riechmann, had gone to Bayside where they listened to Brazilian music and drank cocktails. It was dark when they left, and as they drove through the shadowy streets of Miami, Riechmann made a wrong turn and became lost. When he saw a man standing near some parked cars, he asked for directions.

"I asked, 'Where is Biscayne Boulevard?' " he later told the *Herald*'s reporter. "I know if I stay on Biscayne Boulevard, I find my home. He say he wants to give help."

Instead, the man leaned close to the passenger side of the car, and Riechmann saw that he had something in his hand. The man shot Miss Kischniok twice in the head. Riechmann hit the accelerator on his rented Ford Thunderbird and sped desperately through the dark Miami streets, but by the time he came to a police car his girlfriend was dead.

The police concluded that the motive was robbery, but the killer didn't even get Miss Kischniok's purse. It was still on the seat next to her dead body.

The *Herald* story ended like this: "Riechmann and Kischniok were to return to Germany Wednesday. Now Riechmann is going home alone with a question: 'Why do I earn this, coming here?' "

I clipped the story out of the *Herald* and slipped it into my briefcase. I had a hunch that I could somehow use it for this book, though that seemed improbable. The Kischniok murder was unlike the ones I was dealing with, and it was, sadly, not even an unusual crime. But still I kept the clipping. I'm not sure how I hoped to use it.

There are many such tragedies every day in America, and as I went about the business of researching this book, people often asked me why I had settled on this one. Surely I could have written a book about the well-respected doctor who murdered his wife and put her body through a wood chipper, or the four-star general whose Ivy League son was knocking off gas stations and liquor stores, they said. So why did I want to write a story about such ordinary people as a waitress at a pancake house and her boss and a couple of guys who worked at a gas station?

I live in Massachusetts and I first learned about the story when my brother, who lives in Miami, sent me a clipping from the *Miami Herald*. It was a small and sketchy story about a woman and three men who had been sentenced to death for killing a Florida restaurateur and his mother. The things that most fascinated me about the story were the fact that the woman, Dee Casteel, and one of the men, Allen Bryant, had buried the victims in their own backyard and then somehow impersonated the dead man and sold off his yacht, his stocks and bonds, his house, and other property. How had they done that? I wondered.

But I wondered as a reader, not as a writer. Certainly there was not enough in the newspaper article to make me want to fly to Miami and start writing a book.

I sent for more newspaper clippings. But as bizarre as the story was, there really hadn't been much written about it in Miami, where murders are easier to find than parking spaces. For several days the story haunted me. I wanted to know more. Finally, I put on my reporter's hat and started making phone calls until I came up with a woman who knew Dee Casteel.

"Tell me about Dee Casteel," I said to her. "What sort of woman is she?"

"Dee Casteel," she said, "is the nicest person you could ever want to meet."

I was hooked. The nicest person I would ever want to meet was going to the electric chair for two murders.

I made more phone calls, talked to more people. I spent many hours with Dee Casteel and her daughter, Susan. I interviewed Dee's lawyer, the state's prosecutors, Allen Bryant, policemen who investigated the case, waitresses at the pancake house, relatives of the murderers, people who were victimized by the fraudulent sales of Art Venecia's property.

I decided I wanted to write this book, not for the questions it would answer, but for the ones it would raise. Those questions were, for me, provocative. What exactly is alcoholism? Where do we draw the lines of responsibility for alcoholics? On the scales of justice, should alcoholism weigh as much as postpartum depression, or schizophrenia or psychosis? Is being in love a mitigating circumstance? Does being abused in childhood excuse abusing others in adulthood? And what about the death penalty—whom do we give it to and why? And if the appeals process can last for years, even decades, do we end up executing a very different person from the one who committed the crimes?

And there were other questions, less abstract than

those. I wondered, for example, if a waitress and a manager at a pancake house and two guys who work at a gas station are willing to commit murder for relatively low wages, how many other potential executioners are out there? What about the woman at the diner who served me eggs and home fries this morning? What about the fellow at the gas station who filled my tank yesterday? What about my dentist? What about you? What about me?

We are used to thinking that murderers are strangers to us and that murders are planned in sleazy places—bars, bowling alleys, pool rooms. But these murders were planned in a pancake house, an ordinary, wholesome place, where you take the kids for strawberry waffles on Sunday morning. For the people I interviewed, the memory of that pancake house was perhaps the memory of an illusion being shattered. The illusion is that if we watch our step, if we stay in the right neighborhoods, if we go only to the safe and familiar places, then we will not be where the murderers are. But if the murderers can stand behind us, filling our tank with gasoline, or in front of us, wearing cute little aprons and pouring our coffee and serving our pancakes, then they can be anywhere.

As I went about the business of researching the book, naturally, I did a lot of thinking about what is true. Truth, I find, comes in layers, not in chunks, and the degree of truth in a book depends on when the writer stopped asking questions and started writing his book. Of course he has to stop researching sometime, but no matter when he does, he knows that one more day of probing would change the truth a little bit. In writing, as in science, the truth is only what we know so far.

There are a few things you should know about this book and the truth. One is that when four people commit murder together, their stories tend to diverge, and there are times when at least three of them have to be lying. I have tried here to choose carefully when to tell you about differences in stories and when not to. I don't want to bore you with the information that one person says a meeting took place at ten o'clock and another is certain that it was ten-thirty. But I do want to give you different versions on matters that seem important. You'll have to trust me to decide what's important.

You also have a right to know that several names have been changed. There are innocent people who are embarrassed, and in some cases frightened, because of their connection to the murders. So I have used pseudonyms for them. The following names used in this book are not the real names of the individuals depicted: Jim Garfield, Henry Ramos, Tommy O'Connor, Anne Chepsiuk, Gail Mincer, Bobby Ross, Harry Osterman, Lester Wallace, Bob DeSalvo, Jay Reed, Marty Eagerman, Charlie Jannsen, Ramona Feldman, and Ronald Patano.

Also, you should know that from various memories of what was said, I have tried to reconstruct accurate dialogue. Rarely does an interview subject remember the exact words that someone spoke a year or two before the interview. In those cases where someone does remember the exact words that were spoken, or when the words were recorded somewhere (such as in a deposition), I have repeated them verbatim. In all other cases, dialogue is based on my general knowledge of what was said and of the person who said it.

But remember that no matter how truthful a writer tries to be, his story can only be as reliable as his sources. In this case my primary sources are forty volumes of trial transcript, twelve volumes of court file, an eighty-eight-page police file, and more than a hundred interviews. The files, of course, say what they say. But interviews say a good deal more. The writer must ask the same questions over and over of different subjects until one answer seems to be the right one. When he is done, he has volumes of transcribed interviews. For some questions there is an ultimate authority. For others there is not, and all the writer can do is give the reader his best conclusion. Sooner or later the writer has to believe somebody.

So these are the things I thought about as I went along with the business of researching my book, and from time to time I thought of throwing away my newspaper clipping about the German tourists. It didn't really seem to speak to this particular book.

But one of the people I interviewed was John Parmenter, a Miami homicide detective who had worked on the Venecia-Fischer case. One morning several months after my first visit to Miami, we talked in his office about the case, and in time our conversation broadened to the subject of murder in general. "Let me ask you something," I said. "What are the chances of catching a murderer who has no connection to his victim, you know, one of these random murders you read about every day?" And just to clarify my question I said, "For example, a while back there was a story about a German tourist who was driving around one night and—"

Parmenter interrupted me. "I know the case," he said. "He confessed."

"Who confessed? They actually caught the guy?"

"The boyfriend did it," Parmenter said. "Riechmann. He brought his girlfriend to Miami and murdered her. He made up the story about the man by the parked cars. He had been to Miami before and he knew about our crime rate, and I guess he thought the story would play well here."

So there it was. The truth, as I knew it, had changed because I'd asked one more question. Things were not what they seemed to be. If I hadn't had that conversation with Parmenter, I might quite sincerely have told you the story about the poor German man whose girlfriend was murdered by a stranger in the dark, and left it at that.

Disconcerting as it was to realize that I had come that close to telling a story all wrong, I took some satisfaction in this turn of events. It proved, at least, that my writer's instincts were in good working order. My crumpled newspaper clipping did have something to say to readers of this book, after all, something about truth. And the victim, Kersten Kischniok, did have something in common with Art Venecia. While she was staring out the car window, perhaps watching for dangerous strangers on unfamiliar streets, the real danger was right there in the car with her in the form of someone she loved. That's what happened to Art, and this is the whole truth, as I know it.

1

The Prisoner

Your name is Dee Casteel. In October of 1987, after three years in the county jail, you came to death row in Fort Lauderdale, America's playground. There wasn't even a cell for you. Death row was full. So for eight months you lived in a small brick box of a cell in another part of the Broward County Correctional Institution. You took your daily exercise hour with the three other death-row inmates. Your laundry went out with death row's laundry. And the return address that you neatly printed in letters to friends had an ominous "D/R" tagged onto it. But you didn't actually live among those women with whom you shared such a peculiar circumstance. You lived instead in the echoic world of pissed-off women shouting at each other through the bars. The smell and the feel of the women was all around you, but you weren't one of them. They were going home someday.

But that wasn't the worst of it. The thing that you really hated, the thing that most blackened your despair and made the electric chair seem sometimes like the lesser of two evils, was that your cell had no window.

In June of 1988 when another condemned woman had her death sentence whittled down to "life, mandatory twenty-five," it was your turn to live in a death-row cell among your own kind. When you were led into the cell, possibly the last home you will ever have, you saw the window and it made you cry.

A window is no slight thing when you have to stay alone in your cell for twenty-three hours a day, especially to a woman like you who loves the outdoors, who used to fish and go camping in the Everglades, who used to dig her fingers in the garden soil. Now you can stare through your window and see an expanse of brilliant blue Florida sky, a small man-made lake, and best of all, the raucous daily volleyball games between teams of young women who, convicted of lesser crimes, will someday be walking out the front door.

But a single square window is not enough to maintain your sanity. To do that you must be able to turn the bare walls of your cell into a screen on which you can project the memories of what it was like to walk down a street, to buy a dress, to make love with a man. You must convince yourself that a life beyond the cell waits for you somewhere. You do this, but inevitably the memories lead like a tunnel to the awful crimes, and you are shaken by the tough questions. What have you done to the lives of your children, Susan, Todd, and Wyatt? How will you ever make them understand what you did, and why? How can you make them understand when you don't even understand it yourself?

The questions are too painful and you push them away. You crochet. You watch television. You read. You play solitaire. And as best you can, you groom yourself. You are fifty now and the years in prison have etched more deeply the lines on your face, but no gray has yet invaded the long strawberry-blond hair that used to turn the fellows' heads. But these distractions can take you just so far. And when you have used up your allotment of yarn, when you can't bear to watch another episode of *General Hospital,* when your eyes are too tired to read, and your brain too wired for sleep, there is nothing else for you to do but face the past again and wonder what in the name of Christ happened.

2

The Plan

Dee Casteel was an ordinary woman. Everybody says so. Take Calie Maitland, for example. Calie lived a couple of doors down from Dee in South Miami back in the late 1970s. Their kids played together and Calie used to walk over to Dee's house between loads of laundry, and the two of them would smoke and drink coffee and talk.

"We didn't talk about politics or philosophy or anything cerebral," says Calie, "just the kids and housework. The price of detergent, the best place to get shoes for the kids. The children were small then, and those were the things women talked about in those days. Dee worked as a waitress, and she was a housewife. She kept the cleanest house I have ever seen. Dee and I were never really close, but I liked her a lot. She was always there with a favor, always anxious to help you out. After I moved away I never saw her again. When I read in the papers that she had been sentenced to die in the electric chair, I was stunned.

Dee Casteel was the nicest person you could ever want to meet."

If you had dropped in on them back then, you would have thought the two women were alike. Both were bright. Both lived in a lower-middle-class neighborhood. Both were in their late thirties. Both raising kids and trying to keep up with the price of bread and milk. But there must have been some differences, because today Calie is an advertising executive in Miami and she gets to fly to places like Las Vegas on business, while Dee the prisoner has no travel plans except to the Florida State Prison in Starke, where they keep "Sparky." That's the state's electric chair, which, incidentally, is the busiest one in the country.

Dee started that trip toward Starke on May 29, 1983, Memorial Day weekend, in an unlikely setting for treachery and murder: the International House of Pancakes in Naranja, Florida. The Naranja International House of Pancakes, IHOP for short, is like all the others around the country. It's a family restaurant, A-frame with a blue roof, a lot of flags and hanging plants, great pancakes, pitchers of coffee on the table—a cheerful, nice place to eat.

Naranja is an unincorporated area of Dade County about thirty-five miles south of downtown Miami. You can call it Miami because people all over Dade County loosely refer to their communities as Miami, even when that's not correct. But Naranja is definitely not part of "America's Casablanca," and it's not the sort of place where you'd run into Don Johnson. It's a pretty bland area, a low-income area. Lots of pickup trucks and Chevys, not many Porsches and Jaguars. A lot of Naranja people work at the nearby Homestead Air Force Base, or at farms in The Redlands or in shopping malls along Route 1. It's not a big tourist area, but it is on the way to Key West, and the Monkey Jungle is not far away, so there are some tourist dollars flowing into the local economy.

At a little before two in the afternoon on the

twenty-ninth of May, Dee was working at the IHOP and saw the company-owned Lincoln Town Car pull into the parking lot.

Dee was working the six A.M. to two P.M. shift, instead of her usual night shift. It was a typical Sunday, busy as hell, with customers, mostly families, coming in wave after wave.

Dee was carrying her umpteenth plate of pancakes to a customer when she saw the car pull in. By this time the plate felt heavy in her hand. She was approaching the end of her shift. Her feet ached, as usual. She watched the car pull to a stop in front of the window. It was a typically hot May day in southern Florida, and waves of heat rose like cigarette smoke from the just-washed surface of the car. It must be Allen, she thought, feeling a little bit nervous and excited.

"Gail, will you watch my station," Dee called to another waitress as she rushed into the ladies' room to primp.

Dee always liked to look her best when James Allen Bryant was around. Other employees at the pancake house had noticed that whenever Allen entered a room, Dee seemed to stand a little taller, smile a little more brightly, speak more slowly. Those who knew Dee well found this surprising, not because Dee was forty-four and Allen was twenty-five, but because Dee had always filled her life with large, stormy men, real macho numbers—women-beaters for the most part—and Allen was not only small, but gay. For eight years Allen had been the lover of the restaurant's owner, Arthur Venecia. Venecia, a successful businessman who had made his money in real estate, had bought the IHOP franchise in Naranja specifically for Allen to manage.

Some of the waitresses who worked at IHOP then say that Dee Casteel was already in love with Allen. But Dee says no. She says she was just insecure around him. During the nine months that Dee had been working at the Naranja IHOP, Allen had seemed cool with her; he didn't seem to flirt with Dee and fawn over her in his girlish way, the way he did with the other waitresses. Dee thought Allen didn't like her. That worried her. Sometimes, for no reason, she would get it in her head that he was going to fire her, and that was about the worst thing she could imagine.

When she got into the ladies' room Dee coaxed her hair into place and pressed fresh lipstick on her thin lips. She avoided a careful study of herself in the mirror. She knew she was gaunt these days. She had once been a very pretty girl, with guys tripping over each other to get near her, but she had squandered her good looks on alcohol and she regretted that as much as anything. She glanced at her hands to be sure they weren't shaking.

When Dee came out from the ladies' room, Allen Bryant had already come into the restaurant. Dee went first to check on her customers. At each table she stopped and smiled. "Is everything okay? Would you like more coffee?" Then she went to Allen. He stood behind the glass counter that was just inside the door. Allen had on a blue boat-neck shirt and tight white jeans, and some expensive-looking loafers. Nice clothes, good quality. Allen was always well dressed. He leaned over the cash register, and with frantic little motions of his long, slender fingers he snatched bills out of the cash drawer as if he were snatching cheese from a mousetrap. Allen was a willowy young man, about five foot eight, and in 1983 he still wore his light brown hair in a carefully shaped Beatle-style perm, which seemed a bit old-fashioned, but still inspired occasional nasty comments from Florida rednecks.

"Just getting some gas money," he said to Dee. He stared down into the cash drawer as if he were contemplating his next move in some game. Dee watched him for a few seconds. And then she saw it. The goddamn oregano bottle was on the floor next to the wall safe.

All day long Dee had been sipping from a tall glass that contained iced coffee and Scotch whiskey. The whiskey supply, which she smuggled in every day, was kept in the jumbo-sized Durkee's oregano bottle that she always kept hidden in her pocketbook by the cash register. Now the bottle was on the floor, just a couple of feet away from her boss.

After she was hired as a waitress at IHOP, Dee had gone several months without drinking on the job. But it had never been easy. By the end of her shifts her hands would be shaking, her vision would sometimes blur, and she often felt as if she were walking on loose planks. She always envied the alcoholic cook. Jim Garfield was his name. From his position in the kitchen, surrounded by walls on two sides, and shoulder-high counters on the other two, Jim could sneak drinks at work anytime. Being able to drink at work was a major survival issue to Dee and the other alcoholics she knew, a lot more important than raises and vacations and paid medical insurance.

Dee had managed to work sober until about March, when one day she damn near crumbled right there in front of all those families. IHOP was running a pancakes promotion that day, so the breakfast trade was nearly overwhelming. Lunch was just as busy, and by the time Dee had gone seven hours without a drink, she was on the verge of fainting. She tried to pick up her beverages for a party of four, and her trembling hands knocked two of them over.

"Are you okay?" a customer had asked as the glasses went crashing to the floor. Dee ran to the ladies' room. She splashed cold water on her face and took deep breaths. She was just barely able to pull herself together. Like a diabetic who had gone to work without insulin, Dee told herself she would never let that happen to her again. That's when she began smuggling in Scotch in the oregano bottle. Jim Garfield knew about it and Dee often shared her booze with him.

Damn Jim, he's going to get me fired, she thought now as she watched Allen Bryant count money from the cash register. On this particular day Jim had been in real bad shape, and after he had sucked down his own supply of alcohol, he had been nipping at Dee's Scotch all day. But instead of putting the bottle back in Dee's pocketbook after his last nip, he had left it on the floor by the safe. Now as Dee stared at it, she could easily imagine Allen's picking it up and sniffing it. Oh, God, she prayed, please don't let Allen see it.

"How's it going?" Allen asked.

"Busy," Dee said nervously, her eyes shifting from Allen to the bottle, from Allen to the bottle. "It's starting to quiet down now. You want me to send one of the girls home?"

"No. Let them stay," Allen said. Dee watched him as he dealt out the ten- and twenty-dollar bills like playing cards on the glass counter. Suddenly the oregano bottle seemed to be the largest object in the restaurant.

Allen meticulously turned all the bills so that they were facing the same way. Why doesn't he just take the money and go? Dee thought. She glanced around the restaurant, hoping to find a table with small children. "Look at the darlings," she could say, and Allen would go right to them. Allen was great with kids. It would be a distraction. Then she could pluck the oregano bottle off the floor and shove it in her pocketbook. But no such luck. The families had pretty much cleared out, headed for the beaches or the arts festival in Cutler Ridge. Only couples were left sitting at tables.

"I love Sundays," Allen said. He folded several bills and slid them into the pockets of his tight jeans.

To Dee, it seemed that Allen had been robbing the restaurant blind for months. His arrangement with Venecia, according to him, was that he drew no salary but would take expense money from the cash drawer as he needed it. That was probably true. But Dee knew that Allen's expenses included things that Art Venecia didn't know about or didn't have in mind, like cocaine and boyfriends. Now she glanced through the window into the parking lot to see if Allen had a boyfriend waiting for him in the Lincoln. Not this time. Everybody, including Art Venecia, knew that Allen had been cheating on Art with a succession of lovers, always young, usually Cuban. In fact, Allen had gotten quite blatant about his infidelity, often joking around the pancake house that Art, who was the same age as Dee, was turning into an old fuddy-duddy and couldn't keep up with him.

Lately, though, Allen's promiscuity had waned. He was in love. The new object of his affection was a strikingly handsome young man by the name of Henry Ramos. Sometimes Allen would show up at the restaurant with his young Latin lover and the transformation would be extraordinary. Allen, the temperamental boss, would suddenly become Allen the fawning queen, patiently attending to his young man's every whim . . . "More coffee, dear? Is the toast dark enough?" . . . like a new bride.

Dark-eyed and dashing, Ramos set aflutter not just the heart of James Allen Bryant, but the hearts of several IHOP waitresses who suspected that Henry was not gay at all, but just a gigolo whose charms would work equally well on females, especially females who had access to a goose as golden as the IHOP cash register.

"If Art asks, tell him I took a few bucks," Allen said.

"Sure," Dee replied, feeling puffed up by Allen's trust in her and relieved because he was getting ready to leave. Dee was confident that she would never have to lie for Allen. Art Venecia would never ask her how much Allen had taken. He would figure it out himself when he came to do the accounting in the upstairs office, which was practically the only time Dee ever saw Venecia in the restaurant. Art hardly ever came to the pancake house anymore, because whenever he did, he and Allen would end up quarreling.

During the time that Dee had worked at the IHOP, the relationship between Allen Bryant and Art Venecia had been volcanic. Dee, like the other waitresses, often felt as if she were tuned in to some perverse soap opera. More than once Art had come by with cuts on his face and bruises on his head, which everybody knew had been inflicted in battles with his younger lover. Sometimes it was Allen who showed up with a bruised cheek or a cut over the eye. On one occasion the two men came to fury in the restaurant's upstairs office. For twenty minutes the waitresses and customers listened to the muffled curses and the crashing sounds of Allen and Art shoving each other around in the cramped office until finally an enraged Allen streaked down the stairs, rushed out of the building, and screeched off in the Lincoln, which Art had bought for him.

Even before that incident Allen was inclined to gossip to the waitresses about his quarrels with Art Venecia, and he often said things like, "Sometimes I could just kill Art." But none of the women made much of it. They were inclined to say the same sorts of things about their own husbands.

"You want some coffee, Allen?" Dee said.

What the hell was she doing? She bit her lip. The longer Allen stayed around, the greater the chance that he would find her alcohol, and here she was inviting him to have a cup of coffee. Christ, why not get him a plate of blueberry pancakes, too, and say, "Oh, by the way, Allen, that's my oregano bottle full of Scotch on the floor over there." Dee didn't understand her compulsive need to please Allen any more than she understood her relentless craving for alcohol. But it was a feeling that was always there.

"No time for coffee," Allen said. "Got to run. Art wants me to go to one of those tedious organ recitals." He made a face, then headed for the door.

Dee was relieved. She didn't think to hide the oregano bottle. She would get to it later, she thought.

A few minutes later Dee was standing by a table at the back of the IHOP where a guy named Tommy O'Connor sat all alone. O'Connor, who was proud of telling everybody that he had once pitched for a Red Sox farm team, was a lonely old guy who had retired from a fifty-year stint as a bell captain in Miami Beach. Now he came into the IHOP every afternoon so that he could have a cup of coffee and someone to talk to. Good waitresses tend to have their own following, and Dee had known Tommy when she worked at Sambo's and again at Denny's. Over the years she had befriended a lot of Tommys. Now when things were quiet, Dee always sat with O'Connor for as long as it took to smoke one Benson and Hedges cigarette, and they'd swap troubles. O'Connor would tell Dee about his wife, now gone thirteen years, and Dee would tell Tommy about her husband, Cass, who she wished would go away and stay gone. From time to time in recent years Dee would dig into the pockets of her apron and lend Tommy some of her tip money, which he promised would come back to her tenfold on the back of One Smart Cookie or Major Garonovitch, or some other promising thoroughbred at Gulfstream Park. Tommy never paid Dee back and she never expected him to.

"That the boss?" Tommy asked now.

"Huh?"

Tommy pointed to the front of the restaurant. "The young fellow. The one who's a little light on his feet. He the boss?"

Dee turned, and there was Allen. He had come back in, and now he stood behind the glass counter with his back to her. He was sniffing the oregano bottle.

Dee felt sick. She was sure she was going to be fired.

But Allen didn't say anything. He didn't even turn

and give her a look. He twisted the cap back on the bottle and placed it back on the floor where it had been. Then he left.

Still, a few minutes later when her shift had ended and she got into her old Buick, Dee was worried. She drove south on South Dixie Highway. Allen was as unpredictable as a tropical storm. She knew he could charm her today and fire her without regret tomorrow. What would she do? she wondered. How would she get by? She held the steering wheel tightly, thinking that with all this alcohol on her breath, she didn't want to get stopped for a ticket.

Dee had been an alcoholic for years, perhaps since birth, but only in the last few years, the Cass years, did things seem to be getting out of control. Cass was her husband, and the fragile bond between them had been built not on love or romance, or even sex. It floated on, it swam in, it drowned under, alcohol. They were drinking buddies long before Cass moved in with Dee, and when they drank, which was almost every night for eight tumultuous years, they were like a couple of hand grenades rolling loose across the floor, reckless and destructive. Cass was a nice enough fellow when sober, but when he was drunk, he was abusive and obnoxious.

Now, sinking into depression because she expected to be fired, Dee wished she had Cass to talk to. Cass was gone. He had gone like this before, dozens of times, on desperate, hateful binges, and always she had thanked God for taking him away, prayed that he would not come back, and cried because he was gone. Maybe he would come back this time. Maybe not. But for now, as far as men were concerned, Dee was alone. "Alone again, naturally," she sang out loud, remembering the song from the early seventies. She fidgeted with the radio dial, but she couldn't get anything worth listening to. Alone again to scratch out a living for herself and her boys, Todd and Wyatt, in a small house on Southwest 170th Street. Even with the $225 or so she was bringing home every week, the bills were piling up. To lose her job now would be devastating.

Dee couldn't afford to be fired again. She had been thrown out of just about every restaurant on that strip of Route 1 between Homestead and Cutler Ridge. She had been fired from Denny's because she had staggered in drunk on New Year's Eve and told her boss that whether he liked it or not, she wouldn't be working that night. She had been fired from Wag's, another chain, for drinking on the job. And she had been fired from Kelly's Kitchen because she couldn't even function on the breakfast shift without a couple of drinks to get her through the morning. Sambo's had closed, and the Naranja IHOP was now the only chain restaurant that hadn't evicted her for drinking and was still in easy driving distance from Dee's house in the city of Homestead, five miles south on Route 1. Dee knew that she drank too much to be driving any long distance to work every day. She was sure that she would kill herself in a smashup or get bagged for DUI and lose her license. So in her mind the Naranja IHOP was her only chance to earn a living for herself and her two teenaged sons. Even if Cass came back, she knew it wouldn't be for long. The marriage was deteriorating faster than she was. To Dee the Naranja IHOP was the end of the line.

As she drove along South Dixie that day, it seemed to Dee that she was too sad even to feel sad. Her whole life had come to this; she was nothing but a boozer, a lowlife with a high IQ. For a moment she tasted the memories of a time when she was pretty and had good jobs and could be seen dancing every night with some of the richest and most successful men in Miami. "I coulda been a contender," she said to the dashboard, and sadness filled her again when she remembered that Marlon Brando was just playing a part in a movie, but she was really living her life. On the steering wheel her hands were shaking, a harsh reminder that she was falling fast and far toward something dreadful.

Monday and Tuesday were Dee's days off. She spent Monday with her daughter, Susan. Susan, who was just a few days shy of her seventeenth birthday, lived in Fort Lauderdale. Susan, unable to bear the sight of her mother being beaten, had moved out at age eleven, when Cass moved in. Now she recalls Dee's visit that Monday as being one of the "good ones."

"That's how I have to think about my mother," Susan says. "This good time, that good time. The times when she was sober. When my mother was sober, she was the most wonderful woman in the world. We were the best of friends. When she was drunk, I hated her."

At sixteen, Susan was in most ways mature beyond her years. She was a pretty and deceptively wholesome-looking girl. With hair the color of honey, and tiny freckles sprinkled like nutmeg across her dimpled cheeks, she might have been a guide at Disney World. But Susan was not the girl she appeared to be. Few people can go through the grinder of life with an alcoholic and come out undamaged. Susan was not one of them. By the time she turned sixteen Susan's self-esteem had been squashed so close to the ground that she trusted no one who offered love. A kind heart and a gentle touch made her uncomfortable.

On this Monday in 1983 Dee was sober and she and Susan were the best of friends. That afternoon they met in town at the Bayfront Park and drove over to northwest Miami to shop at a fabric warehouse. Then they found a Kmart where they picked out sneakers for Wyatt, the younger of Dee's two boys. After that they took a scenic drive across the MacArthur Causeway to look around at the newly restored "Deco district" in South Beach with its famous etched glass and pastel buildings and art deco architecture. Later mother and daughter ate at Denny's on Biscayne. Susan, as usual, had insisted they go to a place that didn't serve liquor.

"I'm afraid that Allen is going to fire me," Dee confessed over coffee.

"Oh, Ma, why would he do that? You're a great waitress."

"He found my drink. The oregano bottle I keep my Scotch in."

Susan said nothing. She glared at her mother. It was a look that spoke for all the years of this cursed mother-daughter relationship.

"Well, then why don't you stop drinking?" Susan said. "You can do it. You've done it before."

Though she had been hospitalized twice for alcoholism, Dee still believed she could give up drinking without professional help. In fact, she had done it. On more than one occasion she had bet someone that she could stop drinking for thirty days. Then she had gone the thirty days, and gotten drunk on the thirty-first day. This ability is not unusual in an alcoholic. The road to alcoholic ruin is rarely straight downhill; it is usually a roller-coaster ride: you're on the booze, then you're off the booze. In fact, about half of all alcoholics are dry at any given time, but over the long haul very few can fight the relentless craving for alcohol.

"You're right. I can do it," Dee said.

"That's the spirit, Ma," Susan said. Susan's greatest dream in life had always been that her mother would stop drinking, and now she was as capable as her mother of fooling herself into believing that this would be the time it would stick.

"I think I can. I know I can," Dee said. "I'm like the little train that could." She smiled. She had read that one to the kids years ago. I have to, she thought, my life depends on it.

After she left Susan that day, Dee did not touch alcohol. That night Cass was home and she played penny-ante poker with him and the boys to keep her mind busy. Tuesday, Dee spent the morning weeding the small garden at the back of the house in Homestead. Then she read Stephen King on the couch. Her bottle of Clan MacGregor Scotch was handy and she reached for it several times. But she was always able to push it away with the thought: my life depends on this. Around two o'clock Dee was cleaning her kitchen cabinets with Pine Sol when the phone rang. It was Allen.

"Dee, can you come down to the restaurant this afternoon," he said. "I want to talk to you about something."

"Sure, Allen. What time?"

"Would four o'clock be convenient?"

"Sure. I'll be there."

She hung up. The son of a bitch had betrayed her, she thought. She was sure that Allen had used the two days to find another waitress before firing her. For the first time that day she opened the bottle of Scotch. She poured a slug of the whiskey into a coffee cup and swallowed it, reasoning in typical alcoholic fashion that if she was going to get fired, she deserved a drink.

After that, Dee ironed her clean waitress uniforms and folded them neatly so that she could surrender them in the same condition she had received them. By this time Todd and Wyatt were home from school, but Dee didn't have the heart to tell them what was going on. She stopped in the bathroom to check her appearance in the mirror, then hurried out of the house. Even driving off to be fired, she didn't want to keep Allen waiting.

When she got to the International House of Pancakes, Allen was standing just inside the door, pacing. "Hi," he said. He sounded nervous.

"What's up?" Dee said, trying to sound nonchalant. She had left her uniforms in the car. No sense making it easy for him.

"Come on," he said, gently taking her arm. "I want you to go for a ride with me."

Allen led Dee across the parking lot to the Lincoln. Stopping at the passenger side, he opened her door for her, waited until she was seated, and then closed it for her. Dee settled into the front seat of the new Town Car. It felt luxurious.

Allen steered the Lincoln out of the IHOP parking lot, turned north on Route 1, and drove in silence while Dee tried to figure out why they had to drive anywhere for him to fire her.

"Where we going?" Dee asked.

"No place," he said.

Clearly something was on his mind. This was not the sort of place where you go for a scenic drive. Route 1 south of Miami, also known as South Dixie Highway, is one of those hopelessly unimaginative strips of low buildings and congested parking lots that sprawl across the outskirts of all major cities. Three lanes, as flat and straight as bowling alleys, point south; three lanes point north. Between them is a median strip of unmowed grass. Only the ubiquitous palm trees and the occasional cracked coconut rotting on the sidewalk assure you that you're not near Pittsburgh or Buffalo or Seattle. If you were to wake up unexpectedly on South Dixie Highway, you would think you had died and gone to fast-food heaven. Wendy's, McDonald's, Kentucky Fried Chicken, they're all there, each cloned several times up and down the highway. The closest you will come to fine dining is the pork chops at Denny's or the international omelets at IHOP.

If there is anything more prevalent than eateries on South Dixie Highway, it is businesses dedicated to the automobile. Dealerships, muffler shops, auto parts stores, and service centers abound along with a gaggle of Gulf, Texaco, Shell, and Amoco stations. There is nothing here to lift a spirit, particularly one that had fallen as low as Dee Casteel's had.

"How was the organ recital?" Dee asked, not able to stand the tension of the silence any longer.

"Dull as piss," Allen said. And then, "Art's

driving me nuts. He's so jealous and possessive. It's like living in a prison."

"Sorry to hear that," Dee said.

In the alcoholic gloom that made up much of her daily life, Dee had become disinclined to analyze things. It didn't seem important that Allen was talking about something other than the business at hand. She would simply wait for him to announce that he was getting rid of her and then she would try to talk him out of it.

"Incidentally, I know about the oregano bottle," Allen said.

"Huh?"

"The one with the booze in it. It is yours, isn't it?"

"Yes."

"I thought so. Anyhow, I don't want you to worry about it. I'm not going to tell Art about it. He'd fire you in a minute if he knew. But I understand. Really, I do. People like you and me, we got to stick together, you know."

Dee felt as if she could breathe again. She wasn't getting fired. That's what mattered, and it didn't seem important that Allen, apparently, wanted to talk to her about something else.

Allen is all right, she thought. She had misjudged him. He's a nice person. Though he sometimes had a temper. She liked him. She liked him a lot, and for the first time she thought that maybe he liked her, too.

"I'm going to give it up," she said.

"How's that?"

"The alcohol. It doesn't do anybody any good. Should have given it up a long time ago. I owe that to my kids."

"Good," Allen said, patting her knee, "good for you."

His hand was like a small bird on her knee. It was a comfort to her, and Dee was hoping that Allen would continue to touch her. But in a moment the delicate hand flew away, back to the steering wheel, where its grip was tense, angry.

"Got to make my break from Art," he said. "He's making me crazy."

They drove for a few miles, through Cutler Ridge, into Perrine. The communities, each as flat and unremarkable as the next, spilled into one another. If it weren't for the signs along the highway, you would never know that you had left one place and entered another.

They drove past restaurants where Dee had worked. They drove past several bars where Dee and Cass had gotten drunk. Between the wedges of silence Allen would bitch and pout about some behavior of Art's. He tapped the steering wheel. He turned on the radio. He turned it off. Dee listened to him, not quite hearing every word, but feeling bad for him because she, too, had lived with brutal men. Not knowing Art well, Dee had no way of knowing that Allen was full of shit, that Art Venecia was, in fact, quite a nice man. Finally, Allen took a U-turn and headed south again.

"You ever eat at Monty Trainer's?" Allen asked.

"Monty who?"

"Monty Trainer's," Allen said. "It's a restaurant in the Grove."

"No."

"It's quite lovely," Allen said. "We ate there after the recital. I'll take you there sometime."

Dee couldn't believe what she was hearing. Instead of firing her, Allen was inviting her to a fancy restaurant in Coconut Grove.

After they had passed the Cutler Ridge Denny's for a second time, the one where Dee had made that awful scene on New Year's Eve, Allen cleared his throat nervously, like a boy about to ask for a date.

"You know what someone told me once?" he asked.

"What's that?"

"It sounds crazy, but somebody said you know a guy who could take a contract."

"You mean murder somebody?"

"Yes, for money."

"Who said that?"

"I don't know," Allen said. "One of the waitresses. What's the difference who?"

"Must have been talking about Mike," Dee said.

"Mike?"

"Mike Irvine. A friend of mine. Whoever told you that must have meant Mike."

"Who is he?"

"Friend of Cass. I met Mike when I was working at the Saga Lounge. He works at the Amoco station up on Three Hundredth Street."

"So, would he?" Allen asked.

"You mean actually kill somebody?"

"Sure. Would he really do it?"

"Not Mike, no. Mike's a teddy bear, a real sweetheart."

"So he's not a criminal?"

"No. I think he sells dope sometimes, but he's gentle. He would never do anything violent. He's a real sweet guy."

"So it's not true?" Allen said. "He's not a hit man?"

"A hit man? Christ, no. Not Mike. He's a kidder. He always says to me, Dee, if you and Cass ever decide to split, don't bother with a lawyer. I'll take care of it for you cheaper."

"You mean he would kill Cass?"

"Yeah, but he's only joking about it."

"Damn," Allen said.

"Why? Are you really thinking about having somebody killed?"

"Forget it," Allen snapped. "Just forget it."

They drove in silence for a long time. Now Dee felt sad. She had let Allen down.

"No," she said. She sat up straighter in the car.

"I can't imagine Mike Irvine killing anybody. I just can't picture it." She stared out at the pastel blocks, the stores, the shops, the fast-food joints that went whizzing by, and she sensed that Allen was asking her to do something that was really important to him.

"Just can't picture it," she said again, as if to convince herself. "But . . ."

"But what?" Allen said.

"But he might know somebody who would."

So that's how it began. Dee Casteel and James Allen Bryant went for a ride on South Dixie Highway, and the plan to murder Art Venecia was born in the front seat of the Lincoln that Art had bought for Allen. Simple. But not understandable. And a year later when the murders were discovered, people all over south Dade County who had known Dee as a friend or a waitress or as the woman down the street with two sons and a daughter, people who thought of Dee as "the nicest person you could ever want to meet," and "a woman who would do anything for you," these people would read about it in the *Miami Herald* and they would wonder what in Christ's name was going on in Dee's mind. Why didn't she just tell James Allen Bryant to fuck off? Why did she go along with it?

3

The Meeting

During the second week of June, a few days after Allen took her for a ride, Dee drove to Yappell's Amoco station on Route 1 in Homestead. That's where Mike Irvine worked as a mechanic. Allen had asked Dee to find out if Irvine would really do a murder, or if he knew somebody who would take on the job. Allen had also asked her to get a price. Dee says she went because she was still worried about losing her job. Anxious to please Allen, she wanted to meet with Irvine so that she could go back to Allen and honestly report that she had asked him about doing a murder.

In fact, Dee's work situation had already improved. Before this time she had waited on tables at night during the week, working the more desirable morning shift only on weekends. But after their drive on South Dixie Highway, Allen switched Dee to the six A.M. to two P.M. shift, which is by far the most lucrative daily stint for a waitress at a pancake house. The only catch was that Dee had to pick up and drive home Jim Garfield, the alcoholic first-shift cook. Garfield, who also lived in Homestead, had just had his license yanked for driving under the influence.

Allen told Dee he was making the schedule change so that she would be free to meet with Mike Irvine, who worked nights. But the switch to a shift she had always wanted had another effect on Dee: it showed her that cooperating with Allen could be rewarding.

Mike was not at the Amoco station the first night, so Dee went back the next night. She pulled into the gas station right at midnight, hoping to keep the conversation short and get home quickly. But Mike still wasn't there. These fruitless errands were stressful for Dee because Cass was currently in residence with her. Cass was a jealous man, and he had beaten Dee several times. "Where are you going?" Cass would ask. "Who are you meeting? When are you coming back?" The questions were constant. In fact, Cass had already given Dee grief over the fact that every morning she was picking up Jim Garfield and driving him to work. "Who is this Jim guy, anyhow?" Cass had asked suspiciously. He had harassed Dee about it until Dee brought Jim into the house one morning and introduced the two men. Cass had later put his stamp of approval on the arrangement with a good-humored, "Oh, hell, he's just another faggot."

When Dee finally caught up with Mike Irvine, it was at three-thirty in the morning. It was not unusual for Dee to be up in the middle of the night. Like other places she had worked, the Naranja IHOP was a twenty-four-hour restaurant, so between night-shift work and all-night drinking binges, Dee had seen plenty of blurred sunrises. When she drove into the Amoco station, Mike was alone, and he was happy to see her.

"Hey, babe," he said, "how you doing?" He shoved the gasoline hose into the tank of her Buick and came around to talk to her. He leaned his six-foot frame over, placed his elbows on the car door, and smiled at her, his big brown country-boy eyes full of mischief.

"You still married to that son of a bitch Cass?" he asked with a smile.

"Not for long," Dee said.

"Good. You finally seen the light, huh?"

"I seen the light a long time ago," Dee said.

"Then you must be about ready to have me kill the bastard?"

"Don't tempt me."

"Don't waste money on a fucking lawyer," Mike said.

"No chance of that. I'm lucky if I can pay the rent."

"I'll take care of Cass for you," Irvine said. "Is the bastard ready to die?"

"I doubt it," Dee said.

"Doesn't matter. You just give me the word and I'll kill him for you. We'll grind him up in a trash compactor or something."

Though Mike knew that the Dee-Cass marriage was falling apart, he was only kidding. In fact, Mike and Cass had been friends for years, even before Dee came on the scene. Mike had worked at Kiernan's gas station when Dee had worked at the Saga Lounge, and both Mike and Cass would come into the Saga from time to time and sit at the bar shooting the breeze with Dee. This hit-man stuff had become a running joke between the three of them. It was this familiar banter that Dee had mentioned to another waitress a few weeks earlier, and that had led Allen to believe that Dee might know a bona fide hit man.

Dee was sure that Mike Irvine had done some small-time drug selling. In fact, he had once offered her an opportunity to be a "mule" on one drug deal. She turned it down, but the offer did not detract from her fondness for Mike. She saw him as a gentle man, an innocent, a penny-ante player at best, a country bumpkin who sometimes told tall tales but would never hurt any living thing.

Dee kidded with Mike for a few minutes while he filled her tank. He asked about Susan. Mike had always been fond of Dee's kids.

"Is her car running okay?" Mike asked. It was a car he had given to Susan after her own broke down.

"Fine," Dee said.

"You tell her if she has any trouble with it, bring it to me. I'll fix it, no charge."

"Thanks."

Another car pulled in, got gas, and left. Dee glanced around to be sure they were alone.

"Can I ask you something, Mike?"

"Anything, sweetheart."

"You're always joking about knocking somebody off."

"Yeah."

"Would you really do it?"

"Kill somebody?" he asked.

"Yes," she said.

"You mean for money?"

"Yes."

"Why?" he asked.

"I know somebody who wants somebody killed," Dee said. It was still unreal to her. She felt as if she were a kid acting out her part in a game. Now Mike would say no, and the game would be over.

"Who?" Mike asked.

"Just someone I know," Dee said. Bryant had insisted that she not mention his name to anyone.

"Not me," Mike said, "I'm no killer."

"Didn't think so," Dee said.

"But I have a friend who will do it."

"Really?"

"Sure," Mike said. " 'Course, we wouldn't want your friend to know who we are. We'd have to deal through you."

"Can you give me a price?"

What the hell am I doing? she thought. *Can you give me a price?* I sound like I'm buying a used car. I'm asking for a price on a murder; this is crazy. But she also thought: Allen will be pleased, he'll be proud of me.

"The price would depend on who the person is," Mike said. "How hard he is to hit, a lot of things."

He's trying to impress me, Dee thought. Good old Mike, always liked to make it sound as if he were a big-time criminal.

"I don't even know who he wants killed," Dee said.

Mike stood up and went to the back of the car to pull out the gasoline hose.

"Twelve bucks," he said loudly, as if there were somebody there who had to hear that they were conducting normal business. Then he leaned on the door of the car again and grinned. He smelled of gasoline. He was big and broad across the chest so that he almost filled the window space, but even in the sulfurous yellow light of the Amoco station, he looked harmless to Dee, a regular teddy bear. "I bet it's that queer bastard you work for and he probably wants his lover knocked off," Mike said.

Dee, momentarily lost in thought, stared out at the few cars that drove up Route 1. Where the hell are they going? she wondered. Sometimes she wished she could get on the highway and just . . . go.

"Maybe you're right," she said, paying Mike for the gas. She was weary. She needed a drink.

"You bet I'm right," Mike said. "Shit, it don't take no genius to figure that out."

Of course, he's right, Dee thought. Allen wanted to kill Art so he could be with Henry. Now it seemed so obvious that she wondered why she hadn't realized it before.

"My friend would need some information first," Mike said.

"Like what?"

"Like who's going to be hit? Where does he live? What are his habits? What kind of car does he drive? When is he normally at home?"

Jesus, Dee thought, maybe Mike does know a little bit about this sort of thing.

"Anything else?"

"We'll need a photo."

"I'll see what I can do," Dee said, and she drove home thinking that if the game continued, she could get in so good with Allen that she could have her job and her bottle, too.

4

The Teddy Bear

If there was going to be a murder conspiracy, Dee's friend Mike Irvine was almost as poor a choice to join in as Dee was. Mike was a mechanic, not in the Charles Bronson sense of the word, but in the Goober Pyle sense of an auto mechanic. He was just a guy who worked at a gas station. Just as Dee could be traded for any waitress in the country without alarming anybody, Mike Irvine could easily be the guy who fills your tank and asks you if you want your windshield wiped.

Certainly if Mike Irvine had to apply for the job of murderer, he would have been turned down. Especially in a town like Miami where thousands of highly qualified applicants walk the streets. For one thing, Mike had no experience. He also lacked aptitude. According to friends, there was never the smell of violence about Mike, never a hint that a murderous instinct might be festering inside of him. He was, everybody agrees, a gentle man. And funny and friendly, too. Donna Hobson, another of those waitresses who has worked at eateries up and down South Dixie Highway, remembers, "Mike was a great guy. He'd come in for coffee and tell a few jokes and flirt, and he always left a good tip." Pat Swanson, a lady friend whom Mike was in love with, says, "Mike was a kind, good man. I don't believe he would ever hurt anybody." Another friend, Natalie Stewart, who describes Mike as "someone I would trust my life with," tells this story:

"Mike used to live next door to where we used to all hang out at one time several years ago. Mike would never lock his door, and he always had a cigar box full of money on top of his refrigerator. It was just a habit of his, and everybody knew Mike had money in the house.

"Like I say, he would go to work. The door would remain open. You needed something, you could go into Mike's apartment, take it, and tell him you took it. Fine. Okay.

"Somebody ripped him off one day, took all the money, left the box there. All Mike said was somebody must have needed the money more than he did, and nothing was ever done.

"I was with him when he discovered the money was gone, and I didn't even see him lose his temper. He never did anything about it. His attitude was 'that was that.' It was gone, period."

Several of the women who know Mike underline the relationship between Mike Irvine and their children. The children, in every case, adore Mike. He played with them, he helped them with their homework, and as they got older and got involved with automobiles, it was always Mike who would come over to get a stalled engine started.

Of course, keep in mind that just as 90 percent of the people in prisons "got framed" or "didn't do it," 90 percent of the friends of prisoners will tell you that Tom, Dick, or in this case Mike "couldn't possibly have done it."

But even with that, it seems that a crime of violence by Mike Irvine required a sudden and dramatic swerve from the path of life as he lived it. Mike was, everybody says, "just a country boy." The ones who don't use that phrase say "farm boy" or "good old boy." Some echo Dee's "teddy bear" description. Even Jay Novick, the state prosecutor whose job it was to convict Mike of cold-blooded murder, acknowledges that Irvine had no history of violence and says, "Mike was just a country bumpkin."

In fact, Mike Irvine *was* a country boy. He grew up in the rural outskirts of De Kalb, a small city in north-central Illinois, best known for its production of barbed wire. Until Mike was approached by Dee Casteel about a murder contract, his life, it seems, had mostly been gas stations and women.

Irma Sorrell, who married Mike twice and divorced him twice, says Mike was a nice enough fellow, but she had to get herself unhitched from him because "he liked his girlfriends." Still, Mrs. Sorrell, like the others who know Mike Irvine, cannot imagine him taking a life. Sorrell says she has never seen Mike raise a fist and can hardly remember him even raising his voice.

"I have only seen him raise his voice maybe twice to the kids" (referring to her kids by an earlier marriage. Mike had two daughters, also by an earlier marriage). "That was because they had come in after dark and he was worried and upset. He might raise his voice until he realized that it's not going to do any good, then he'd calmly sit down and talk to them and they'd understand."

Mike, by all accounts, was a nice, easy-going fellow who liked to read westerns, watch football games on television, and go fishing. Like Dee, he was the type who couldn't say no. When people asked him for a favor, he did it. Though he denies ever killing anybody, he once told Pat Swanson that he did tell Dee he could find someone who would commit the murder. This seemed pretty outrageous to Pat, and when she asked him why he had done that, he said, "Dee was a friend and she needed a favor."

There were less savory aspects of Mike, however, that were clear to Dee and others but hidden to his close friends. Mike, for example, was a dope dealer. Or at least he claimed to be. Dee knew him as somebody who was involved in occasional drug deals, and the one time he offered her the opportunity to be a mule, bringing drugs up from Key West, it was for a lot more money than she could collect in tips. The extent of Mike Irvine's involvement in selling drugs is difficult to gauge since he was the type of guy who, if he made a $2,000 deal, might try to puff up his own importance by inflating it to a $20,000 deal by the time he bought a round of drinks, or bragged about his score to the fellows down at the Amoco. In other words, Mike was a bullshit artist.

It's tempting to say that Mike was a harmless enough fellow, but obviously he wasn't. Still, the idea of Mike Irvine committing murder is tantalizing. Why would he do it?

It's unlikely that alcohol influenced Mike Irvine's decision to commit murder.

"He never touched liquor," says Pat Swanson. "I never once saw him touch alcohol. Mike drank milk. He drank about a gallon of milk a day."

It's not quite true that Mike never touched alcohol. Certainly he used to hoist a few down at the Saga, and some people say he went on a thorough bender about once a year. But that was about it. Irvine was not an alcoholic, like Dee.

So it wasn't booze that was causing Mike to sign on. Homophobia, perhaps?

According to Pat Swanson, Mike had no particular antigay feelings. "Mike believed in live and let live," she says.

The money? Mike had a job. He had the occasional dope deal. He had friends in Florida. He had relatives in Illinois. They could certainly have come up with a few thousand bucks if he needed it. So what the hell was he doing sneaking around in pancake houses, agreeing to murder people for what turned out to be relatively small change? Was he just acting out some cowboy fantasies of being a big-time criminal?

We have to assume that Mike Irvine was not exactly the man his friends describe. He must have had a dark side that they had never seen. Either that, or we are left with the more disturbing conclusion that many of us, if handed the right script and pointed in the right direction, are capable of participating in bloody murder just for the thrill of it.

5

The Gun

The day after her first late-night meeting with Mike Irvine at the Amoco station, Dee reported her conversation to Allen at the pancake house. Allen was as pleased as she had hoped he would be. "Good girl," he said, giving her a pat on the shoulder, a kiss on the cheek. He dashed upstairs to the office. A minute later he returned with a passport photo of Art Venecia.

"So it is Art," Dee said.

"Huh?"

"That you want killed."

"Well, of course, dear, who else would I want killed?"

Dee returned to the Amoco station and brought Mike the photo.

"It's the faggot's boyfriend, just like I said, isn't it?" Mike said proudly.

"Yes."

"Just as well. Save you some money."

"How's that?"

"Well, if it was a prominent individual, we'd have to charge you more."

Prominent individual, Dee thought. Mike's trying to make it sound as if he occasionally knocks off governors or cabinet members.

"We'll need half the money in advance," Mike said.

"No problem."

At a third meeting at the Amoco station she gave Mike the information that she had gotten from Allen. Art Venecia's address was 21900 Southwest 134th Avenue. Art owned two cars, the Lincoln Town Car and a 1980 Plymouth pickup truck. He usually drove the Plymouth; Allen drove the Lincoln. Art was usually drunk by eleven at night, and that would be the best time to murder him.

Though Dee had heard rumors that he was a heavy drinker, she had never seen Art Venecia drunk.

Mike Irvine said he would pass the information along to his friend.

The next morning Mike strolled into the IHOP, a big grin on his face. Wearing baggy khakis and a blue short-sleeved workshirt, he looked a lot cleaner and neater than he had in the unflattering light of the gas station at midnight. He flirted with one of the waitresses as he made his way to Dee's station on the Route 1 side of the restaurant. "Morning, Dee," he said. He slipped into a booth, gave her a wink, and ordered a cup of coffee. They made small talk for a few minutes, then Dee went to other customers. When she came back to refill Mike's coffee cup, he winked at her and flipped his napkin over as if he were flipping over the final card of a straight flush. Dee stared down at the napkin, hoping that the wink meant what she thought it meant.

On the napkin Mike had written "$1,250"—the price for the murder.

After Mike left the IHOP that morning Dee told Allen the price. Again, Allen seemed pleased with the work she had done for him. "Okay," Allen said, "tell your friend it's a go."

Dee made another late-night trip to the gas station, this time to tell Mike that Allen would pay the money. She asked Mike when the murder would happen.

"We don't give you a time until we have the upfront money," Mike told her. Though Mike had originally told Dee that a friend of his would do the murder, he had never mentioned the friend's name, and by this time he had slipped into the habit of referring to "we" and "us." Dee, for her part, had made the same mistake, always talking about "Allen and I," instead of just Allen.

Another day or two went by before Allen reappeared in the restaurant one morning.

"Let's go for a ride," he said to Dee.

It was a slow weekday morning and by this time the breakfast rush had ended. Dee was pleased that Allen wanted to be with her.

"Where are we going?"

"Fort Lauderdale," he said.

"For what?"

"Not here," Allen said. "I'll tell you outside."

"What are we, going swimming or something?"

"Not today, dear," Allen said. His fingers were tucked into the pockets of his tight jeans and his thumbs tapped nervously against his beltline. Dee sensed that whatever Allen wanted, it had something to do with Art. Allen needed her help. She asked one of the waitresses to take over for a while. Then she pulled off her apron and draped it over a chair at the back of the restaurant. Before going out the door she grabbed her pocketbook, which contained a small bottle of Scotch.

"Allen, what's this all about?" she said when they got to the parking lot.

"We're going to buy a gun," Allen said.

"A gun?"

"I've been thinking it over," he said. "Why should we pay your friend all that money? We'll do it ourselves," Allen said. "Besides, that way there'll be less people that know about it."

"What's this 'we' business?"

"I'm going to do it, dear. But I need you to go with me."

"You're crazy," Dee said. "You really are thinking of killing him."

"Well, of course, I am. What do you think, this is a game?"

"I don't know what to think."

Whatever her misgivings might have been, the fact is that Dee, still wearing her IHOP waitress uniform, and fortified with a couple of swigs of Scotch, got into the car with Allen and drove to Fort Lauderdale.

One reason Allen wanted Dee was that she had some knowledge of firearms. There had been a time when guns were a part of her life. Though it had been fifteen years since Dee had handled a gun, she knew how to fire one and how to make one safe.

They took I 95 north to Commercial Boulevard in Fort Lauderdale where they found a small gun shop located in a dilapidated strip of stores not far from the exit. Dee had consumed much of her Scotch on the drive up, and by this time the idea of shooting Art had taken on a dreamlike quality. It wasn't real, she thought, and if it was, it didn't seem like that big a deal.

At the gun shop Allen acted strangely. He moved about the store, looking down into the glass cases that housed a small armory, but he kept a certain distance, as if buying a gun were the last thing on his mind. He turned to Dee often as if she were the customer and he was the one who had gone along for the ride.

Finally, they picked out a .32-caliber pistol, a small holster, and ammunition.

Florida is notorious for gun laws that seem designed to make murder as easy as possible, but even in the Sunshine State the gun buyer is required to show some identification. In anticipation of needing his identification, Allen searched carefully in each pocket of his pants, even his shirt, but he couldn't seem to find his wallet.

"Damn it, I forgot my wallet. We'll have to come back," he said.

But when they got outside the store, Allen said, "Dee, this is silly. Why should we come back? You can buy the gun."

Though he didn't have his wallet, Allen did have the cash for the gun. He handed it to Dee, who was happy to do him a favor, and within minutes the pistol was purchased in her name.

Around eleven o'clock that night Dee was at home watching the late news when Allen called.

"Come on," he said. "Let's go out and buy a couple of bottles and learn how to shoot this thing."

This was the beginning of a pattern in which Allen would ask Dee to do something, then sweeten the pot by including alcohol.

Dee was torn. She didn't want to turn him down, but she also didn't want to ignite the ire of the ever jealous Cass. In the end Allen convinced her to tell Cass she had to work the graveyard shift at the pancake house. Dee put on some makeup and donned her waitress uniform. She stuffed some street clothes into a paper bag and rushed out, telling Cass she'd be home early in the morning. In her car, she changed into the other clothes.

Dee knew about a place called The First and Last Chance, a bar and package store that she had gotten drunk in once on the way to Key West. So she and Allen drove toward Key West.

Along the way Allen talked about Henry. He carried on like a lovesick schoolgirl. "He's the man I've been waiting all my life for," Allen told her. "We have something special. I just hope he realizes how good I am for him. God, Dee, I love him so much that it hurts sometimes." For mile after mile in the dark of Route 1 it was Henry this and Henry that. Did Henry love him or would Henry leave him? What could he do to make Henry happy, to keep Henry in his life? He talked about the house they would live in, how he would decorate it, the meals he would cook for Henry, the places they would go. He was obsessed, and after a while it got on Dee's nerves.

Though Dee was unaware of it at the time, other employees at the restaurant saw her as no less of a lovesick schoolgirl with regard to Allen. One waitress who worked there then says, "With Dee it was 'Allen this and Allen that' all the time. As far as Dee was concerned, Allen could do no wrong."

During this drive Allen confessed to Dee that his main reason for wanting to get rid of Art was so he could be with Henry. Dee, either because she'd been drinking, or because she didn't want to annoy Allen, didn't point out that Allen could be with Henry simply by moving out of Art Venecia's house. They didn't talk about Art's money in so many words, but Dee knew it was the only conceivable motive for murdering Art.

At The First and Last Chance they picked up a bottle of Scotch for Dee and a bottle of vodka for Allen. Allen, who had an ulcer, did not consume the vast quantities of liquor that Dee did, but when he drank, at least with her, it was usually vodka.

For an hour they tooled along the flat, narrow roads of the Florida Keys, guzzling alcohol from the bottles and firing the pistol out the car window. Allen drove and the two of them took turns shooting at trees and road signs. The darkness and the booze bore down on their inhibitions until the idea of shooting Art Venecia had been reduced to the level of Halloween mischief, and finally, around two A.M. Allen swung the car out onto Route 1 again, facing north. He turned to Dee and said, "I'm ready. Are you?"

Dee, now totally stoned, said that she was ready.

They drove back to The Redlands, to Art's house. This was Dee's first visit to the property. They drove up a dark and very long gravel driveway to a clearing with a small house. There were no lights glowing, and Dee could make out little except that it was brick and ordinary looking. The surrounding property was substantial and it was thick with tropical plants. Spots of moonlight seemed to dance like spirits on the ground between the shadows of trees. Allen pulled the Lincoln up next to the attached garage on the right side of the house. "Wait here," he said. He got out and walked into the house through the door on the side of the garage.

Dee, feeling the need to be free of the car, staggered out and sat on a big slab of concrete that served as a foundation for an air-conditioner handler. Inhaling the cool night air, she felt a dreamy nostalgia for the days when she used to hunt and fish and camp. Her dad used to take her camping. Later, her husband, Les, used to take her. She couldn't imagine Allen tramping in the woods doing manly things like that, but someday she would ask him if he'd like to go camping. Sadly, it seemed there had been no time for outdoor activities lately. Got to take the boys camping soon, she thought. As often happened, thoughts of the boys, Todd and Wyatt, put Dee into a maudlin mood. She had been a piss-poor mother lately and she knew it. The job. The alcohol. She was neglecting them. Wyatt was thirteen, Todd fourteen, and they needed more attention and love. She made a vow that the next time the kids wanted to go to the mall, which seemed to be their thing lately, she wouldn't just drop them off and hand them a few bucks the way she usually did. She'd go with them, play some of those crazy video games, then maybe take them bowling and show them what a bowler their mother was. She hadn't bowled much since Todd was born.

Minutes later Dee was sound asleep.

She woke up to something terrifying. In the dark some sort of big black animal had climbed on top of her. She could feel its weight and its warmth against her; she could hear its deep growl. She let out a shriek that sounded loud to her but was apparently not heard inside the house. In a moment the animal moved, and she realized it was Art Venecia's Doberman, Shadow.

"Just a damn dog," she said to herself.

If she had been sober, she might have been more afraid.

A few minutes later Allen came out of the house.

"Come on, forget it," he said. "We're not going to do it. We'll let your friend take care of it."

Dee never found out what conversation, if any, occurred in the house that night. And she's not sure who had the gun then. She thinks she did and she wonders if Allen would have shot Art if he'd gone in with the gun.

"He may or may not have gone through with it," she says. "I certainly could not have done it. But this is when I knew that this guy was not playing games. He really wanted to kill Art. I don't understand myself why I didn't just tell him to take the job and shove it, but I didn't. Back then, if Allen called and said meet me in ten minutes, I did it. It doesn't make much sense. My men were always real macho types and they never intimidated me. I never jumped for those guys. So why did I do it for Allen? Maybe it wouldn't have made any difference who it was, as long as it was the person who said I can work or I can't work. All I really cared about was my job and my bottle, and in my mind they were almost the same thing."

Shortly after the gun fiasco Allen told Dee that he couldn't go through with murdering Art on his own. He wanted to have Mike and Mike's friend do it. By now the pretense of Mike as go-between only had been dropped. It was "Mike and his friend" who would be contracted with. Sometimes Dee wondered if there really was a friend.

A couple of days later Allen gave Dee half the money, and in the middle of the night she delivered it to Mike at the gas station. Again she asked Mike for a specific date because Allen wanted to arrange an alibi for that time. Mike didn't want to give a date because he said he and his friend didn't want anybody to know when there was going to be a hit. Dee pushed the point and Mike said okay, he would come up with a date.

If this scenario were fiction, it would not work. What is the character's motivation? critics would ask. Why is she doing this? It doesn't make sense. There would seem to be a missing piece. Why would a woman who is "the nicest person you'd ever want to meet" be skulking around in gas stations at three in the morning, working out a deal to murder a man she hardly knew?

There are three possible explanations. One is that Dee was so mesmerized by Allen and so afraid of losing her job that she would do anything to please him. Another is the compelling argument that the Dade County district attorney would eventually adopt, that greed was the motivation, that Dee planned to share with Allen in the proceeds from Art Venecia's death. And the third possibility is Dee Casteel's own equally persuasive argument: she never really believed there was going to be a murder, until it was too late.

"I never thought Mike would be involved in a murder," she says. "There was always the kind of wink of an eye that said to me, 'We're not really going to do this.' One time I asked him if he was really serious. He laughed. He said, 'No, I'm not serious.' He said he was going to get a friend to go with him and all they were going to do was shake Bryant up. They were going to scare him, make him think they were going through with it, but just rip him off. There would be no killing, they would not go through with anything like that. A lot of times Mike referred to Allen as 'the little fag,' and there was always this sense of 'we're just going to rip the little fag off.' "

Was there indeed a subtext in all of this, a wink of the eye or a special tone of voice that said, "We're not really going to murder anybody?" Did it all just somehow get out of hand? There's no way to prove Dee is right or wrong, but the literature on alcoholism suggests that the answer probably lies somewhere in the middle.

In his book *Understanding the Alcoholic's Mind* (Oxford University Press, 1988), Arnold M. Ludwig, M.D., writes:

> Often the mind of the abstinent alcoholic is so devious as to come up with a number of seemingly innocuous decisions, sometimes beginning days, weeks, months, and even years in advance of a lapse, which eventually place the individual in a situation in which a return to drink becomes inevitable. Through a complicated, often intricate series of mental maneuvers, designed mainly to outwit himself—to slip his real but perhaps unconscious intentions past the gullible sentry in his mind—the individual unwittingly ensures that he will be seduced into drinking. After getting himself into a position to be tempted, the alcoholic, like Oscar Wilde, who could resist anything but temptation, inevitably succumbs. But, if he could be really honest with himself, he would recognize that his lapse was not because of bad luck or fate but because, at some level of awareness, he planned to do this all along. He was unconsciously responsible for his own downfall.

Ludwig is writing here about an alcoholic who is on the wagon, and how he might arrange to fall off without having himself to blame. But given this insight into the complex mental machinery that the alcoholic constructs, and given the fact that alcoholism is by definition a rush toward self-destruction, it takes no great leap of logic to imagine that an alcoholic like Dee would go through the same mental machinations to protect her access to the bottle, i.e., her job.

Ludwig writes:

> In a sense the alcoholic keeps tossing out banana skins which he "accidentally" manages to step on and then slip. His brain keeps coming up with ingenious booby traps and inadvertent pitfalls, arranging for the bad luck to occur. Among the scores of alcoholics I have known, I continue to be amazed at how reasonably intelligent individuals can actually believe their claims of innocence and not recognize the blatant self-rationalizations, selective perceptions, distortions of reality, denial, and self-deception in their slips.

Perhaps Dee never really believed there would be a murder, in the same way that people in Los Angeles don't believe that the smog is doing the same thing to their lungs that it's doing to the paint on their cars, or the way they don't believe that there will be a massive earthquake one day soon. They know these things to be true, but to believe them would be so upsetting and require such upheaval in their lives that they cannot accept the truth.

Whatever the perceptions, the reality was that Mike Irvine scheduled the murder of Art Venecia as easily as he would schedule a lube job and an oil change. He called Dee to tell her that the work would be done on the weekend of June eleventh and twelfth. With that, Allen Bryant arranged to be away, and Dee arranged to be drunk.

During that weekend Dee, as usual, washed her apprehensions down with Scotch. Nothing's really going to happen, she told herself. There's not really going to be a murder. There can't be. During sober moments she played Monopoly with Todd and Wyatt, but it was hard to concentrate, and her boys easily wiped out her supply of make-believe money. She was worried. She talked to Susan on the phone several times. She was tempted to tell Susan some of what was going on, but fearing Susan's disapproval, she kept her secret. On Saturday morning Dee and Cass drove to the Moose Lodge, "The Moose," as they called it. There they did what they always did there: talked, smoked cigarettes, and got drunk. On Sunday morning Dee scanned the crime news in the *Miami Herald*. There had been a murder in Hialeah, another in Opa-Locka, and two up in Broward County, but none in The Redlands.

On Monday morning she drove to work slowly, as if to push back any bad news that was coming her way. Of course they didn't actually murder Art, she thought. The whole idea was ridiculous. People don't just murder people. Murders are committed by murderers, not gas station attendants like Mike Irvine.

Still, the first several hours at work were as tense as a hurricane watch. Not knowing if tragedy waited in the wings, Dee stiffened every time the phone rang. She glanced often at the parking lot, watching for Allen. The plates of food seemed almost to rattle in her hands. Customers came and went. Was Art Venecia dead? The question tormented her and she sipped often from her glass of iced coffee laced with Scotch.

Later that morning she heard her name called and her heart nearly stopped. It was Art Venecia.

He had come in to work on the books.

"Good morning," he said when she turned around. He was dressed in his usual way, work pants, a plain shirt, and dark loafers without socks. Venecia never dressed like a man who had money.

"Good morning," she said. Nice to see you alive, she thought.

Art smiled cheerfully and it was then that Dee realized just how tense she had been. It was as if she had been coiled like a mainspring and now had popped free. There had not been a murder. Just as she had suspected, there wouldn't be a murder. After Art went upstairs to the office Dee went to her iced coffee. After this, she deserved a drink.

Shortly after noon Allen called.

"Did they do it?" he asked.

"No," she told him. "Don't come in. Art's here. I don't know what went wrong."

"Why didn't they do it?" Allen whined. He sounded like a kid who hadn't gotten the new bicycle he expected for his birthday.

"I don't know," Dee said, though it seemed obvious to her that Mike had ripped Allen off. "Call back later."

At around eleven Art was downstairs reading some numbers off the cash register tape when the phone rang. Art snatched it before Dee could get to it. It was the bank calling.

Art listened in silence for a few minutes, then he hollered, "What?" Dee stood by the kitchen counter, slowly loading her pancake orders onto a tray and eavesdropping on the conversation. "What do you mean the money wasn't there?" Art said. "Christ Almighty! How many checks have I got bouncing?"

"I could kill that son of a bitch," Art screamed after he slammed down the phone. "I could kill him." He turned to Dee. His face was red, and his temple throbbed. But in Art's eyes Dee saw not anger, but sadness. The one person Art loved had once more betrayed him, and he was terribly hurt. "Allen," he told her. "He stole the deposit money. I've got checks bouncing all over town. I'll kill him."

This incident was a long way from being the first time Allen Bryant stole from Art Venecia. Betrayal and reconciliation were the main events of their eight-year relationship. People who knew them both say that Allen was stealing from his lover off and on all through the relationship. According to one friend, Allen had even taken Art's car once, sold it, and then reported it stolen.

At noon on that Monday, Art was still smoldering

when Allen showed up at the IHOP, and the two men immediately got into a shouting match in the upstairs office. Art threatened to turn Allen in to the police. They were still at it when Dee's shift ended and she went home. She hoped this would be the fight that would finally tear them apart. That, at least, would put an end to the talk of murder.

At nine that night Dee's phone rang. It was Art. He sounded breathless.

"Dee, did Allen loan you sixteen hundred dollars?"

"Huh?"

"Did he loan you sixteen hundred dollars? He says he loaned you sixteen hundred dollars to get a divorce."

"I don't know what you're talking about," Dee said.

"Well, Allen claims he loaned you the money. He's in the hospital."

"Hospital? What for?"

"He just tried to kill me and he tried to kill himself," Art said.

6

The Lovers

Though Art Venecia was a combustible substance in the presence of Allen Bryant, he was, in the presence of others, as cool and solid as pocket change. He was an excruciatingly private man, and besides Allen, probably nobody knew him well, except his friend Ralph Anderson, who died two years before Art was murdered. But those who knew Art at all have only nice things to say about him.

"God, he was really a nice fellow," says Robert Edward. "I never heard him say anything bad about anybody."

"You couldn't have met a finer gentleman," says Vivian Andre. "There wasn't anything he wouldn't do for you."

"He was a very nice guy," says Steve Fitzgerald. "Very personable, very intelligent."

And so forth.

All of these people were friends of Art's from the South Florida Theatre Organ Society, and though they are quick to tell you what an exemplary human being

Art Venecia was, how helpful, intelligent, well mannered, and talented he was, they are also quick to add, "Of course, I didn't know him very well." The description of Art Venecia that emerges in almost every interview is "loner." He had, it seems, many acquaintances and they laughed at his jokes and happily sang along when he sat down to play the organ, but nobody loved him deeply enough or saw him often enough to take strong notice of the fact that, by the end of June 1983, Art Venecia wasn't around anymore.

Art's father, Arthur Venecia, Sr., had emigrated from Spain during the Spanish revolution. In the 1930s, Venecia Sr. established a rum distillery in Cuba. There he met his wife, Bessie, and they moved to St. Petersburg, where Venecia Sr. started another distillery. Arthur Jr. grew up in St. Petersburg. He was a quiet kid, and his great-aunts, with whom he spent several summers in North Carolina, remember him mostly for his music. Arthur, it seemed, was always blowing into a recorder, rapping on a drum, strumming a guitar, or tapping out a tune on some keyboard or other.

By the time he entered the University of Miami in Coral Gables, where he eventually acquired a degree in electrical engineering, Venecia was able to make a small living playing the piano in cocktail lounges and gay bars. He was, apparently, a more social creature then than he would be during the Allen Bryant years. He had his share of romances, and photos of his life then often show Venecia surrounded by friends. To some people he was an odd-looking character; one friend describes him as "Ichabod Crane–like" because of his thin body and obtrusive Adam's apple. But most of the people who knew Art describe him as an attractive man.

Art's homosexuality remained for the most part private. There was nothing limp-wristed about him, and nobody describes him as effeminate. He stayed in the closet for most people most of the time, and when he did trust an acquaintance enough to open the door and reveal his homosexuality, it almost always came as a surprise. His homosexuality, along with the fact that he didn't work in the engineering field for which he had been educated, became sources of conflict between Art and his mother, Bessie. Bessie, like many mothers, could not believe that a son of hers was gay, and she was inclined to show up unannounced at Art's door, with a marriageable female on her arm.

For a few years Art worked as a salesman for the National Cash Register Company, and later for Burroughs, but still he had the soul of a loner and in time it led him to more entrepreneurial enterprises. He got into real estate, both as a buyer and as an agent. He worked, successfully but unhappily, for a real estate agent for a while and then went on his own. In Hialeah he invested in residential property. And in south Dade County he invested in strip stores, those unimaginative one-storied stone cubes that house, it sometimes seems, about half the retail establishments south of Jacksonville.

According to Art's cousin James Campbell, the accumulation of money only made Art more of a loner.

"He never got very close to people because he didn't want anyone to know that he had money," Campbell says.

Art Venecia was never Bar Harbor or Palm Beach wealthy, but he did well for himself. By the mid-1970s, he owned a beautiful house in Coconut Grove and had stocks and bonds. He was able to live a relatively relaxed lifestyle.

In 1975, when Venecia was thirty-three, he met a young man from the small town of Goshen, Virginia, a slim and effeminate eighteen-year-old who was by turns charming and temperamental. The young man was James Allen Bryant. The two men got together for quiet dinners, and in time Venecia invited Allen to move in with him. Venecia, rebounding from a long romance, perhaps saw in Allen not just a desirable sexual partner and companion, but a project. Maybe from the clay of youthful innocence he could mold something of value. Certainly, it appears, Bryant was in need of a good influence. "He was taking a lot of pills," says one friend. "He was a troubled kid and Art took him in, thinking he could help."

Allen Bryant had come to Miami to visit an aunt. A good-looking kid with angular features and shining eyes that were both mesmerizing and troubling, he was a soft-spoken young man with genteel southern manners, often using the formal "Mr." or "Mrs." even for people he knew quite well. Bryant's parents had gotten divorced when he was young, and he and his two older sisters grew up with a variety of relatives. His childhood, he says, was "normal. We did the things that kids did."

Bryant, by his own assessment, matured early.

"I was never one who played with toys or read comic books," he says. "I always channeled my energies into more mature things. I had an aunt who was sickly and I spent a lot of time with her, doing the cooking and the housekeeping for her."

Allen's uncle owned a small restaurant, where Allen worked making sandwiches, and it was there that he developed his love for the restaurant business.

As for the alleged drug problem, Allen says it's not true.

"I have never had a drug or alcohol problem," he says. "Oh, sure, just like everybody else, I've smoked a reefer, and I've done a little cocaine and taken a Quaalude, but I've never had a problem with drugs."

The pairing with a younger man made Venecia not more sociable, but less so. During their years together Art and Allen went to occasional parties but had few houseguests.

Art was not intimate with many people, but neither was he a hermit, and there were significant parts of his life that did not involve Allen. The center of Art Venecia's social life was the South Florida Theatre Organ Society. The group, dedicated to preserving theater organs in their original installation, was formed in 1968, and Art Venecia was there, says one member, "right from the very beginning."

For years the group's major project was the restoration of the irreplaceable Wurlitzer pipe organ at the Gusman Cultural Center in downtown Miami. That organ had been installed in the theater, then a movie palace called the Olympia, in 1925. Like many such organs, its prominence was eclipsed by the arrival of talking pictures in 1929, and over the years leaky roofs, pests, old age, and neglect took their toll.

Venecia had a deep, palpable love for such instruments, and he was prominent among the forty people who stripped and varnished the instrument, replaced air-driven parts with transistors and diodes, removed and cleaned the organ's 1,035 pipes, laid cable, and in all, put 100,000 man-hours into the restoration. It was a project in which he took enormous pride, and one which gave some balance to his life. While Allen Bryant was a fiery and reckless ingrate who often threw Art's love back in his face, the old Wurlitzer was manageable; it improved with loving care and attention.

The people who worked beside Art on those evenings and those long weekends down at Gusman Hall liked and respected him. He joined in at buffets, concerts, and parties. Even to some of those who call him a loner, he seemed often witty, gregarious, and well stocked with friends. "I remember how he would come and help us clean and help us set up chairs and tables," Vivian Andre says. "He was a very busy man but he would always come by and ask if we needed any help. And oh, such talent. He and Ralph Anderson were such gifted men. They would sit at the organ for hours and hours with no sheet music and they would play tune after tune. They knew all the old show tunes, and you could sit and listen to them and people would enjoy it so much." In 1977, Venecia was elected president of the society.

Occasionally Art brought Allen Bryant to the society's social events, and Allen recalls going to theater organ conventions in Chicago and other cities. But none of the society's members have strong memories of Allen, except as a "younger man who didn't say much."

Reid Welch, another friend from the organ society, remembers, "Once Art brought Allen to a party at my house. It was strange. No matter where I went in the room Allen would turn his head the other way and kind of cover his face with his hand, as if I might recognize him from someplace and he didn't want to be spotted."

During their early years together they lived in the big house in Coconut Grove. Art sold real estate, Allen worked in restaurants. For five years they went together to Venecia's AA meetings. Like Dee, Art Venecia was an alcoholic.

"Sometimes he would drink all day," Allen says. "But he was never mean or nasty. When Art drank, he was too sweet, he couldn't say enough nice things about you."

Also during these years, Allen encouraged a reconciliation between Art and his mother, who by this time had been estranged for five years.

"It was me that got the two of them together again," Allen says proudly. "I grew up in a small town with strong family ties and it didn't seem right, a mother and son not talking to each other."

By 1981, Art had grown tired of the house in Coconut Grove and disgusted with the high taxes on it. The two men decided to move.

"We were just driving through The Redlands one day," Bryant says, "and I saw this piece of property for sale. It was five acres, just woods, not even a road onto it. It was so dense you couldn't even walk in it, but I knew it would be perfect. Art wanted to raise orchids and plants, so we bought it."

The Redlands, which gets its name from the red

clay in the soil, is a fascinating area in south Dade County. If you come down Route 1 and take a right turn anywhere south of Perrine, in less than a minute you will feel as if you've been transported from urban glut to rural Georgia. The Redlands, stretching all the way to the Everglades National Park, is farmland. Avocados, citrus fruits, corn, beans, mangoes, and other crops stretch for dozens of square miles, with not a motel or a fast-food chain in sight. This area is one of the world's biggest suppliers of indoor and outdoor plants, including everything from Christmas poinsettias to the palm trees that surround restaurants and hotels all over the world.

Though there are several big operations and packing houses in The Redlands, most of the area's ten thousand or so residents own five or ten acres of property, and many of them run plant nurseries. The property that Allen had spotted was five acres of undeveloped land, lush as a rain forest, crowded with Dade County palms, palmetto, and pine trees.

"It was all overgrown," Allen says. "We had to get a bulldozer just to make a road for us to get into the property."

Art, who had designed the house in Coconut Grove, now designed a small guesthouse, in which he and Allen would live until they were sure they wanted to stay in The Redlands. Then they would build a bigger house. The house, which they hired a friend to build, was plain and small. A red-brick building, one story, it had a long bedroom on one end, a large middle room that sectioned into a dining room and a living room, and an attached garage. There was also a small kitchen, and a Florida room that stretched the length of the house at the back. It was no bigger than an apartment really, and Art filled it with the heavy, masculine furniture that he favored. The house, surrounded by five acres of property, situated far from the road, and hidden on all sides by pine trees and palms, was the perfect place for a murder.

Art named his place Pine Acres Nursery. With Allen's help he hacked away at the relentless brush that encroached from the edges of the property on all sides. He cut down trees, pulled out stumps, cleared the interior, and put up three greenhouses. There he grew his orchids as a hobby, and indoor foliage plants that he sold to a wholesaler. At the front of the property, but still hidden from the road, he built a metal barn that looked as if it could be a hangar for small aircraft. This was to house the parts for an enormous theater organ that he had bought, and that someday he hoped to reconstruct and play for friends.

Life, perhaps, was looking good to Art right about then. He had his house in the country, his orchids, his organ. And if his young lover seemed a bit lost, well, that could be remedied. Art bought the Naranja International House of Pancakes franchise, a ten-minute drive from The Redlands house, and turned it over to Allen to manage.

If Allen Bryant and Arthur Venecia's social life was a bit dull, their sex life, apparently, was adventuresome.

Warren Woods, who lived on the property behind Venecia's, tells this story:

"Art had cleared some junk on his property and pushed it onto mine. So I had a bulldozer out there pushing the stuff back one evening. Had a big redneck fellow driving the dozer. So Allen comes out to see what we're up to. He comes walking up to the bulldozer and says, 'What do you think you're doing?' Then he just stood there watching. He was wearing a black dress and black high heels. The redneck looks at me and he says, 'Should I shoot him or run him over or what? He's making me nervous.' "

Some IHOP waitresses report that Allen occasionally showed up at the restaurant in drag.

"I hate to say this," one of them says, "but when Allen put on his wig and dress and high heels and everything, he made a beautiful woman. I'm sorry, but he did. You couldn't tell Allen was a man. He talked just like a woman. He'd come in the restaurant all gussied up and his own customers wouldn't know him."

As Allen Bryant tells it, he never had a homosexual experience until he met Art Venecia. Maybe. Perhaps Allen was an innocent from Goshen, Virginia. Or perhaps he was, in the parlance of the homicide police who would later arrest him, "a chicken." That is, an attractive young homosexual who was sexually and romantically available to older men in exchange for material goodies. Certainly he was selfish and he was demanding. It's a harsh assessment, yet nobody who knows Allen contradicts it.

If "loner" is the word most commonly applied to Art Venecia, the one most frequently employed to describe James Allen Bryant is "liar." In fact, more than one person who knows him feels "pathological liar" is even more accurate.

"Pathological liar" is a precise psychiatric term. A pathological liar is compulsive about lying or telling tall tales even when there is no advantage that can be achieved. Such compulsive lying is found among alcoholics, swindlers, impostors, con men, and others who sometimes do not seem to feel or understand the nature of a lie.

Only a professional could determine whether or not the term "pathological liar" can correctly be applied to Allen Bryant, but the fact that so many of his acquaintances think it fits him well says a good deal about the young man.

"I reckon Allen was a pathological liar;" says Anne Chepsiuk, an IHOP waitress. "Let me put it this way. If everybody in Miami got a piece of rug every time Allen told a lie, nobody would need to buy any rugs."

State prosecutor Jay Novick puts it this way: "If James Allen Bryant told me it was three o'clock and I looked at my watch and it said three o'clock, I'd think my watch was broken."

Others put it less colorfully, but just as forcefully.

"Liar," "damn liar," "goddamn liar," "two-faced liar," and "lying son of a bitch" are frequent answers to the question "How would you describe Allen Bryant?" The cook Jim Garfield, when asked what he remembers about Allen, says, "Only that he was an asshole," then quickly adds, "and a liar, of course."

None of which is to say that Allen Bryant was universally disliked. Not at all. Allen Bryant was a young man of considerable charm and persuasiveness, a fellow who might have made quite a name for himself in the used-car business or the insurance industry. "He could sell you anything," says waitress Joanne Rivera. At times he could be as slick and sweet as pancake syrup, and the people in his life, particularly the women, lapped it up. The waitresses who worked for Allen adored him.

"Some of these girls worked for Allen a long time," says Gail Mincer, another IHOP waitress. "Jackie, Brenda, Cheryl. Many of them would have walked through fire for Allen. Allen loved Cheryl and her little girl. Allen was great with kids, and if Cheryl had nobody to take care of her little girl, Allen would always be there. 'I'll baby-sit,' he'd say. These gals saw Allen at his best and they saw him at his worst, but his best far outweighed his worst."

Even Jim Garfield, while he recognizes Allen's faults, says, "I always liked Allen. He always treated me well."

The people who speak well of Allen and the people who don't all admire his abilities in the restaurant. Dee Casteel says, "Sometimes when it was busy at the restaurant and the kitchen was all bogged down and the cooks couldn't keep up with the orders, Allen would come in there for a half an hour and he would have every order turned out, every customer served.

He was a whiz in the kitchen and he was a wonderful waiter. He could have succeeded at anything, and he could certainly turn on the charm."

Allen Bryant was, to say the least, a young man who stirred up conflicting feelings, and nowhere was that more apparent than in his relationship with Art Venecia. From the beginning their affair was as charged as a frayed high-tension wire. Allen was drawn by the comfort, the stability, the love, and he was repelled by the paternalism, the commitment, the fidelity. Allen and Venecia fell into a familiar pattern for unhealthy individuals. Allen would somehow betray Art's trust. Allen and Art would fight. Allen would leave Art. Allen, unable to manage his life in the style he was fond of, would make himself available for reconciliation. Art, as grateful as a puppy, would take Allen back and buy him nice things. Allen would get bored with Art, perhaps have an affair. It seems fair to say that if Art were blameless and emotionally healthy, this pattern would not have continued. It takes two sick people to carry on a sick relationship. Art was apparently a man who, to use the phrase made famous by author Robin Norwood, "loved too much." He was forever buying Allen things, trying to get his loyalty, and Allen was forever betraying him.

7

The Motel

If the love affair between James Allen Bryant and Arthur Venecia is a drama of turbulence and trauma, then the penultimate scene was played out on the night of Monday, June 13, 1983, the night that Art called Dee and told her that Allen was in the hospital.

Earlier that evening Kenny Baldwin, a Princeton fireman assigned to the rescue squad, had responded to a call from a kid who worked for Art at the nursery.

"I went out," Baldwin recalls, "and Mr. Venecia was on the road waiting for us, all disturbed. He had red marks on his neck and he said this guy Allen had tried to kill him. He just had on a pair of shorts and tennis shoes. I said, 'Why did he do it?' and Venecia said, 'Well, he's been stealing money for years out of my restaurant.' I said, 'Where's Allen now?' and he said, 'He's locked himself in the house.' So I'm a fireman, we're not into breaking down doors when there's no fire, so I call the cops. The cops came and they talked to Allen through the door, and finally he let them in and he said he had taken a bunch of pills.

He was crying. He had on a nice outfit, nice shirt, nice slacks, he was pretty sharp looking. We figured these guys were lovers. The cops had to talk baby talk to Allen to get him to tell what pills he had taken. 'Come on, Allen,' they teased, 'now tell us what pills you took,' and like that. Allen was real mad, real upset about the way things didn't turn out, and having all the cops and firemen around.

"The thing that struck me, though, was we're putting this guy Allen in the ambulance, and his lover, Venecia, the guy Allen had just tried to kill, was all worried about him. 'Why are you taking him to the hospital,' he says. 'Well, because he took a bunch of pills and we don't know what he took.' 'Where will you take him? Will he be okay?' He was really concerned about Allen."

It was later that night that Art called Dee to ask if Allen had lent her $1,600. Art also told her that Allen had tried to kill himself.

"And he said he loaned me sixteen hundred dollars?" Dee said.

"Yes."

"Wait a minute," Dee said. "Calm down. I don't want to get in the middle of this. I'll meet you at the restaurant."

After she hung up the phone she looked in on the boys, then wrote a short note for Cass, in case he should rise from his stupor.

Suicide. Poor Allen, Dee thought. She knew he was high-strung sometimes, but suicide? Why would he want to kill himself when he had Henry to live for? She remembered that the bottle of Scotch she kept in the car was empty, so she grabbed one from the house, took a quick swallow, and tucked it into her pocketbook.

When she got out on Route 1 a layer of clouds screened out the moonlight, and the highway was slick with late-night rain. Dee had sense enough to stay in the right lane and drive slowly, knowing that if the rain caused an accident, the alcohol on her breath would still get the blame. Damn Allen, she thought. She wished she didn't care so much about him. He was a good friend, but why couldn't he just leave her out of it? He must have used some of the stolen money for his payment to Mike. The worn-out windshield wipers scraped back and forth, but the road in front of her remained as murky as everything else in her life.

When she got to the restaurant, Art was already there. Wearing loose slacks, loafers with no socks, and a blue denim shirt that was misbuttoned, he looked as if he'd been rushed out of a burning building in the middle of the night. He looked frightened, wide-eyed and vulnerable, like a small woods creature caught in the glare of a headlight.

Art's hands moved frantically through the air as he stood by the kitchen counter talking to the night cook and Donna Hobson, the only waitress on duty.

Donna remembers well her conversation with Art that night.

"He came in and said he needed to talk to me. He'd had a fight with Allen and he wanted me to take over as manager. I said I didn't want to, I couldn't make as much as manager as I could working the floor. He said, 'I really need your help, I've had Allen arrested.' And the last thing he said to me was, 'I'm afraid of him.' "

When Dee came into the restaurant Art was telling both Donna and the cook, "Allen is fired. He is not to enter this building again, and if he does, don't let him near the cash register." He spoke firmly, poking at the air for emphasis. This time it's really over between them, Dee thought.

Art led Dee to a table at the back of the restaurant, near the rest rooms.

"After all I've done for him, I can't believe the way he treats me," Art said, shaking his head. Dee noticed then that Art had scratches on his neck and a bruise on one cheek. They sat down. Dee wished she could pull the bottle out of her pocketbook and pour herself a drink. Where does this leave me? she wondered.

"So Allen is out as manager," she said. She knew what it meant. One implicit bonus for her conspiracy with Allen had been that she could now drink on the job as long as she did it discreetly. With Allen gone that all-important privilege would surely be lost.

"He's out as everything," Art said. "He's out of my life. God knows, I've loved that boy and tried to do everything for him. I don't know why he doesn't love me. I've given him everything. But no more. I'm giving up."

Though Dee had never felt close to Art, had in fact thought of him as distant and uncommunicative, she reached across the table now and awkwardly patted his arm. She was touched by his sadness. She had lost at love a few times herself.

"What's this about sixteen hundred dollars?" she asked.

"He stole sixteen hundred dollars," Art said. "He took it out of the receipts. That's why I've got rubber checks bouncing all over Dade County."

"He admitted it?" Dee asked.

"Oh, he lied and lied at first. Then he finally admitted taking the money, but said it was to help you. He said you were his best friend."

"He said that?"

"Yes. He said you needed the money for a divorce. But it's not true, is it?"

"No," Dee said. "I mean, the divorce part is true. I definitely need a divorce. But no, Allen didn't lend me any money." She felt as if she were betraying Allen, but it was his own fault. He should have cleared the story with her first.

"I didn't really think so," Art said. "He's such a liar. So we fought. He tried to choke me."

"Choke you?"

"Yes, he had his hands around my throat. And he

was squeezing. He would have killed me, I swear it. I was scared to death. He said he hated me. I punched him. He slapped me and clawed at my face. It was awful. We were spitting and kicking and screaming at each other. I don't know what would have happened if Barry hadn't called the police.

"When Allen saw the police cruiser pull up in front of the house, he ran into the bathroom and swallowed everything in the medicine cabinet," Art said.

"Do you think he really wanted to die?" Dee asked.

"Who knows? He gets so hysterical."

She wanted to go to Allen. She wanted to take care of him.

Art told Dee that Allen had been taken to Coral Reef General Hospital, where they pumped his stomach, and then he had been transferred to Community Health Institute on 216th Street.

Before leaving that night, Art emptied the cash register and reminded Dee, Donna, and the cook that Allen was no longer the restaurant manager. After he was gone Dee felt as if she'd just watched the final episode of the long-running soap opera that had become so much a part of her life.

She stayed at the restaurant for another hour or so drinking coffee and smoking cigarettes like one of those loiterers who sometimes came in off the street with no more than the price of coffee. Then she drove to the Amoco station, where she found Mike Irvine stretched out on a dolly under someone's Cadillac. She told him that the murder was off. "Just as well," Mike said. "Allen sounds like a fucking loony." Besides, Mike told her, he and his friend had gone out to do the murder, but his friend had gotten scared and wanted to put it off for a while.

Driving home, Dee felt relieved. Maybe now, she thought, she could give up drinking.

At ten o'clock the following morning, Tuesday the

fourteenth, Dee was saying good-bye to one of her regular customers when the phone by the cash register rang. It was Allen. He told her he had checked himself out of CHI and into the Naranja Lakes Motel, just a few miles from IHOP. He told Dee that he needed to talk to her and asked her to come to the motel with a toothbrush and deodorant, and a few other grooming supplies. Also, he told her to pick up a bottle of vodka for him and a bottle of Scotch for herself.

Despite everything, Dee was pleased that Allen was turning to her, and when her shift was over, like a dutiful wife she drove to the nearest Eckerd's and bought the things Allen had asked for. Later that afternoon Dee arrived at the motel with a paper sack full of grooming supplies, and another bag containing the two bottles of booze.

Allen was frantic. In his eyes there was a reckless quality, a wildness that frightened Dee. Jesus, she thought, he really is a mental case.

"Did they kill him?" Allen demanded to know as Dee laid her bags down on one of the twin beds. "Did they kill him?" He paced tigerlike across the worn carpet of the small motel room.

"No," Dee said. "I got the things you asked for."

She started pulling items out of her bag, hoping to please him. "See, I brought you soap, too. And shaving cream."

"Why not?" Allen screamed. He was furious. "Why didn't they kill him? I paid for it."

"Mike's friend wanted to postpone it for a couple of days," she said. "But now it's off permanently."

"Permanently?"

"I told Mike to call it off."

"You did what?" Allen screamed.

"I called it off."

"Are you crazy? How could you do this to me?"

"I don't understand," Dee said.

"You're supposed to be my friend," Allen said. "How could you stab me in the back like this?"

"But I talked to Art," Dee said. "You and Art are divorced. I wish it was that simple for me. You and Henry can live together now."

"On what?" Allen asked her, his hysteria mounting. "You think I want to work as a waiter at some HoJo's on the Florida Turnpike? How could you do this to me? You had no right. It wasn't your money. You had no right to stop it."

"I didn't know what else to do," Dee said. She told him about her conversation with Art.

"Oh, great," Allen said, no longer shouting. "Just believe everything Art tells you. Don't listen to me, I'm just your friend, that's all."

"I thought I was doing the right thing," Dee said. "I was trying to be a good friend."

Allen looked exasperated. "If you want to know the truth, we didn't fight just over money. We fought over the fact that I was going to leave him. He said he was going to tell my mother that I'm gay."

"Well, what's the difference now? It's over, isn't it?"

"What is?"

"You and Art?"

"Of course it's not over," Allen said. "We've had dozens of fights. This doesn't mean anything."

"It doesn't mean anything that you tried to kill him?"

"Not a thing, dear," Allen said. "Not a thing." He waved a hand at her as if he were flirting and Dee smiled. Finally, he was calming down.

In the bathroom Dee found two plastic cups. She poured vodka for Allen and Scotch for herself. The alcohol felt good going down. She liked the smell of it, the taste of it. But mostly she liked the fact that it made her feel as if her life were under control.

The vodka seemed to agree with Allen, too, and soon his more personable side rose to the surface. Before long they were talking about things down at the restaurant, as if Allen had been gone for weeks and Dee were filling him in on the latest gossip.

"Okay, okay, everything will work out fine," Allen said when the glass was empty. He tipped the vodka bottle into his glass for the second time. "We'll offer them more money."

"Who?"

"Mike and his friend," Allen said. "We'll offer them whatever they want. It will be worth it."

Perhaps Dee wanted to say "*you'll* offer them more money." Perhaps she was uncomfortable with this "we" business, as she says. Perhaps she just said nothing because she didn't want to reignite Allen's temper. Perhaps a lot of things—but certainly the result of this turn in the conversation was that the murder of Art Venecia . . . or the rip-off, if that's how Dee imagined it . . . was suddenly back on the front burner.

"But it's got to be done right away," Allen said.

As more and more booze leaked into his bloodstream, Allen became more and more mellow. He talked, as Dee knew he would, about Henry. Things would be great as soon as he and Henry could live together. Art was a bore, Allen said. Art never wanted to go out. Art never wanted to do anything except play his organ and pot plants in his greenhouse.

"He wants too much from me," Allen said. "I mean, I can put in twelve or fourteen hours at the restaurant and that's all well and fine, I'm running the business. But then it's 'Where are you? I want more time with you.' I mean, God, there's just so many hours in the day."

But Henry was great, Allen said. Henry loved to party. Henry and he could do things together.

"But we have to kill Art," he told Dee. "We have to kill him so that I can support Henry the way I want to. I want to buy him things. I want to take care of my man."

There was no phone in the motel room, so at

eleven-thirty P.M. Dee and Allen, both slightly drunk, walked out to the pay phone in the parking lot. Dee dialed Mike Irvine's number at the gas station. She said hello to Mike, then turned the phone over to Allen. Though Mike and Allen had seen each other at the pancake house, they had never been introduced before.

Allen started by telling Mike that he didn't care what the job cost, it had to be done. He would pay $5,000, but he wanted it done right away. Mike said he'd have to talk to his friend. He told Allen to call back at three A.M.

Dee and Allen went back to the room where they drank and talked. They cranked open the jalousie windows. The sounds of traffic out on Route 1 mingled with the buzz of bird and insect life in the trees nearby, and soon the night became one of those pale and dreamlike moments that we all have a few of, when two well-lubricated souls begin to mesh, to swap secrets, to admit fears, to suspect that they understand about each other things that the rest of the world does not. Allen told Dee that he was afraid of Henry's ex-boyfriend, a fiery-tempered Latin who had sworn to castrate Allen with a switchblade for poaching his lover. "Poaching," Allen said, trying to laugh off his fears, "that's what he calls it. It's one of about ten English words that he knows, poaching." Dee told Allen that once when her husband was hospitalized, and out of work for a year, she embezzled $15,000 from her employer to pay the bills. She'd gotten caught and fired. It was the last secretarial job she'd ever had, and she had worked in nothing but bars and restaurants ever since. "Up to then I always had good jobs," she said. "If it hadn't been for that one mistake, who knows what I might have become." Then she told Allen about her lifelong dream of becoming a police officer, and they both found that amusing.

At three o'clock, now thoroughly loaded with Scotch and vodka, and feeling like fast friends, the two again walked out to the pay phone and called the Amoco station. Mike Irvine had talked to his friend, and they had agreed to the $5,000 price. But they couldn't fit the job in right away, Mike said. It would have to wait until the following weekend. Allen agreed.

There was one more condition. They wanted Allen to go with them.

"But I can't do that," Allen said.

"You have to. It's part of the deal."

Allen put his hand over the phone and tried to convince Dee to go also. Dee refused. Finally, Allen told Dee that he would agree to go, but that he wanted Dee at the restaurant that night, to call the police in case he didn't come back. Dee agreed, though even in her drunkenness she could see what an absurd idea it was. What was she going to do, call the police and say, I'm worried about my friend, he went out to do a murder and he hasn't come back?

"Okay, I'll go with you," Allen told Mike, and the murder was on again.

By this time Dee was too drunk to drive. She called Cass and told him she would be spending the night at the motel with Allen. She and Allen went back to the room, where they passed out on separate beds.

At six on Wednesday morning, with less than three hours' sleep, Dee was shaken from her dreams by the sound of pounding on the motel door.

"Dee, let me the Christ in there." It was Cass. "I want to know what's going on!"

Allen, perhaps thinking that Henry's switchblade-wielding ex had tracked him down, leaped from his bed and dashed into the bathroom.

Dee opened the door to the room. Cass stormed in. He was fuming.

"Who are you with, goddamn it. You're with a man in here. I know it. Where is he?"

"I told you who I'm with. It's Allen, for Christ sake."

"Allen, huh?"

"Yes, Allen. Now why don't you get the hell out of here? You probably woke up half the motel."

"Where is he?" Cass demanded.

"He's in the bathroom."

"He is, huh?" Cass said. "Well, I'm staying right here until that door opens, and there had better be a faggot in there or there's going to be hell to pay."

Allen finally came out, smiled sheepishly, and said, "Hi, Cass, how you doing?" The emergency was over.

Cass left. Dee called IHOP and said she'd be late for work. She drove Allen back to CHI because Allen didn't want Art to know he had checked out. Then Dee called Susan and gave her the gossip about the Venecia-Bryant fight. She was tempted to tell her little girl about the phone calls to Mike Irvine also, perhaps hoping that Susan would make her call the whole thing off. But in the end, not wanting to risk Susan's disapproval, Dee said nothing.

Incredibly, but not surprisingly, by noon Art Venecia had picked up Allen at the hospital, forgiven him, told him he loved him, reinstated him as manager of the IHOP, and welcomed him back into his life, his home, and his bed. It had barely been forty-eight hours since Art had gotten the call from the bank. Art didn't know it, of course, but he had just forgiven Allen one time too often, and it would cost him his life. In fact, the only reason Art wasn't already dead was because a man named Bill Rhodes had, in his own words, "chickenshitted out."

8

The Joker

The man Mike Irvine had enlisted as an accomplice was Bill Rhodes, also called Joker, a nickname he picked up while playing seven-card stud with his Air Force friends in South Vietnam. Rhodes, who liked to spell his name Bil, with one "l," was not the sort of man you'd want to share an elevator with. While it's tough to figure Dee Casteel and Mike Irvine into a murder scenario, the idea of Bill Rhodes committing murder goes down very easily. In fact, at one point in the negotiations, Mike Irvine told Dee, "My friend has done twenty-five murders." Dee believed that Irvine was simply trying to impress her with his connection to such a dangerous character. Probably she was right, for Rhodes certainly didn't act like an experienced killer when he and Mike headed off to murder Venecia the first time.

"I got nervous and I shitted out," he says. "I told Mike to turn around."

Nonetheless, Rhodes was, to some people, a chilling presence. Small and muscular, Rhodes at thirty-four had a police record and he also had a razor knife that he kept tucked into his pants. Rhodes worked part-time at the Amoco station with Mike. He lived across the street in Webster's used-car lot where, ironically, he had been given use of a camper in exchange for being in the lot at night to protect it from criminals. Rhodes, who had done four years in the Air Force, had also done time in prison in Decatur, Illinois, for breaking into a bar and stealing everything in sight.

Rhodes was a Christian. He grew up in a rural area near Springfield, Illinois, where family life for him and his six brothers and sisters centered around Our Redeemer Lutheran Church. He lived in a home that emphasized good Christian values and forbade smoking, drinking, and cursing, but did allow child abuse.

"Bill was the first born," says his sister Sally Hicks, now of Indiana, "and he was always expected to be perfect. He was beaten severely and thrown down stairs many times for doing nothing at all. Bill was never a bad kid. He was kind and sensitive, but he took a lot of beatings. He was always trying to be the best in Mom and Dad's eyes, but he could never be perfect, the way they wanted."

Even as a child Bill loved engines. "He was always interested in cars and motorcycles," Hicks says. "Anything that had a motor, he would tinker with it." Bill, according to his sister, had a normal enough adolescence. He liked Jimi Hendrix and the Beach Boys. He liked to ride horses. He loved automobiles. And he stayed out of trouble. Sally Hicks remembers well the day that Bill came to her high school to tell her he had enlisted in the Air Force. Until then she had never seen anything dark or violent in her brother, and she thinks the Vietnam experience drastically changed Bill.

"Bill's friend Rick also went to Vietnam. He was killed there. When Bill came back from Vietnam, he was different, moody. He wasn't mean or bad, never, but he was different. I can't explain it. But even before Vietnam, Bill often said he wanted to be a loner. I never understood it. He had friends. Everybody liked Bill."

Bill got a job as a mechanic. He married his longtime sweetheart, who had waited for him while he was in Nam. They lived in Laredo, Texas, for a while, had a son, then they got divorced. Bill got on drugs. "Snorting," his sister says, "whatever snorting is."

While Sally was the closest to Bill, and still believes in his goodness and innocence, his other siblings have a less sympathetic view. Over the years he has been a burden and an embarrassment.

"He did a robbery in Springfield," his sister Paula says. "It was at a bar. The Platter. He ran then and he was gone for about two years before they caught up with him. He ran because he had broken into the place and the guy had tacked on every bit of damage whether Bill did it or not. Mother said if I loaned Bill money, she'd disown me. I had done enough for him, because there was a previous time when he was in the Decatur Correctional Center, he had a work-release program and he stayed with us. We went in debt trying to help him out. We thought he was sincere."

After getting out of jail for the bar robbery, Bill drifted from state to state, job to job. He ended up in Dade County, Florida. By the time Mike Irvine met him, Rhodes was working in a junkyard and doing whatever mechanic work he could get.

From his years in Florida there emerges a picture of Bill Rhodes, not as some stone-hearted killer, but as a friendly, often sensitive man, who must have been deeply troubled.

"I waited on Bill several times at places where I worked," Donna Hobson says. "At Sambo's and IHOP. I never got the impression that there was anything evil about him. Bill was short, lot of hair, dirty blond, kind of a baby face, a quiet man. I would never have thought of him as a psycho."

Nor would Eve Merino, perhaps Bill's closest friend in Florida. During the time of the trial Merino wrote a letter to the judge, in which she said, "I've known Bill for many years, and for a large part of that time he lived in our home as part of our family and as a very real part of it. He was there for all of us. My Sandra (Merino's adopted, retarded daughter) is slow but she knows much about love, and a lot of that love is for Bill because he always made her feel that she can contribute much to society even though she is handicapped. Sandra doesn't trust everyone. Before she came to us thirteen years ago she met many bad people who used and abused her, but she recognized a quality in Bill that she trusted implicitly and still does. She refuses to believe anything negative about him.

"I have a sister ninety-three years old who also cares for Bill. He used to treat her like someone so special and with such loving attention. Bill has always had the ultimate respect for women. I'm not saying that Bill is a Boy Scout, but he is not a vicious killer. I know a boy who was into cocaine badly, and even though Bill was trying to kick his own habit, he tried very hard to help this boy. He convinced him to go to Christian Retreat in Bradenton, Florida, where the boy quit drugs completely.

"I'm not saying Bill is an angel but he has good qualities. He has always worked very hard, was never a bum, and always had a job. As for me, he treated me like a thoughtful son would treat his mother. He was a joy to have in my home and I love him as I do my own children.

"I talked to him once about his childhood and he said he must have been a rotten kid, for one of his parents to beat him so much, and he always felt he must have deserved it. All of this left Bill with feelings of low self-esteem."

In more technical terms, Bill Rhodes suffers from an "inadequate personality development syndrome," according to Dr. Jethro Toomer, a psychologist who was assigned to evaluate Rhodes.

Toomer says that Rhodes suffers from the syndrome "as a result of his life experiences. It means that as a result of certain trauma experienced early on, the individual does not develop the necessary controls in terms of making decisions relative to right and wrong."

Toomer, apparently, is saying that Bill is nuts as a result of getting beaten and thrown down stairs at an early age by people who were supposed to love him. Perhaps if Bill had been treated more kindly as a kid, Art Venecia would still be alive. Perhaps not.

9

The Realization

On Wednesday, June 15, Allen handed Dee an envelope containing $2,500, half of the new contract price of $5,000. (Apparently, because the earlier contract had been canceled, the advance payment was forfeited like a nonrefundable airline-ticket deposit.)

That night when Dee delivered the $2,500 to Mike Irvine, he reminded her that Allen would be expected to go on the hit.

"Why do you want him to go?" she asked.

"Me and my friend want him along for the ride. It will give us an edge," Mike said knowingly, as if he'd done this sort of thing a dozen times. "He knows the house. He can get us in without problems."

Dee thought she detected the familiar wink of the eye, the quote marks in the tone of voice, and from this she again got the assurance she needed that this was no murder in the making. It was a rip-off, pure and simple.

Yes, she thought as she drove home that night, it was all so clear. Mike and his friend want Allen along because they probably think he'll have the second half of the $5,000 on him. They can trap him in the car and steal his money without even driving to Art Venecia's house.

Under this new scenario Dee's story about what she believed makes even less sense than it did the first time she made a down payment for the murder of Art Venecia. Her argument, after all, is that since she had something on Allen, he would be unlikely to fire her. Perhaps. But is setting your boss up for a mugging and a rip-off really the best way to ingratiate yourself to him? And furthermore, Dee was very fond of Allen. Why would she allow him to be robbed and possibly beaten? It doesn't make any sense at all. Nonetheless, Dee's story is probably true. For the alcoholic, things don't have to make sense; they just have to protect the liquor supply. Dee was still "tossing out banana skins," still doing what alcoholics routinely do: rearranging reality, mentally editing conversations, turning logic on its head, doing whatever she had to do to ward off real or imagined threats to the pipeline of booze.

On Thursday, June 16, Dee's phone rang around midnight.

"Hi, Dee. Mike."

Jesus, what the hell is he calling me here for, she thought. She was drunk, and exhausted from fighting with Cass, who was passed out on the couch. The last thing she needed was Cass's getting jealous over some mysterious phone call from Mike Irvine.

"Saturday night," Mike said.

"Okay," she said. "Fine." She started to hang up.

"Don't you want to know what time?"

"Sure. What time?"

"Me and my friend we'll come by the IHOP between eleven-thirty and midnight."

"Okay. I understand. See you then."

"The homo will be there?"

"He'll be there," Dee said, laying the phone down softly so as not to awaken her husband.

On Saturday Dee cooked spaghetti. The boys had been begging her to. Preparing the sauce, setting the table, she remembered how much she liked to cook. It seemed as if more and more these days she was out of touch with the small family pleasures. Too often now they would all go out for McDonald's or Kentucky Fried Chicken. Even worse, she thought regretfully, the boys were having to do for themselves at suppertime.

Cass was away, so Susan came down and joined them for supper. It was like old times, the four of them teasing each other around the kitchen table. Old times that had been too rare between the fights and the drinking, Dee thought.

"How's Kim these days?" Susan asked Todd, and everybody laughed. It was an old joke. When Todd was ten, Susan and Wyatt had claimed that Kim, a fourteen-year-old girl, had seduced him. Todd got embarrassed every time Kim's name was mentioned, so the joke had endured. Where were we living then? Dee tried to remember over supper. She couldn't recall. There had been so many places, so many.

They talked about the boys' schoolwork for a while, Susan drifting into the role of mother—"You do your homework, Wyatt" and "Todd, don't you give the teachers any back talk"—as she had done so much over the years. She's been a better mother to them than I have, Dee thought.

After supper the boys cleared the table and headed out for a final game of Wiffle ball before the sun went down. Dee and Susan stood by the sink, washing dishes.

"So Jack came over and we did a line and just hung out," Susan was saying as they put the last of the dishes away. Dee liked things put away, in their place, neat.

Dee realized her mind had been wandering. She

had been thinking about tonight and feeling nervous about not knowing exactly what was going to happen. Susan had been talking for some time. What was a line? Dee wondered now. Didn't it have something to do with drugs? Dee had always been very naive about drugs and fearful of them, but she didn't want to ask Susan. It would only lead to a fight. And who was Jack, anyhow? God, she was losing touch with her kids' lives.

Late that night after Susan was gone, and the boys were watching television, Cass came home. Dee told him that she had to go to work. She drove to the pancake house to stay with Allen while he waited.

Only one waitress worked the floor and things were quiet. Dee and Allen sat at the back of the restaurant in a section that was reserved for employees when things were quiet. This was normally a comforting place for Dee, this narrow cubicle that led to the rest rooms and the upstairs office. On coffee breaks she would sit in a chair with her back pushed against the wall and hike her weary legs onto another chair. She liked to smoke there, leaf through the pages of the *Miami Herald,* and sip her spiked iced coffee. Sometimes, during the dead part of the second shift, Todd and Wyatt would hitch a ride up Route 1 and sit there with her, wolfing down pancakes and telling her the latest.

On this particular night the area felt as if it had been strung with high-tension wires. Allen, bristling with nervous energy, seemed to take up the whole area.

Allen smoked his Marlboros one after the other, announcing with each crushed-out cigarette, "I'll be able to quit smoking after this is over." His ulcer was acting up, he said, and he'd have to improve some of his habits.

He glanced out the window. He tapped his fingers.

"What do you think of the decor in here?" he said. "You think I ought to change it?"

"It's okay," she said. She kind of liked the flags from other countries and the hanging plants and the fact that this IHOP looked pretty much like every other one in the country. Besides, she knew Allen wasn't listening for her answer. He was just asking questions to keep his mind off "it."

"Maybe," Allen said, "but I'll tell you one thing I'm going to change. The waitress uniforms. They're too boring. I'll get you girls something with a little style." He pressed his face against the window. "What kind of a car does Mike drive?"

"Who knows?" Dee said. "He works in a gas station. He takes whatever he's working on."

For a long time they talked about the restaurant, the weather, the dog races. They talked about Christo, the environmental artist who just a month earlier had circled eleven islands in Biscayne Bay with pink plastic sheets. Allen found the whole thing interesting; Dee thought maybe the man was nuts. They talked about everything except the business at hand.

Damn it, where was Mike? Dee wondered. She decided that if "it" somehow got called off again, that would be it, she would bail out. No more renegotiating. It would be over.

"Did you ever think you'd like to have a kid?" Dee asked. It was an odd question, but they had gone too many seconds without talking, and the realization of what was really going on had almost overtaken her. Also, she'd been thinking about her own boys. She was amazed, sometimes to the point of tears, at how much Todd and Wyatt loved her even though she had not been the greatest mom to them.

"I've got a kid," Allen said.

For a moment Dee thought he would shock her with some secret. But then he explained. "My niece," he said. "My sister's daughter. I raised her for five years."

In fact at one time, Dee knew, Allen had come surprisingly close to having a baby. Through one of the IHOP waitresses he heard about a baby that had been mistreated and was being put up for adoption. He took the child in, nurtured it, and in time got the recommendation of the grandparents to be the adoptive parent of the baby. The authorities came to the house, looked things over, and put their stamp of approval on Allen. Art, however, was against having a child, and the baby was put up for adoption somewhere else.

Allen was talking wistfully about what might have been if he'd had a kid to raise when Mike Irvine walked into the restaurant. It was eleven forty-five P.M. Irvine stood just inside the door and shuffled his feet as if he'd come for a handout.

"There's my ride," Allen said. He stood, and Dee stood with him. "See you later." He tried to sound jovial, but he looked as if he were walking off to a firing squad. He kissed her cheek.

Dee peered through one of the little square panes of window and watched them get into the car. She couldn't see the third man, but Allen got in the backseat of Mike's car, so she knew there must be one. After they pulled out of the parking lot Dee reached for her pocketbook, which was on the floor under her chair. She pulled out her friend, Scotch, and poured an especially large helping into her glass of iced coffee.

She stared blankly down the length of the restaurant toward the windows that faced Route 1, the highway that would lead the men to Art's house. The reflections of headlights floated by like some sort of Hovercrafts out of the science fiction movies she and Susan sometimes watched. That's where I should be, she thought ruefully, on another planet.

Inside the restaurant two or three tables were animated by the sounds of late snackers, and a single waitress darted about, trying to keep everybody happy. But Dee felt so alone that the waitress and the customers might as well have been a thousand miles away.

In the stuporous moments that followed, there is a point at which Dee's "I didn't really think there would be a killing" story begins to ride on the same track with the "premeditated, cold-blooded murder motivated by greed" case later to be made by the state attorney. Whatever her beliefs up to now, Dee Casteel admits that when Allen and Mike walked out that door, when she sat down and poured more Scotch into her coffee, when she stared out the IHOP window into the murky Florida night, a single chilling realization gained on her with far greater speed than her ability to ward it off with alcohol. She knew with ironclad certainty that they were going to kill Art Venecia.

It was as if an alarm that had malfunctioned all these weeks suddenly had its wires soldered together, and now with only minutes left, it shrieked the warning it should have shrieked all along. Dee says she even thought of calling the police. "But what could I say? 'There's going to be a murder and I'm involved'? Hell, I didn't even know where Art Venecia lived. I'd only been there once, and that was in the dark."

So Dee didn't call the police. Instead, she drank alcohol and tried desperately to think of other things. But she couldn't go home. Like someone who had missed the last ten minutes of a movie and wanted to find out how it ended so badly they waited through an entire second show, Dee waited at the restaurant. At one point she went to the phone, thinking she would call Susan. Not to tell her what a monstrous thing she'd gotten involved with, but just to hear her little girl's reassuring voice.

Ten minutes went by. Twenty minutes. Thirty minutes. Forty minutes after the men had left, Irvine's car pulled up. Allen got out. As he walked into the pancake house, Dee had the presence of mind to scan him for clues. There was no blood on his clothes. That was good. But he looked like a zombie. His eyes were unfocused and his body seemed limp, as if he could easily be rolled up or tied into knots. Dee tried to have a conversation with him, but he seemed unable to speak more than a few words. Mostly he just nodded his head up and down. "It's over," he said. "They really did it." Dee, not wanting to know anything else, didn't press him. She drove home, blessedly drunk and unwilling even to imagine what had happened.

10

The Victim

Your name is Art Venecia. You're lying in bed. It's almost midnight and you can't sleep. The bed feels too big, too empty You wish your lover, Allen, were home. Where is he, for God's sake? If only he were with you, pressed warmly against you, holding you, telling you that things will improve. Things have been awful lately. The relationship has been stormier than ever and you are terribly sad about that. Allen is so good in many ways, but he is so selfish. You hate it when the two of you fight. The things that are said are so painful. And then he cries and it rips your heart out. But there are the tender moments, too. You remember them now and you melt.

Allen's just a kid, you tell yourself. Twenty-five. You remember when you were twenty-five. He's just a kid and he'll grow. Someday he'll realize that love is what's really important. You feel bad because you know it's not all Allen's fault. Sometimes you are so jealous, so demanding. You could lighten up a bit. But

Allen just doesn't understand how frightening it is to think you might lose someone you love.

You miss him. Where is he? In the dark of your bedroom the clock that glows on the dresser says it's ten minutes to midnight. Where is he? At the restaurant, perhaps. Or with his boyfriend, more likely. You hope that he will come home soon, that he will be in a good mood, that he will come to bed with you and he will be loving, as he sometimes is.

In the dark you like listening to the music of the woods around the house. You still love this place, away from the traffic and the stores. It's so quiet, it's like living in the country. Sometimes it reminds you of North Carolina, those summers with your aunts, the pond, the old rope swing in the yard. The murmur of the woods reminds you of tunes stored in your memory. Damn Allen, if he would just grow up, life could be so great.

You try to think of things that make you happy.

Suddenly your thoughts are broken by the sound of a car driving up the long road to the house. Allen is home. Finally. As the car pulls closer, you hear a pinging from the engine that you never heard before from the Lincoln. And the weight of the car rolling over the gravel makes a crunching noise that sounds different from the one you are used to. In a moment you hear the distant quiet thud of the car door being closed on the other side of the house. But then, surprisingly, you hear another car door close. He's not alone, you think sadly. He's got someone with him. Oh, God, don't let it be his Cuban boyfriend. You couldn't bear that. Don't make a scene, you tell yourself. Just stay in bed, in the comforting darkness. Besides, maybe he's just with Dee or one of the other waitresses.

From the garage area you hear whispers that seep softly through the living room and into your bedroom. Then you hear a soft bump or two, as if somebody unfamiliar with the house is working his way through the living room in the dark. Then nothing. Did they get something and then go out again? There is silence. You lie in the dark wishing Allen had come home alone.

Suddenly you become aware. Somebody is standing in the dark by the door. Waiting. Waiting for what? you wonder. Your heart starts to pump faster. Waiting for what? Waiting, you suddenly realize, for their eyes to adjust to the dark. Nothing could be more startling. Now the mental fear takes physical form; it is like a cold liquid suddenly careening through your veins. The person in the dark is not Allen. It's an intruder.

"Please," you cry out, "take what you want, but don't hurt me." Your voice is sucked into the silence and nothing returns.

Then you hear it, the shuffle of feet moving across the bedroom toward you. In an instant somebody is upon you. There is the weight of a man. His leaden hands pound on you and around you. He is trying to sort out what is you and what is blankets and pillows. He says nothing. Your heart is pumping furiously. You can hear it pounding. You push at the violator, you struggle, you smack the heel of your hand against his temple. He groans and you struggle out of the bed, but your body is caught up in the bedspread and you drag it with you as you move away from the bed. Who is this person? What is going on? You are feeling the kind of fear you have only imagined. "Who are you?" you shout. "What do you want? Take what you want." The figure moves toward you. Now with the light of the moon coming through the bedroom window and falling on him you try to see his face. His eyes are haunting. Patches of milky skin move toward you in the dark, getting clearer, clearer, as if his face is being brought up from the bottom of a river. He is hairy, a dangerous-looking person. He is—and it is a terrifying realization—a total stranger. Something sparkles in the moonlight. Jesus, he has something in his hand.

He pounces on you again. You fight with all your strength. You are so scared, you feel like a child. "Don't hurt me," you cry again. "Please don't hurt me." You can feel his face against you. You didn't do anything wrong but he wants to kill you. He gets you from behind. You stab your elbows back into him as furiously as you can. "Faggot," he whispers in your ear. You want to run for the door, but the bedspread is tangled around your legs. He grabs you again, gets an arm around your chest, an arm around your neck. You squirm, you battle. The shiny thing moves closer to your face, but he can't control you.

"Mike!" he shouts. "Get in here and help me with this dude."

Oh, God. There are two of them.

Another man comes in, a big man. He gets behind you, locks your arms. You can smell him. The first man moves in front of you. He's going to do something awful. The fear is like paste on your skin. You're not even a person anymore, just a form of life following the primal instinct to rage and battle against extinction. But you can't break free. You feel as if you are in a straitjacket. The hand with something in it moves closer to your neck. You know you're about to die. First there is a sting at your throat, as if nothing much really happened, and then a volcano of pain. It's a razor. He has slashed your throat with a fucking razor. You feel as if your chest has been set on fire. You feel the wetness of blood seeping out of you. Only a second has passed since he dug his razor into your throat. You gasp for another breath, but breath doesn't come. You are choking on something. What is it? It's your own blood. You swallow it, thinking air will come next, but all that comes is more blood. You are suffocating. I didn't do anything wrong, you think. The panic is absolute now. Your body convulses, but still this creature holds you in the lock of his arms. You cannot breathe. The razor has dug deep into you and the blood is spilling out of you and pouring down your throat. Everything is getting darker. Thoughts take longer to come. There is only the cold fear, and as the wave of merciful unconsciousness sweeps closer to you, just before you pass into darkness, you are able to hold a single thought: Allen did this to me.

11

The Woman

Because Dee Casteel was, by all accounts, a very nice person, it is tempting to think that her story might be one of those traditional tragedies that made such engrossing movie fare back in the 1940s and 1950s. A young girl grows up on the wrong side of the tracks. She never has anything, not even a chance. She is used and abused, neglected and rejected. Gradually she grows tough, and finally, hard. Then one day she does something shocking. And as she is led to the gallows, people say, poor thing, she never had a chance.

But it's not like that with Dee. Certainly she was handed her ration of pain. But she also was given opportunities. She could have been something. If only she had not so recklessly brought into her life two destructive forces: men and alcohol.

Dee was born Dee Hostutler on June 5, 1938, in Tampa, Florida. Born at the center of an emotional triangle and cast immediately into a real-life soap opera, she did not get off to a great start with the opposite sex. Her father, Tom Hostutler, was from the east coast of Florida, where he lived with his wife, Ona. That marriage had sorely been frayed, and Tom had stepped away from it long enough to drift westward to Tampa, where one careless night he knocked up his girlfriend, Peggy. Since Tom and Peggy were both alcoholics, there's a pretty good chance that they were both drunk when Dee was conceived.

When Dee was born, Tom divorced Ona so that he could marry Peggy and make Dee legitimate. Tom and Peggy stayed together for about a year, then Tom divorced Peggy, drove east, and remarried Ona. Peggy, who suffered from tuberculosis as well as alcoholism, could hardly take care of herself, never mind a little girl. So when Dee was still a toddler, Peggy was sent to a sanitarium in Texas, and Dee moved in with her maternal grandmother in Tampa.

Dee's grandmother was still in her thirties at the time, and she would have preferred to go out dancing, but she enthusiastically took the girl in and was every inch the mother to young Dee. Mama, Dee called her, and they used to play together. Mama would buy her dolls and Mama would run a brush through Dee's long hair, and Mama would tie it up in yellow ribbons. Sometimes Dee would hear Mama griping about being tied down with a child again, but she knew that Mama loved her, and Dee would always feel that Mama was the one true nurturing relationship of her life. "Mama," she would often say, "was the only person who ever loved me." For Dee it was a very happy childhood. If Mama failed Dee at all, it was only in being too lenient with the girl. Dee was spoiled. If Dee wanted something and Mama could afford it, Dee got it.

By the time Dee was eight years old Tom, now a navy man, had returned from the war in Europe. Like many returning soldiers he longed for the comfort and the stability of a family. He wanted his daughter. So he and Ona, who during the war years had come often to visit Dee in Tampa, took Dee to live with them.

The separation from Mama must have been traumatic, but Dee doesn't remember it that way.

"I just got my things together and we drove to Miami," she says. "I guess I thought I was going on vacation."

Ona was a good mother, but Dee missed the yellow ribbons. Four years passed before she saw Mama again.

Now Dee, the girl who had always had things her own way, had a mother and an ill-tempered father to answer to. There were no other children. The family lived in a duplex in comfortable, middle-class Hialeah. Hialeah, famous for its horse track, was Dade County's second-largest city. Tom and his brother, who lived in the other half of the duplex, ran their own business as electrical engineers.

When Dee was very young, she didn't know the word "alcoholism," but she knew that her father spent hours on end at a nearby bar tossing back drinks with his brother. When Dee was in her early teens, Tom gave up drinking, and after that he had little tolerance for people who did drink.

Dee's stepmother, Ona, also had a drinking problem.

"She was a closet drinker," Dee says. "After I would go to bed at night she would sit at the table and drink and drink."

Much of the time things were tranquil between Dee and her father. Tom took Dee fishing. He taught her how to bait a hook and cast a line and pull in the big one. He introduced her to the sky and the trees, the feel and the smell of the great outdoors. Dee was awestruck by the wonders of nature, and from these exhilarating days with her father she developed an abiding love for the woods.

Dee loved her daddy. She loved him, she would sometimes say later, "maybe too much." But Tom had a very short fuse. If he sliced his golf ball, he'd slam his three iron into a tree. If he missed a spare, he'd scream at his bowling ball. From his daughter he expected the same obedience that he expected from his sports equipment. And Dee was her father's daughter. So when father and daughter disagreed, it was like lighting a match at a fireworks factory.

Though Tom was not generally abusive, at least not physically, there was one incident in Dee's adolescence that burned so deeply into her memory that she could never forgive nor forget it.

She was fourteen years old and her chest was still as flat as the kitchen door, but the boys had started coming around. She was a pretty girl then, with long hair and a sparkling personality. One summer day she was ironing clothes in the breezeway while her father sat in the living room watching television. It was a brutally hot day, and this was in the days before everybody in Florida had air-conditioning. Dee wore shorts and a halter top. A boy named Bobby Ross came by to talk with Dee. For an hour he sat talking while Dee ironed clothes. They talked about bowling. Dee, under her father's tutelage, had taken a great interest in bowling. (Eventually she would become one of the top women bowlers in the state, as well as a crackerjack pool shooter.) And they talked about music. What songs would be featured on *Your Hit Parade* this week? they wondered, and they argued over what song would be number one. Bobby was very musical and Dee liked to listen to his impressions of Frankie Laine and some of the other top male singers of the day.

When Bobby left, Dee's father called her into the living room. Just the tone of his voice was enough to warn her of an impending explosion, but she couldn't imagine what she had done wrong. She walked into the living room and stood at a distance from her father. "What?"

"Come here," he said.

"What?" she said again. She felt like crying. She wanted her father's approval more than anything, and it always seemed as if he was mad at her when she hadn't even done anything wrong.

"Come here," he shouted.

She walked closer to him. In his eyes she saw that bewildering anger. What, she wondered, could she have possibly done wrong?

Tom's hand came up, fast and hard, and he slapped her across the face.

"Look at what you're wearing," he shouted.

Dee glanced down, looked herself over. She still didn't understand.

"Dressing like a damn slut for the boys," Tom shouted. "It's indecent. You're as cheap as piss."

Then he beat her.

Later Dee often thought that she could forgive her father for the beating. That pain went away; those wounds healed. But when he had said "You're as cheap as piss," it had been like slicing her open and gutting her soul. Nothing before or since has ever hurt Dee that much, and until the day her father died Dee never forgave him for that.

Despite the frequent friction with her father, Dee had a happy adolescence, or at least one as happy as those torturous years from thirteen to seventeen can be. In many ways she was the standard model for what a girl should be during those Eisenhower years. She was a pretty girl in whose presence young boys turned goofy. She was a smart girl, whose marks were some of the highest in the high school. She was a fast, agile, and graceful young lady who played on just about every girls' sports team. She was a cheerleader, and she sang in the glee club.

On her sixteenth birthday Dee asked for a car, and on her seventeenth birthday she got it, even though Tom and Ona had to go into debt to buy it.

During these years Dee did some drinking, but she probably consumed no more alcohol than many other kids her age in the 1950s. When she was thirteen, her parents drove her across the state to Tampa for a big New Year's Eve bash. There she was allowed to play bartender. Dee felt so adult pouring the rum and whiskey and vodka, mixing the drinks with soda or fruit juice, dropping in the little swizzle sticks, and handing people their drinks without spilling a drop. She liked mixing the drinks, and if there was no one at the bar to order, she'd mix one for herself. Before long she was stinking drunk.

She liked the way alcohol made her feel, and back home in Hialeah she took to drinking with her friends. But unlike most of her friends who had tried drinking too much too soon, Dee did not get sick.

She never had the puking, the headaches, the "why did I drink so much, I'll never do it again" hangover.

"Maybe," Dee says now, "if alcohol had made me sick, I could have stayed away from it, but it never did. I always liked it. I liked the taste of it, the smell of it, I liked the sweet burning sensation of it going down."

During these years Dee had boyfriends, but her first love, and the boy who was by her side much of the time after age twelve, was Harry Osterman. Harry was the first boy she slept with, and though Dee cared deeply about him, she never thought that he was the sort of person she would want to marry.

A few months after her seventeenth birthday Dee started putting on weight, filling out. Because she was an athletic girl, always slender and vital, the sudden weight gain disturbed her. In early December she made an appointment to see a doctor. Though she'd been having sex without precautions, in the innocence of the times it did not occur to Dee that she could be pregnant.

Of course she was. The news scared the hell out of her. She held on to her secret for days. When she finally told Ona, Ona's first words were, "Oh, my God. Your father is going to kill you."

When Dee told her father she was going to have a

baby, Tom blew his stack but did not hit her. "How could you do this to us?" he screamed. "You're going to ruin your life" and "I'll kill the son of a bitch" followed quickly. And finally he announced, "You'll get an abortion."

Dee was terrified. What she knew of abortions then was putrid old men wielding jagged coat hangers in back-alley flats. She refused. Tom called a doctor, but when the doctor learned that Dee was three and a half months pregnant, he refused, saying it would endanger her life. Dee, it was decided, would have the baby.

"Needless to say, it ruined Christmas," Dee says.

Finally it was settled that Dee would marry Harry. Harry agreed. The kids got a blood test, and a marriage license. On the day of the scheduled ceremony Dee drove her car to Harry's house to pick him up, but instead of being greeted by a glowing groom, she was met by an older buddy of Harry's who stood out in front of Harry's house like a sheriff waiting for a lynch mob.

"Harry's not going," the buddy said.

"Huh?" Dee felt her heart drop.

"He's not going. He's not going to marry you."

"Why?"

"He doesn't want to ruin his life. And if you take him to court, I'll testify that I screwed you and I can get five other guys to say the same thing. We'll say that you don't know who the father of the baby is."

Dee was stunned and heartbroken. She was no more anxious than Harry to get married, but it cut her to the bone that Harry would treat her so cruelly.

When Dee's father found out what had happened, some pressure was arranged and the kids ended up getting married after all, but not living together. On Dee's eighteenth birthday, one year after Ona and Tom had given her a car, she presented them with a baby boy. She named him Tom, after her father, and called him Tommy.

From the day she left the maternity ward Dee accepted the fact that Tommy would never be her baby. Ona and Tom made the baby their own, and though Dee enjoyed taking care of him, she also enjoyed the fact that she didn't have to, that she could go out, date, drink, bowl. Her relationship with Tommy became more like that of a sister, and in fact, for years Tommy believed that Dee was his big sister.

The period after the birth was a blissful one for Dee. More than ever she felt as if she was really part of a family. She felt loved and she felt secure.

In the 1950s pregnant girls were about as welcome as lepers in high school, and they were not encouraged to stick around. So Dee, ostracized by the parents of "nice girls" and pressured by the school administration, had dropped out before Tommy was born.

After Tommy was born Dee enrolled in summer school and took the courses she would need to get her diploma. There she learned shorthand and various secretarial skills. When she was graduated in August, she went right to work as a secretary–clerk typist for the city of Hialeah. And she came under the influence of Henry Milander, one of the most colorful politicians in the history of the county and the state of Florida.

Henry Milander, then almost sixty, was the mayor of Hialeah. Milander was one of those flamboyant rascals who are to American political folklore what Robin Hood is to English literature. Always praised for his kindness, always forgiven his sins, Milander was made of Teflon long before that word was applied to Ronald Reagan. Everybody in town had a story to tell about Henry Milander. Though often ill-tempered, he was a local hero. Charming and lovable, he was also, few would deny, corrupt. In 1970, after Milander had been mayor of Hialeah for a quarter century, the *Miami Herald* wrote:

> A sharp-shooting businessman, Milander has made millions in real estate . . . Hialeah real

> estate. He has an uncanny knack for buying property which, after a rezoning or two, turns into a shopping center, an industrial area or an apartment complex. And yet, through it all, he's still the man who really does like children, who at the crack of dawn is working in his meat market and who, at 70, still has an eye for pretty girls.

Dee had been one of those children that Milander really liked. She used to run errands to Milander's neighborhood butcher shop, a shop in which the millionaire mayor worked all through his years as the king of Hialeah. And by the time Dee was out of school and ready for work, she had certainly blossomed into one of those pretty girls for which, said the *Herald*, Milander had an eye. At age eighteen Dee became Milander's secretary.

Milander, a married man who perhaps was more interested in being seen with a pretty girl on his arm than he was in more intimate arrangements, kept things platonic with Dee. He was like a father to her. He was her mentor and it was through him that she met many of the well-placed people who populated her social life for the next several years. And perhaps more significantly, she learned from Milander that "money talks and bullshit walks." When she got a parking ticket, it was fixed. When, at nineteen, she was hauled into the police station for driving under the influence of alcohol, it was "taken care of." Milander was a rich and powerful man, but just as he spent his money on other people, he used his clout to get his friends jobs, suspended sentences, and tickets out of town. These were the kind of favors he could do as easily as he could chop a side of beef. So Dee learned quickly that if you knew the right people, everything could be fixed, paid off, swept under the carpet, or ignored. To this day Dee is convinced, and she's probably right, that if Milander were alive or if she still had friends like him, she would not be sitting on death row.

Henry Milander introduced Dee to Claude Pepper, the longtime Florida congressman. He also introduced her to millionaires and the sons of millionaires, heads of industry, future governors, and occasionally men whose professions were clearly something you didn't ask too many questions about. Gone soon were the callow youths, the cheap dates, the pitchers of beer, and the marriage to Harry Osterman, which had never been more than a technicality. Now she dated men who were ten to fifteen years older than she, men who had yachts parked in the Miami Beach marina and suites at places like The Fontainebleau and the Eden Roc, men who were rich, powerful, and in some cases, famous. Her only rule: they had to be single; she would not date a married man. "Perhaps I'm looking for a father figure," she said to a friend at the time. "Who knows? I'm not a psychiatrist."

These men took Dee to elegant places; they bought her expensive things. They made her feel like a queen. This was the beginning of the party years for Dee, and in her dating, a pattern was asserting itself, but it was a pattern she would not recognize for several years. It was this: if she went out with a man and the two of them ended up drinking, she went out with him again. If they didn't end up drinking, he would seem dull, and she would avoid him.

When she did go drinking with a guy, chances were he would get lucky. Alcohol made Dee sexually compliant, and though the result of one unwanted pregnancy was at home getting his diapers changed by Ona, Dee screwed recklessly. Not surprisingly, she got knocked up again.

This time the father was a man that many women in Miami would have been thrilled to get knocked up by. Rich, handsome, and not quite thirty, he had recently been voted the most eligible bachelor in Miami. He was the charming youngest son of a Dade

County family that was plugged into power sources everywhere, a family that still owns certain entertainment facilities that are known all over the world.

On her first date with this man, Dee had gone to his luxury apartment at the prestigious Jockey Club on Biscayne Boulevard, where they got soused together and made love. It was there that Dee got her first taste of Scotch. She liked it, and Scotch became her closest friend for the next twenty-five years.

Dee had few illusions about her relationships with upper-class men. She knew they probably saw her as someone to have fun with, an easy mark, a girl with a baby, no husband, emotionally immature. And so it never occurred to her to ask this man to marry her. She felt that she was not in his class. She decided she would ask only for the money to get an abortion. But she couldn't find the father.

He liked to fly to wherever the thoroughbreds were running, and at the time they happened to be running at Santa Anita in California. So Dee turned to old reliable, Henry Milander. Milander gave her the five hundred dollars for an abortion.

"I was too far along for the normal method," she says. "So the doctor used a plastic tube to insert air into the uterus to cause abortion. I had to wait for it to happen. I had a girlfriend, Mary, and she and I went downtown with the kids on Saturday. We went to Burdine's. This was when you went downtown to shop, before every subdivision in Miami had its own shopping center. I went into labor right there in Burdine's, right next to ladies' shoes. We went home and I walked the floor up and down, up and down. The pain was excruciating. On Sunday night I finally lost the baby. I just flushed it down the toilet. I guess I thought it would just be a ball of stuff. But it was a baby. A baby. What a horrible experience. I will never get that moment out of my mind.

"Ona heard it when I broke my water. She came in when I was on the toilet. 'You all right?' she said.

'Yes,' I told her. But she knew. The next morning she came in. 'You lost a baby last night, didn't you,' she said.

"I was still in a lot of pain. I called the family doctor, and when I went to see him, he said it was a good thing I got there in time. The afterbirth, the placenta, still hung inside me, and I would have been dead within twenty-four hours."

By this time Dee had changed jobs. She had become executive secretary to the Hialeah branch manager of Florida Power and Light, an impressive job for a twenty-year-old. All indications were that if she could stop getting pregnant, Dee would make something special of herself.

After the abortion Dee stayed out of work for several weeks, and when the folks at Florida Power and Light found out about the abortion—because Dee, naively believing that honesty was the best policy, had told them—they fired her. Dee was heartbroken. She had done such good work for the company, everybody said so, she couldn't believe they would just fire her. The rejection stung her terribly, but she found that after a few drinks it didn't hurt so much.

Before the first pregnancy Dee had harbored hopes of becoming a pediatrician. Now her aspirations had been scaled down. She dreamed of becoming a police officer. And she also dreamed of being a wife and mother, of someday having a loving husband and a little girl in whose hair she could tie yellow ribbons just as Mama had for her.

There was one other surprising career opportunity that was almost offered to her during this period: professional bowler.

By the time Dee was fully recovered from the abortion, she was bowling in five leagues a week, and she was the best woman bowler in all of them. Locally, she had been elected to the board of directors of the Women's International Bowling Conference, the youngest person ever to receive that honor. Her name got around and professional bowling scouts came to watch her. They liked what they saw. But the big companies that sponsored bowling tournaments wanted not just great bowlers, but people of high moral character who would fortify the game's image as wholesome family recreation. When the scouts started asking questions about Dee's personal life, they were told simply, "She drinks." And that dream was quickly discarded.

As it turned out, Dee didn't have to worry about getting pregnant again. Though she didn't know it, the abortion had screwed up her innards so badly that pregnancy was impossible. It would be many years and many medical procedures later before she would be able to get pregnant again.

When Dee was twenty-three years old, she was at a cocktail lounge one afternoon when she spotted an interesting-looking man sitting alone at the bar, nursing a drink that she had never seen before.

She walked over to him. "What's that?" she asked.

"A margarita," he said. "Would you like some?"

"Sure," she said. The man lifted the glass to her lips, and Dee took her first sip of the tequila drink.

"I like it," she said, and she left.

This taste of alcohol was a fitting beginning for her next romance.

The man was Lester Wallace. Les was a handsome man, well dressed and exotic looking, with his head shaved bare like Yul Brynner's. He was big, tall, muscular, and unquestionably masculine, just the way Dee liked her men. About a week after she sipped his margarita, Dee ran into Les again and before long she was head over heels in love with him.

Like her father, Les took Dee hunting. Dee and Les would drive out to the Everglades with Les's buddies on weekends, and there they would shoot turkey and camp out. Dee liked the smell of coffee over a campfire, and the sight of a fiery sun falling off the horizon in a blaze of color. And after dark she liked to nestle in Les's arms and listen to the night sounds, staring up at the stars and dreaming her dreams of a perfect marriage, of a baby with yellow ribbons in her hair, and of a career in law enforcement. With another man she might have had all this. But unfortunately, Les, like her father, was an alcoholic.

Oddly, Les was only a full-moon alcoholic. Sober three weeks out of the month, he would in the light of a full moon turn instinctively to the bottle, like a baby to a nipple. He would become drunk, then abusive, then violent, then sick, and finally, remorseful. During the three weeks per month of sobriety, Les was quite the health-conscious individual, a regular Jack La-Lanne, and during these periods he urged Dee to give up cigarettes and alcohol.

Dee and Les got married and bought a house in Hialeah. Les, like many men, wished to impose a more conservative set of standards on his wife than he had on his girlfriend. He asked Dee, more strongly now, to stop smoking and to give up drinking. If she couldn't give up drinking, she should at least have the decency to confine her drinking to home. He didn't want his wife drinking in bars. Dee was somewhat compliant. At this point she was still a happy drunk, an alcoholic who didn't know she was an alcoholic and certainly didn't see alcohol as any sort of problem in her life. So she was able to choose when and where she would drink. If it made Les happy, she would stay out of bars.

Though Les adhered to most of the typical sexist assumptions of the day, and was violent during his drinking spells, he was at other times a decent enough husband. He occasionally brought flowers or candy, he earned a good living selling real estate, and he was a satisfying lover. Overall, Dee felt that her marriage was as stable as the one next door, and when she and Les both wanted a baby, there seemed no reason not to have one. By this time the internal damage from her last abortion had been surgically corrected. Though Dee was in many ways the traditional wife, an appendage to her husband, she was in other ways her own woman. Dee was working at Sweet Paper Company then and she had her own money, her own checking account, her own savings account, and it was out of these that she paid the expenses of having a baby.

In June 1966, when Dee was twenty-eight, her daughter, Susan, was born, and Dee, more than at any time in her life, was happy. In fact, she was ecstatic. She quit her job and stayed home with her baby. Les was a wonderful, loving husband, and doting father. When Dee looks for a picture of past happiness to frame in her mind, she thinks of herself and Les stretched out on a blanket at Flagler Beach, the Beatles singing "Sergeant Pepper's Lonely Hearts Club Band" over the transistor radio, the smell of Coppertone rising from their backs, and little Susan grabbing fistfuls of sand and giggling as she ran the sand endlessly through her tiny fingers.

Susan was a lovely girl, and perhaps because of the happiness she brought into her parents' lives, Dee went a year without drinking. Les was happy, too, and for a while it seemed that booze and violence had been exterminated from their lives. But whatever emotional or genetic imprinting had caused them in the first place still festered just beneath the smiling surface they maintained, and in time the old patterns reemerged. Les would frequently stay out until two or three in the morning, drinking or catting around. Dee would complain bitterly. Les would shout, defend himself, tell her to mind her own business. Dee would drink more; things didn't hurt so much when you drank. Les would drink, would get stark raving drunk, and start breaking things. Dee would rail against him. Les would beat her. Dee would curse him. Les would get more violent. Dee would warn him, "If you ever hit our baby, I'm gone."

"Then one night," says Dee, "we went out. On

our way home Les wanted to stop at one more lounge for another drink. I said we can't, we had to get home to the baby. We fought. Finally he drove me home. He got out of the car and ran into the house ahead of me. I sat out in the car for a while. I was afraid he would beat me. I wasn't worried about Susan. He had never hit her. By the time I went into the house Les had paid off the baby-sitter and sent her home. He had taken his clothes off. He was sitting in the kitchen in his underwear, holding the .357 magnum pistol I had bought him for his birthday. 'You say one word,' he said, 'and I'll blow your head off.' I knew the gun had a hair trigger and the safety was off. I was scared to death, but I didn't let it show. 'No problem,' I said. 'Can we leave?' He said, 'Yes.'

"I took Susan and got the hell out of there and called the police. It took the Hialeah cops three hours to get there. All of the baby's things were in the house. The police made Les leave so I could go in and pack my things. I had to swear out a warrant for Les's arrest. By this time it was around four in the morning and the sergeant asked me, 'Have you been drinking?' 'Yes,' I said, 'about four hours ago.' 'Then we can't take your complaint,' he said. I knew Les had gotten to them, but I wasn't going to let him get away with it. Les had the local police, but I had the mayor. I called Henry Milander and I told him I wanted the son of a bitch arrested. Henry called the police and told them he wanted it done now and he didn't want any paperwork shuffled. Henry called me later and he said, 'Do you need anything else?' 'Yes,' I said, 'I need a job.' "

Henry Milander got Dee a job as a police dispatcher for the city of Hialeah. It was her second encounter with police work. Back when she had been a secretary, word had gotten around among the officers that she could take shorthand, and she had gotten calls at all hours from cops who wanted her to take statements of suspects they had just arrested. Dee, always willing to do a favor, never said no. A cruiser would appear at her house and off she would go clutching her stenographer's pad in her hand. Now, as a dispatcher, Dee found again that she could get excited about work in law enforcement. She liked being one of the guys down at the station, and the guys liked her. She was, says one ex-cop, "good old Dee, the nicest gal you'd ever want to meet."

As usual, Dee excelled at her work and was well liked by her fellow workers. Before long she was ready for a step up. But there was nowhere for her to go in Hialeah so she took another dispatcher job, a higher-paying one, with the Dade County police in the city of Miami. She still dreamed of being a police officer, but by this time the dream was like a candle that had burned all night, and soon, she knew, it would flicker out.

In 1969, Dee's biological mother, Peggy, urged her to bring her little girl and move to Tampa. Peggy, still a practicing alcoholic, had gotten married to a police officer, Bob DeSalvo, a moody, wife-beating alcoholic who, before he became a heavy drinker, had been one of the top homicide investigators in the state.

Dee, tired of the penny-counting, often lonely life of the single mother, and knowing how much Peggy wanted her company, drove to Tampa for a two-week visit. There she lined up a police dispatcher job. She had decided to drive back to Miami, pack up her life, and move to Tampa. On Sunday morning before she left Tampa everybody was smiling. Bob told Dee how happy he was that she would be moving in. He held little Susan in his arms and bragged about the fine things he would buy his adorable granddaughter for Christmas. Though Dee knew that Bob had brutalized Peggy during drunken rages, she hoped things would change now. Bob had always been such a depressed sort, and it was nice to see him happy.

That Sunday evening in Miami, Dee got a call from her mother. Bob had committed suicide, shot himself in the head.

In the light of later events it is interesting to note that Dee has never been fully convinced that Bob pulled the trigger on himself. She has always suspected that Peggy might have been beaten one time too often and had turned Bob's police revolver on him and cured him of his depression once and for all.

Dee, who once thought that Mike Irvine "wouldn't hurt a flea," now says, "I think that anybody is capable of taking a life."

By this time Dee had known a good many men, and though she was not big on self-analysis, there were at least two patterns in her relationships that were difficult to ignore. One, as already mentioned, was that she only gave a second date to men who filled her with liquor on the first date. The other was that at the beginning of a relationship she was a traditional subservient woman, willing to do anything to please her man. But there was a limit to how much she would surrender, and soon her independent instincts would emerge and she would rebel. Sparks would fly and the relationship would go down in flames.

Just as knowing that you are an alcoholic doesn't necessarily help you to stop drinking, knowing these things about herself and men didn't stop Dee from jumping right back into an unsatisfactory relationship.

After Bob's suicide Dee decided against the move to Tampa and went back to her old job. But Peggy pleaded with her to come. Dee's instincts told her it was a mistake, but Peggy was lonely and Dee wanted to do something for her. So in December, Dee, who had always had a hard time saying no, loaded her clothes and her little girl into her car and moved to Tampa.

At a party a few weeks later Dee was introduced to Charlie White. She got drunk that night and slept with him. Charlie was just her type, an alcoholic.

Dee, who had already decided that moving to Tampa was a mistake, now compounded it by marrying Charlie. She did it, she says, because everybody told her she should, and she felt pressured into it. A psychiatrist or an expert on alcoholism might say she did it because Charlie was an alcoholic and marrying one made it easier for her to be one, even though she didn't acknowledge that she was one. In any case, things did not work out in Tampa, so before long they were back in Miami. By the time Susan was six, Dee had given birth to two sons, Todd and Wyatt.

Charlie was an alcoholic but he was a working alcoholic who made a good living installing air-conditioning equipment, and he never raised a hand to Dee. In fact, Dee was always able to dominate Charlie, which might explain why she got bored with the marriage so quickly. When Dee wasn't working or parenting, she spent her time with Charlie and friends drinking at local bars. Though her social life revolved around alcohol and had for years, Dee still had no sense that she was doing anything unusual or problematic.

In her book *Goodbye Hangovers, Hello Life* (Ballantine Books, 1987), Jean Kirkpatrick, an alcoholic and the executive director of Women for Sobriety, talks about her own continuous and destructive social drinking in words that could describe Dee or most other alcoholics:

> None of this behavior seemed strange or unusual to me. Of course, I knew that not everyone was drinking in the same way, but my behavior did not disturb me, and I just can't understand why it didn't. Perhaps it was because there were always others who joined me; that they were always different persons evidently made no impression on me. It seems totally unbelievable to me now. But then? It seemed perfectly normal. Drinking to the alcoholic never seems abnormal.

So they were drinking buddies, Dee and Charlie, but there was no real passion in their relationship, and

Dee always wanted something more, some unnamed emotional connection. There was, there had always been, it seemed, a hole in her life, some nameless longing that booze always obliterated. It never occurred to Dee to have an affair. She had never cheated on Les; she would never cheat on Charlie.

If she couldn't have a man, Dee decided, she'd have a career. Maybe that would make her feel complete. It was time to pursue her dream.

By this time the first waves of feminism had swept across the country, and communities in every state were being persuaded, protested, or sued into enlightenment. For the first time the city of Miami was accepting female applicants for the job of police officer. Dee applied for training and was quickly accepted. She passed the background tests, the physical tests, and the intelligence tests easily. After two weeks in training Dee stood at the top of her class. She was well on her way to becoming one of the first lady cops in Miami.

Halfway through the six-week training program each recruit came up for oral review; that is, an evaluation and a grilling by three senior officers. The review was a winnowing process during which those deemed unfit to serve as police officers could be dismissed without recourse. Dee was not concerned. After all, she was the best in her class.

But questions, apparently, had been asked. Friends had been spoken to. Somehow the review board had learned something about Dee that she didn't even know about herself. They had concluded that Dee was an alcoholic. She was washed out of the program.

It was an embittering experience for Dee. Since the days of Henry Milander she had suspected that it was not what you knew, but whom you knew. This only proved she was right. The rejection, this heartless bombing of her dream, was a killer, but Dee had an antidote for this sort of pain. Her friend, Scotch. A half bottle of Scotch and nothing seemed so terribly important.

Dee's next job was at the Miller Gas Company. As usual, she was given a responsible position and was considered a top-grade employee. She regretted not being a police officer, but she loved her job at Miller Gas as much as anything. She and Charlie weren't madly in love, but they made a life together for their family. The kids were happy. Things were okay.

Then Charlie got sick. He had bad kidneys. He was taken to the hospital. He had surgery. He was told not to work for a year. Dee's salary was barely enough to pay off a pair of car loans, let alone pay the food, mortgage, and household bills to support two adults and three kids. And so she did something that would become a fatal turning point in her life. She started "borrowing."

In her job at Miller Gas Company, Dee accepted gas-bill payments, many of which were in cash. She entered the payments into ledgers, which in turn would periodically be entered into computers. Miller Gas customers were divided into zones, with each zone having a different billing period. Because many people paid their gas bills weeks before the due date, Dee was left with a good deal of cash from each zone that didn't have to be accounted for until that zone's next billing period. She began by borrowing fifty bucks to pay a medical bill for Susan. By the time that money had to be accounted for, Dee was still broke, so she borrowed a hundred bucks from another zone, gave back the fifty she owed, and kept fifty to pay for shoes for Wyatt, dentistry for Todd, clothes for Charlie, food for the family. Each time, she left a check in place of the cash, knowing her check was no good, but also knowing it would not be cashed.

She never thought of this as stealing. She was borrowing. But each time the money came due, she didn't have it and she needed more. So she borrowed greater and greater amounts from zones that weren't up for billing. She replaced the money that had to be accounted for and she paid household bills with the rest. She got away with this for a year, running up a tab of over $14,000. Her nightly prayer was, "Please, God, don't let me get caught."

God let her get caught when she let her own check for $1,000 go through, thinking she would be able to cover it. The check bounced, an audit was done, and Dee was fired.

This borrowing scam might have been the single greatest mistake of Dee's life up to then, more consequential even than the bad marriages and pregnancies, because it effectively pushed her out of the white-collar job market and into the transient world of bartenders, short-order cooks, and cocktail waitresses. Unable to get another secretarial position because of her crime, Dee ended up working as a bartender at the Saga Lounge in Cutler Ridge. Now she could be near alcohol all day long, and it was during this period, the mid-1970s, that alcohol began to take over completely and destroy her life.

But was it a mistake? Was it simply bad luck? Maybe. But the literature on alcoholism is filled with case histories of people who unconsciously slammed and locked all the doors of opportunity, except the one that led to alcohol. The craving for alcohol is not fully understood, but it seems to act like an inner demon, directing an unsuspecting life toward its own ends. Quite possibly Dee's life until now had been a series of decisions whispered in her ear by the craving demon whose only goal was to make the consumption of alcohol easy and excusable.

While she worked at the Saga Lounge, Dee divorced Charlie. But typical of her, she felt sorry for Charlie because he was sickly and out of work, so she let him continue to live with her and the kids. In fact, she gave Charlie the bedroom, and she slept on the couch.

At the Saga, Dee met Cass. He was, to her eye, incredibly attractive and sexy.

Cass was another alcoholic, another wife beater, another poisonous personality who could bring her nothing but pain, so in time she did the only logical thing. She married him.

And she was still married to him, though miserably so, in the early-morning hours of June 19, 1983, when James Allen Bryant came back to the pancake house and said, "It's over." Dee lay beside Cass that night, sipping her good friend, Scotch. Unable to sleep, she drank in the dark, all the time reviewing her life and thinking, No, it can't be true. Art Venecia can't be dead. My life could not have led me to this.

Though it took longer than usual, the alcohol did its job. It mellowed Dee, it relaxed her. It evicted from her soul that growing sense of dread and replaced it with contentment, the feeling that everything was going to be all right. By the time she passed out, Dee knew that the whole thing was a misunderstanding. Of course Art wasn't dead. People didn't just go around killing people.

12

The Stories

Only three people know exactly what happened to Art Venecia around midnight of June 18. Not surprisingly, their stories vary, and none of them in themselves are plausible explanations of what happened.

Here is how James Allen Bryant now describes the night:

"On the night of the murder I got a phone call from Dee. She telephoned me at my home around eleven-thirty and asked me to drive to the IHOP and meet her. I didn't ask what it was about because during the past week we had gotten together a couple of times for a drink, so I didn't find it unusual that she was calling me so late. I drove over and met her at the back door and we walked over to a car, a dark-colored Mustang, I believe. She introduced me to two men, one in the backseat, one in the front. The man in the backseat had a razor or a knife in his hands and they made me get into the car with them. I sat in the front seat. From there we drove to Art's house. The two men didn't talk to me; they talked in, I don't know, street language, I guess you'd call it. I don't know what their conversation was. When we got to Art's house, they turned their lights off as they headed in the driveway. They drove almost up to the actual drive itself, then parked.

"We went into the house. The only light on was the small light in the living room. The man with the razor went into the bedroom. The other man stayed out in the living room with me. Then I heard Art say, 'Please, just take everything that's in the house.' I heard the man's voice. Then I heard a scream. Shortly after that, the man emerged from the bedroom and told the other man, 'Let's go.' I just saw Art very briefly at that point. I saw blood, and just the bottom of his feet lying on the floor. Then one of the men picked up a money bag and some keys that were on the organ bench. We got in the car and drove back to the restaurant. They gave me the keys and told me to take them to Dee. The IHOP was open but I didn't go near the customers. I went in back. I emptied the safe and gave the envelopes full of money to Dee, and she gave it to the men in the car and they left.

"Then Dee and I talked about how the situation was going to be handled. She said things were going to be better for us now, financially. Then I lay on the sofa at the restaurant and cried most of the night.

"The reason I went along with everything and didn't tell anybody was that Mr. Venecia and I had a very serious fight a week or so before that and I had been quite frightened that if any of that should come up that it would all be turned around and it would all be blamed on me because of the fight."

Mike Irvine describes the events of that night this way:

"We went out there that night. We was going out there to rip Bryant off, not to murder anybody. We went in my '75 Ford LTD. I was driving. Bill was in the backseat and Bryant was sitting in the passenger's seat. I knew the way because Bryant gave me directions to the house. When we got there, Allen went up and unlocked the door. Bill and I went in. Bryant went in with us, then he turned around and went out and headed around to the side like he is going out to the driveway. I stayed in the living room while Bill walked down like to the hallway into the next room, and I heard a guy say, 'Don't hurt me.' I turned around and said, 'Let's go, Bill, let's get the daylights out of here,' and I went outside. Bryant was coming in and I said, 'Let's get the hell out of here,' and he says, 'Just a minute.' I went out by my car. I was going to leave but my keys wasn't in the damn ignition. Bill, he comes out and I ask Bill, I says, 'You got my keys?' He says, 'No.'

"A couple of minutes later Bryant comes out. He handed me the keys and we left. I took Bryant back to IHOP and I went back to work. Bill got on his bike and went out. I don't know where he went.

"Dee came up and gave us some more money in an envelope. I didn't open the envelope. I threw it over on the desk and later I gave it to Bill. He gave me half the money. I don't remember how much it was. I didn't call the police because I didn't know what went down out there and I was afraid. I didn't talk to Bill or Bryant about what happened there."

Bill "Joker" Rhodes describes the night like this:

"Mike Irvine and Allen Bryant picked me up at the service station. Mike was driving. I sat on the passenger's side, and Bryant told Mike where to drive. When we got to the house, we all got out of the car. Bryant had a key to the house, he opened the door. Then me and Mike went in and I don't know exactly where everybody was positioned, but I know Bryant came inside the door and he went right back out by the car. Then Mike said to me, 'Come on, let's get it done.' We went in and I went in about three or four steps down like a short walkway into a big bedroom. I walked into the room and over to the bed, and I hit the bed, and the guy came up out of the bed; he jumped up and grabbed me and I felt a pain underneath my arm and I got cut. I tried to get away, keep this dude from cutting me again, and I pushed him down I don't know how many times. It seemed like forever. I was pushing his hands at him, pushing toward the floor. I hollered at Mike, 'What the hell is going on, man?' and the next thing I know me and this guy are tussling, wrestling back and forth. I was trying to keep whatever the hell he had in his hands away from me. I kept hollering, 'Hey,' but there was no answer from Mike. I don't know if Mike ever came in the bedroom because it was dark. The guy stumbled back and forth and I got my right hand loose and I hit the guy once. I don't know where I hit him exactly, but I hit him hard because I didn't want him coming back at me again.

"The next thing I know, the guy went down. We both went down to the floor. I heard gurgling sounds. In the neighborhood I come from, gurgling is when you get one upside the jaw, extra hard, you are trying to catch your breath, you are gasping. The man was hollering and I got up and I ran to get away from him and ran into something, and I made a slight jog and out the door I went.

"Outside I saw the car and Bryant. I didn't see Michael, but I wasn't paying that much attention. I was getting the heck away from the house. I went to the car and told Mike, 'Let's get the fuck out of here, man; they are going to call the cops.' Bryant said he had to go back in the house and get some change, and he went back in the house. After about four or five minutes he came out with a little plastic bag. I got in the backseat and took my shirt off. I was trying to see under my arm because I was bleeding pretty good. Later I burnt the shirt. The next day Mike came by and gave me a $700 payment for roughing up the guy. When he told me that Art Venecia was dead, it made me sick to my stomach."

* * *

There is another version of the murder that, though secondhand, might be the most reliable, since it comes from the one person who does not deny her role in the murder: Dee. She says that when Allen told her about the murder the next day, he said, "It was horrible. Bill really enjoyed his work. He did a nasty job on Art. They cut his throat. Mike held his arms and Bill did the slashing."

13

The Morning After

At six A.M. on Sunday, June 19, Dee Casteel reported for work, as usual. Sunday, she knew, would be a busy day, and the boisterous family trade would maybe be enough to keep her mind off "it."

She had only been in the restaurant a few minutes when Allen came down from the office. Obviously, he had spent the night there. He looked drained.

"Dee, I want you to come to the house with me," he said. Dee glanced out the window, and across the empty parking lot at the rising sun. The sun will come up tomorrow, she thought. That's what people always said when you talked about bad things in your life: "the sun will come up tomorrow," as if that meant anything. Of course the sun would come up tomorrow. So what? Did the sun come up today on Art Venecia? she wondered.

"What happened?" she asked, not really wanting to hear the answer but knowing she could avoid it no longer.

"They killed him."

"No," Dee said. The word came unexpectedly from inside her. "They couldn't have."

"They killed him," Bryant said.

"How did they kill him?"

"Dee, you'll see when you get there, okay? It's a mess, a total mess." He looked edgy. It was clear to Dee that Allen hadn't thought past the point of murder.

"We've got to clean that place up," he said. "It's horrible."

" 'We'?" Dee said. The idea of Art's actually being dead was unreal to her. In any case, it hadn't even occurred to her that she was one of the murderers. "Why 'we'?"

"Come on, Dee. I depend on you," Allen said. "You know how much I need you. We'll get it finished and forget it. You help me dispose of the body and you'll have a job for the rest of your life."

"It's Father's Day," Dee said.

"Huh?"

"It's Father's Day," she said.

"So?"

"I don't know," she said. "I just remembered that it's Father's Day. It seems so sad that this happened on Father's Day."

"Dee, don't fall apart on me, okay," Allen said. "I need you."

It was a busy morning at the restaurant, and it wasn't until one-thirty that Allen felt he could spare Dee from the floor. By then a few tables were empty, and Allen assigned Dee's parties to other waitresses.

Dee had only been to Art Venecia's house once, the night of the gun incident. Now as they drove to the house in the Lincoln, Dee was scared. "If you're in for a dime, you're in for a buck," she joked, but neither she nor Bryant laughed.

"I was just remembering when Art bought this car," she said as they turned off Route 1 and drove into The Redlands. "Do you remember? He brought it over to the restaurant for you and you were showing it off to all the waitresses and busboys and flirting like mad. Do you remember?"

"Yes, yes, I remember," Allen said. "So?"

"I don't know. It's just that I remember looking at Art. Everybody was looking at the car, but I just watched Art's face. He was so happy to see you happy. God, he was beaming like a proud parent who had just bought his kid a great Christmas present."

"Jesus, Dee. You think that's the kind of thing I want to hear right now?"

"Sorry," she said. And then, "Tell me how they killed him."

"You don't want to know."

"Tell me," she said.

"Christ. They cut his throat. It's really a gory mess."

"Oh, God."

"It was horrible. Bill really enjoyed his work. He did a nasty job on Art. Mike held his arms and Bill did the slashing."

"I don't know whether I can handle this or not," Dee said.

"You have to go in with me this time," Allen said. "You have to help me."

Allen had it all wrong, Dee decided a few minutes later. Mike Irvine certainly would never murder anybody. "I'll believe this when I see it," Dee said, but Allen, grim faced as he guided the Lincoln past the flat, sprawling farms, was lost in his own thoughts and said nothing.

When Allen got to the driveway, he turned left and drove up to the house. Next to the house there was a white trailer, close enough to be plugged into the house's electric and phone lines. Dee hadn't noticed it on her first visit.

Allen pulled the Lincoln around to the side of the house. They walked in through the garage door and crossed into the large front room.

"Oh, my God," Allen said, glancing at the window near the front door.

"What?" Dee's heart started thumping.

"Anybody could see in," he said. He rushed to pull the curtains on the window.

"What is there to see?" Dee said. "There's nothing here."

"I mean if the bedroom doors were open, they could see right into it," Allen said.

Which one of us is more rattled? Dee wondered.

Allen gestured toward the thick, wooden sliding doors at the far side of the living room. "The bedroom," he said.

Dee's steps slowed as she and Allen moved closer to the room. Allen pushed apart the large sliding doors.

The tableau that awaited her, tragically brightened by the early-afternoon light passing through the bedroom windows, would forever be etched in Dee's mind. It was a very large bedroom, masculine like the living room, with a king-sized bed, a large desk, a big-screen TV, and VCR. Art Venecia's dead body was sprawled across the floor, half of it on a blue bedspread that he had apparently torn from the bed in his struggle to avoid having his throat slashed. He wore pajama pants but no shirt. The chair that should have been in front of the desk was overturned.

There was blood, what seemed to Dee like gallons of it, all over the floor, but none on the walls.

It was a picture that her brain refused to process into reality. She felt as if she had magically been transported into the celluloid frames of some horror movie. Buckets of blood, she thought. It was a phrase from a horror flick she had seen with Susan. Buckets of blood. This was not, could not be, a real place in real time. In a moment I will wake up and it will be over. But her heart, racing madly now, knew that it was real.

They stood looking at the body for a moment,

then backed out of the room as if something might leap on them if they turned their backs to it. "See," Allen said. He closed the bedroom doors and led Dee into the dining room, which was just a section of the large front room. He poured them each a drink.

Dee sat at the small dining-room table and stared back at the bedroom doors, thinking that if she just waited long enough she could go back into the bedroom and the body would be gone. This would never have happened. It would turn out to be some kind of nightmare, some hallucination caused by her alcoholism. Many of the alcoholics she knew had hallucinations. She'd never had them, but maybe, dear God, this was the first time. But there was a part of her that knew it was real, because her thoughts went to her children. If something happens to me, who will take care of Todd and Wyatt?

"We'll have to go to North Carolina," Allen said.

His voice seemed distant, as if he were speaking to her from the bottom of a well.

"What?"

"Yes, that's it," Allen said. He paced in front of the door that led out to the garage. "We'll put Art in the trunk and drive to North Carolina."

"Are you crazy?"

"It's perfect," Allen said. "Art owns land up there. I know where it is. We'll tell everybody that Art's gone to North Carolina on business. We'll take the body up there and dump it somewhere, then drive back. Nobody will ever know we went. Then when they find the body, it will all make sense. Somebody murdered him up there. It's perfect."

"You really are nuts. You can't put the body in the trunk. What if you get stopped by the state police for a drug check? What about agricultural inspections? They stop cars at the state line all the time to check for plants and vegetables. Jesus, what are you thinking?"

"Okay, forget it," Allen said, "just forget it. We'll burn it."

"Burn it?"

"We'll take him out in the yard, douse him with kerosene, and set him on fire."

"Allen, you're talking crazy. What about the smoke? What about the smell? Somebody will call the police. How do you explain the fact that you're barbecuing a corpse on your front lawn?"

Unable to make a permanent decision about what to do with Art's body, they settled for a temporary one.

"In the garage there was a wooden wardrobe about the size of a 7-Up machine," Dee says. "Allen emptied that out. 'We'll put the body in this,' he said. 'We'll keep it in the garage.' The body was all covered with dried blood, and it was half on and half off the bedspread. When we tried to move the body, it slung the other way and I could see the big gash in Art's throat. Allen was handling the head, but he couldn't take looking at it. So we covered the head with a pillowcase and then Allen took the feet. I just walked behind him, dragging the bedspread. We dragged the body out to the garage. It took a while, but Allen was able to muscle the body into the wardrobe, then I was able to help him move the wardrobe up against a wall. The garage was air-conditioned so we weren't worried about the smell. We had to set the thermostat way down. We got some linens, towels, sheets, whatever was handy, and started soaking up the blood, cleaning things up as best we could, and we tossed the blood-soaked towels into the wardrobe with Art."

After that they went back and sat in the dining room. Allen poured another set of drinks and began talking again about how they could permanently dispose of the body. More and more Dee was accepting the fact that Art was dead and what was required of her was a clear head so she could deal with this tragedy and put it behind her.

They discussed dumping the body in the Everglades, less than an hour away, or possibly dropping it in the Miami Canal, but finally they decided that the safest bet was not to move it far at all.

"I've got five acres here," Allen said. "I could just take it out back and dump it."

"It will smell," Dee said. "Animals will find it. Somebody might wonder why animals are feasting on a corpse in your backyard. Don't you think the best thing is to bury it? You don't intend to get rid of the property, do you?"

"No. I'm going to keep it no matter what happens. Henry and I will probably move out here."

"Fine, then bury Art here."

"When?"

"Well, not in broad daylight," Dee said. "Later."

"Okay, good," Allen said. He seemed to be calming down now that they had decided what to do with the body. "Now, I've got to tell Mrs. Fischer."

"Mrs. Fischer? Who's Mrs. Fischer?"

"Art's mother."

"What are you going to tell her?"

"I'll tell her that Art went to North Carolina on business."

"Won't she think it's a little strange that Art didn't say good-bye?" Dee asked.

"She's practically senile. We'll tell her that Art did say good-bye and she just doesn't remember."

"We" again, Dee thought. "Where does she live?"

"Here."

Dee couldn't believe what she was hearing. She felt an alarm go off inside her.

"What do you mean, here?"

"Right out front, in the little trailer."

"His mother lives here, on the property?" Dee was shouting. She bolted up from the table, knocking her glass of Scotch to the floor. "Right here? You murdered Art right here, twenty feet away from his mother?"

"I didn't murder him."

"Oh, no. You just stood by while somebody else slit his throat with a razor."

Now, fuming with fear and sobbing uncontrollably, she was standing over him, waving her arms wildly.

"Will you calm down? You're getting hysterical," Allen said.

"Hysterical? Jesus, Allen, I can't imagine why I'd be hysterical just because you've got me involved in a murder and the man's mother lives twenty feet away."

"We'll take care of it. We'll take care of it."

"Take care of it? For God's sake, you can't take care of it. The man is dead. Dead. Art is dead. You killed him and you've got me involved. This is not a dream, Allen, we're not going to wake up from it."

"You have to get hold of your friend, Irvine."

"For what?"

"Well, isn't it obvious?" Allen said. "For Mrs. Fischer. She has to be killed, too."

"Oh, my God," Dee said. She had spent her rage, her fear, even her sympathy for the dead man, and now she was empty. She collapsed into her chair, reached blindly for the glass that wasn't there, and finally pushed her face into her hands. The sound that came out of her was like the wail of a wounded animal. "This can't be happening," she said, "this can't be happening."

"Well, it is happening," Allen said. "We've got to finish it."

"No!" Dee shouted. "No, no, no." She pounded on the table. "I didn't sign on for a killing spree. We're not going to kill some old lady."

Allen looked as if he'd been slapped.

"Well, dear, what do you propose we do with her?"

"We let her live," Dee snapped. "How's that for a novel idea?"

"She's old. She's senile. She can't even cook her own meals. We had to shut off her gas because she kept turning on the stove and forgetting to light it."

"I'll feed her," Dee said.

"You'll feed her?"

"Yes, from the restaurant. I'll bring her meals over. Whatever has to be done, I'll do it. Anything, Allen, just don't kill her, okay? I'll take care of her."

"What if she finds out about Art? I could end up in jail. So could you."

"She won't find out anything, I promise."

Allen stared at Dee for a long time. "Okay," he finally said, "but if she starts asking too many questions, we call Mike Irvine. I'm not going to jail because of some old lady."

"Oh, God," Dee said.

"What is it?"

"Where's the bathroom," she said. "I'm going to be sick."

In the bathroom Dee fell to her knees and vomited into the toilet bowl. She knew it wasn't the Scotch that was making her sick now. It was murder. She retched until she was weak and empty, and when she was done, she felt as if she could just barely hold back that sense of panic. She was right on the edge of losing control, and the edge, when she imagined it in her dizziness down there on the bathroom floor, was like a razor blade.

Somehow her mind drifted to all the jobs she'd had, the good ones. The city of Hialeah. Florida Power. Sweet Paper. Dade County. Miller Gas. She had been so . . . competent. Yes, that was the word, competent. She was always so good at what she did, everybody said so. She was sharp then, before the booze came in buckets, before she made a total mess of her life. Give it to Dee, they used to say, she'll do it right. She was neat, she was accurate, she was smart. Now, struck by the symbolism of being sprawled out on a bathroom floor, she knew that her competence was needed again. She had to get back on her feet. She had to get herself under control. Allen needed her to be at her best.

After she finished vomiting, Dee cleaned herself up. She and Allen talked again, whispering in the dining room as if there were someone who might overhear. Now she felt as if she had purged herself of something. They planned. They reasoned. Maybe if they did everything right, this murder could be swept away, forgotten, and she could return to normal life.

14

The Mother

Following Allen's instructions, Dee went to Bessie Fischer's trailer and knocked loudly. Bessie came to the door. She was a short woman, stooped from age. Her silvery-white hair blew in the breeze and Dee could see the pink of the old lady's scalp. It made her look so vulnerable. Bessie peered suspiciously at Dee through round, wire-rimmed glasses.

"Yes?" she said.

"Hi. I'm Dee Casteel," Dee told her. "I'll be bringing your meals while Art and Allen are away in North Carolina."

"Arthur's gone away?" the old lady said. She sounded like a child. "He didn't say anything."

"Sure he did," Dee told her. "Don't you remember, he came over and told you he was going to North Carolina."

It took some time, but finally Dee was able to convince Bessie that Arthur had gone away, that he had told his mother, and that Bessie was simply being forgetful. At last Bessie moved out of the doorway and shuffled back to her wheelchair where she usually sat, by a small wooden table that folded down from the wall of the trailer. She invited Dee in, showed her the small trailer. It was old and somewhat run-down, but Bessie seemed comfortable there.

"Arthur won't let me live in the house," she explained. "He says it's too small."

Dee sat for several minutes while the old lady thumbed through an old photo album. Then she handed it to Dee to look at. "That's my second husband, Mr. Fischer," she said. "And there's Arthur when he was a boy."

Dee turned the pages with sincere interest. She liked looking at photos, especially of families. She tried to hold back her tears, knowing that this woman's son was dead. As the moments passed, Bessie nodded off, but Dee continued to turn the pages of the album slowly. It was something to concentrate on while she waited for the wave of panic to recede. Soon she became aware of Bessie's cat, a big white beast sitting majestically on the Formica surface of one of the trailer's built-in cabinets. Dee felt as if the cat, with its unsettling green eyes, like Allen's, was staring at her, accusing her of something.

"What's your cat's name?" Dee asked nervously, trying to crack the silence in the trailer and vanquish the weird sense that the cat was putting a spell on her.

Bessie opened her eyes. "Cat," she said. She smiled for the first time. "He's my best friend. Except for Arthur, of course."

"Of course," Dee said.

Dee asked Mrs. Fischer what she liked to eat and what times she would like lunch and supper. She felt like a visiting nurse. The schedule would create problems, but it would keep Mrs. Fischer alive. Besides, it was nice to be needed. When she left that day to return to IHOP and get supper for Bessie, Dee felt better knowing she was able to do this favor for Art. She felt partly responsible for his death.

Bessie Fischer, Dee later learned, was eighty-four years old and had been brought over from her home in St. Petersburg a few years earlier, when Art concluded that she could no longer take care of herself. She had had a stroke and a couple of accidents, one of which had left her stranded in her house for five days without help. So Allen and Art had driven to the west coast of Florida and packed up Bessie's things and brought them to The Redlands.

"Mrs. Fischer was not easy to get along with," Allen says. "She was always critical of Art, always nagging him. No matter what he did it was never good enough."

Jackie Ragan, who worked as a waitress at the pancake house long before Venecia bought it, says that Mrs. Fischer was "cantankerous," but she notes that Arthur was a loving son. "He was one of my customers before he was my boss," she says, "and he used to come in and he'd bring his mother. He would help her along. She was real old. And Art would sit there with her and cut her meat for her. He was a dutiful son."

During the days following the murder Allen disconnected Bessie's telephone line, and he dead-bolted the door to Art's house so Bessie couldn't get in with her key. When they'd brought her over from St. Petersburg, she had been "sinking fast," he says. But now she wasn't sinking fast enough for him. Allen was afraid that Bessie would find out about Art.

On Tuesday, June 21, Allen gathered the IHOP employees together and told them that Art had gone to North Carolina on business and would be gone for quite some time. Allen said that he would be spending a lot of time taking care of the nursery and that Dee Casteel would be the day-to-day manager of the pancake house. Her title would be assistant manager.

The fact that this lie went down as smooth as maple syrup, even to a staff that knew Allen had tried to kill Art a week earlier, is not surprising. Art did own property in North Carolina, and the restaurant employees rarely saw Art, anyhow. But more to the point, the IHOP employees had no trouble believing Allen because he was their friend. Most of the employees loved him.

The North Carolina story became the basic explanation for Art Venecia's absence. The story varied depending on who was being lied to. In some versions Art was up there building a motel, or sometimes it was a restaurant. In others, Art, the alcoholic, had gone there to dry out at a sanitarium. In some stories Allen and Art had broken up as lovers. In others, Allen was making frequent trips to North Carolina so he could be with Art.

While the employees were satisfied with the explanation of Art's disappearance, Dee worried about how the story would wash with other people. For the first few weeks after the murder her heart seemed to skip a beat every time the restaurant phone rang. What if it's a friend of Art's? she thought. What if it's a relative? Suspicions would be aroused. Police would be called. But sadly, during the weeks that followed, not one friend, not a single relative, called to see how Art was doing. Art's accountant, George Freitas, called, but Dee was able to stall him with the North Carolina story. She began to relax. According to Dee, Mike Irvine came by one day and she gave him the second half of the $5,000 (although Irvine claims she brought the money to the gas station the night of the murder). In any case, everything was back to normal. They had, it seemed, gotten away with murder.

Of course, Art's body could not be left to decay in his own garage. Both Dee and Allen were worried that Bessie might find it.

"We had to get the body out of the garage," Dee says. "Allen decided it would be better to put it in the metal barn that's on the front of the property, because Mrs. Fischer never went into the barn. He didn't want to take a chance of her finding it in the garage. So I made her a beauty shop appointment. She was very excited about it. I picked her up and took her to the Naranja Beauty Salon and left her. Then I went and got Allen. We took the pickup truck and went out to the property and backed up to the garage. We muscled the wardrobe to the back of the truck and drove up to the front of the barn, made sure nobody was around, and put the body in the barn. There were a couple of pieces of wood, I would say four-by-eight, and we placed them on top of the wardrobe to keep animals away."

With Art's body safely stashed away, Dee did what she could to prevent Mrs. Fischer from becoming body number two. Every day at noon and again at six Dee would place an order at the pancake house, set it on a tray, cover it, and carefully place it on the front seat of her Buick. Then she would drive to Art Venecia's property in The Redlands. The ten-minute drive was always harrowing. She was haunted by visions of someone's discovering the body in the hangarlike barn. Already the body was putting out a stench that could make a grown man puke, and horrifying body fluids leaked from the big wooden box like oil from a junked engine. A stranger coming by, looking for nursery work or whatever, might recognize the smell of death and put in a call to the local police. Dee, bedeviled by the smell of death even when she was far away from it, was always edgy until she had driven over the rise in the entrance road. From there she could see the big metal barn and know that no strangers were snooping around.

For the first several days Dee would see Shadow, Art's Doberman, hungrily scouting the property as if his food had been hidden from him. But the dog never came when she called, and by the end of the first week he was gone. Each day Dee would pull up by Bessie's trailer and for a moment stand outside looking around. "Hello," she would call in case somebody was exploring the property. Then, hearing nothing, she would rap on the trailer door, which Bessie always kept locked. Dee would pull the tray of food from her car and Bessie would let her into the trailer.

Bessie, who spent her days staring at soap operas and game shows, and sleeping almost as much as her cat did, was always excited to see Dee.

"Have you heard from Arthur?" she would ask, even before Dee had set the tray of food down on Mrs. Fischer's small kitchen table. Dee would feel her heart go out to the old lady and she would say, "No, Mrs. Fischer, not today. But he'll be coming home soon, I'm sure." It was always "Mrs. Fischer." Never "Bessie."

"He's a good boy, my Arthur," Mrs. Fischer would say.

"Yes, he is," Dee would answer, and she would sit with Mrs. Fischer while she ate.

For much of the time Bessie dwelled in a merciful senility, a world mostly of girlhood memories. The memories were fragments, but they were well-focused fragments, each misplaced piece as clear to Bessie as last night's dinner is to most people. A gentleman she knew at twenty would somehow end up married to a lady she'd met thirty years later, or the birth of a child would come in the middle of a seventh-grade pageant. She got things mixed up. Sometimes she called Dee "Agatha"; sometimes she described conversations she'd had with Arthur "yesterday," even though a moment later she could wonder out loud why she hadn't heard from Arthur for so long. Half the time Dee couldn't make heads or tails of what the old lady was babbling about, but she listened anyway, and in time Dee grew fond of Mrs. Fischer. The senility helped in one way: when Art had been gone a week, Dee could convince Bessie that it had only been two days.

Though Dee Casteel sincerely believed that she was not responsible for the murder of Art Venecia, the routine of bringing Bessie's meals week in and week out and keeping her company felt, nonetheless, like penance. It tempered the ache of her anxiety about the murder, and in some small way she was doing it for Art, to make up for the fact that he'd been murdered. Still, given Dee's history and the stories of kindness her friends tell, it is likely that Dee would have done as much for any old lady if she had been asked. She was, if you take the word of her friends, doing no more and no less for Bessie Fischer than she had done for a lot of other people.

The compassion Dee felt for Bessie also had a source unrelated to Art and the murder. Dee's grandmother, her precious Mama who had loved and nurtured her until the age of eight, was now near eighty and herself senile. Dee worried about Mama. How was she treated? Was she lonely? Who brought her meals and did they stay and talk with her? There were times when the images of Mrs. Fischer and Mama merged in Dee's increasingly troubled mind, times when they seemed to come in on the same wavelength, when the two women seemed to be one.

Such things preyed on Dee as she went about her life during the summer of 1983. More and more that life was consumed by the demands of her job. She had taken over as assistant manager, but she was not happy. As a waitress she had been making $200 to $250 a week. But as assistant manager she was earning a lot less. In fact, she was receiving no salary at all, just getting money from Allen when she needed it and when he was willing to dole it out. She drank at work more than ever. She kept a bottle in the restaurant, a bottle at home, and a bottle in the car. At first she continued to pick up Jim Garfield and take him home, and almost every afternoon she and Jim would stop at a bar on South Dixie Highway to have a few drinks. But the IHOP, it seemed, wouldn't run efficiently unless Dee put in more and more hours. Soon she was working twelve or sixteen hours a day. Donna Hobson had to take over the job of transporting Jim. Todd and

Wyatt were beginning to seem like memories. Dee hardly ever saw Cass, and when she did, it was usually late at night after both of them had been drinking, and they would fight.

Dee talked to Susan almost every day on the phone. Mostly they talked about their jobs and people they knew. But there were times when Dee's maternal instincts arose.

"What's a line?" Dee finally asked Susan late one night, remembering her remark on the night of the spaghetti dinner. "It's drugs, isn't it?"

"Coke," Susan said.

"Oh, Susan."

"Ma, never mind with the 'Oh, Susan,' okay? You do a hundred times more drugs than me. What do you think alcohol is? It's a drug."

"Yes. But. Honey, I just don't want you to ruin your life."

"The way you've ruined yours?"

"Yes," she said coldly, thinking Susan didn't know how bad things had gotten.

"Sorry, Ma. It's just . . ."

"Just what?"

"It's just I wish you would worry less about me and more about yourself."

At moments like this, when Susan reached out and tried to fortify the emotional connection that had been as much a part of their relationship as the shouting and the fighting, Dee was sorely tempted to blurt out the truth. She knew if she would ever tell anyone, she would tell Susan. She thought she would gain peace if she could just scream it into the phone: "I helped Allen murder Art Venecia. Please forgive me." But to do so would be to risk losing the thing she valued most: Susan's love.

"I'll try," Dee said.

"Love you," Susan said.

"Love you, too," Dee said.

"And it's okay about the coke, Ma. I don't do a lot of it. Honest."

The truth was that things were not okay. Contrary to her claim, Susan was indeed doing a lot of it. Like Bessie Fischer, she was sinking fast.

Despite the drinking, Dee appeared during this period to be very much under control. The drinking, in fact, enhanced her performance as assistant manager of the IHOP, and the job was so demanding that without booze Dee would have folded up in two days. Dee took her IHOP job seriously. The competence, in which she had taken such pride while on the bathroom floor, was called upon daily. She worked from before breakfast to long after dinner. She made out the work schedules, she assigned stations, she did the payroll, she ordered food supplies and cleaning supplies and uniforms, she greeted her regulars when they came in for coffee, now and then deflecting the curious questions about how Art Venecia was doing and what he was up to. And she dealt with corporate IHOP, fending off questions like, "Where the hell is our money this month?" after Allen had gone several weeks without sending a check. This aspect of her job became more and more tense as Bryant recklessly stole money that should have gone to the corporate office. It seemed to Dee that she had been handed a twenty-four-hour job and she felt as if she had no other life. Just as well, she sometimes felt, for it kept her from thinking too much about the cold body in the barn, the midnight razor skating across the throat of Art Venecia, and the buckets of blood on the bedroom floor.

During the weeks after the murder Dee did not see Bryant in the restaurant often. When he did come in, it was to snatch money out of the cash register. Dee estimates that by the middle of July Allen was skimming between two and three thousand dollars a week.

Though Allen had talked about moving into Art's house with Henry, he never did. In fact, after Art was murdered, and the body was stowed in the barn, Allen never entered the house again. It frightened him. Instead, he rented a house in Kendall and moved in with Henry. He bought furniture. He bought a dishwasher. He painted the whole house, floor to ceiling. He put in air-conditioning. He put in carpeting. He hung drapes. And then he went out and bought Henry a new car. And he paid for it all with cash from the International House of Pancakes cash register, and from Art Venecia's E.F. Hutton account, which Allen began plundering the day after the murder.

"The house was beautiful," Joanne Rivera, the waitress, recalls. "Allen's favorite color was blue and he redid it all in blue. He had great taste and he did a fabulous job. He built a deck and everything. He did so much work you'd think he was going to live there forever."

Sometimes Allen didn't even come to the restaurant for money. He just called in for it, and Dee would have one of the busboys bring it up to the Kendall house. The restaurant was as busy as ever; people never seemed to get sick of pancakes, but Dee worried that Allen's pilfering would suck the life out of the business. As much as she worried about Art's body being found, she worried more about the restaurant's going under and her being tossed out on the street. More and more the idea of being without a job felt to Dee like the end of the world.

When Dee did see Allen, he spent much of his time trying to convince her that Bessie's death would be best for everybody. He argued that sooner or later Bessie would come in contact with another person and that would lead to questions and the truth would inevitably ooze out like the vile fluids that were leaking out of the wardrobe. With Bessie dead, he said, there would be no loose ends.

But Dee was adamant.

"Art's murder was horrible enough," she told him once at his new house, where she had gone to deliver five hundred dollars in cash. "It was a dreadful mistake, but it's a mistake we somehow got away with. God knows how. But I'm not going to compound it with the murder of a helpless old lady who hasn't hurt anybody."

"What if she calls somebody up?" Allen said.

"She can't call anybody—you yanked the damn phone cord out, remember?"

"She might go somewhere and call."

"Bessie's not going anywhere. She can hardly even walk."

Conversations like this would push the subject back in its box, but in a day or two Allen would get a case of jitters and he would try to wear Dee down again.

There were times when Dee was pushed perilously close to agreeing that Bessie had to go.

One Saturday, at the end of that first frantic week following the murder, some friends of Cass and Dee's got married. Dee went to the reception at the Moose Lodge. Dee, already drunk, had to leave the reception early to bring Bessie her evening meal. Driving home from Bessie's, Dee noticed a cop car trailing her. Was it really following her, she wondered, or was paranoia finally settling in? She turned left, she turned right. They turned left, they turned right. What do they want? Do they know something about Art Venecia?

When she pulled up in front of her own house, the police stopped behind her. Cass was already home and she could see him watching through the window. She got out of her car. Two cops climbed out of the cruiser. They walked toward her. Oh, God, this is it, she thought. Within minutes she was under arrest—for driving under the influence of alcohol. As the police were loading Dee into the car, Cass came to the door.

"Call Allen," she called to him. Allen had become the person she depended on to take care of her.

In less than an hour Allen was down at the police

station with the bail money. As they walked out of the station, he put his arm around her.

"Dee, you've got to stop drinking so much," he said. "I'm worried about you."

"I can't handle this without drinking," Dee said.

"I understand," Allen said. "Believe me, I understand. What we need to do is get rid of Mrs. Fischer. It's for your own good."

After that Allen asked for daily reports. What did Mrs. Fischer say? What questions did she ask? Did she sound suspicious? He was chipping away at her, and Dee could feel herself getting weaker.

As Dee continued to bring Mrs. Fischer's meals, the mysterious visits to "some old lady" inevitably ignited Cass's jealous instincts. That led to another nerve-racking encounter.

"Who is this old lady? Where does she live?" Cass wanted to know.

Dee explained for the hundredth time that she was taking meals to Art Venecia's mother while Art was away, but Cass was convinced that Dee was meeting some lover twice a day, and he insisted on being taken to Bessie Fischer's trailer and seeing a real live old lady with his own eyes. So one evening Dee took Cass with her when she delivered Bessie's supper. Dee was, understandably, nervous. A jealous man was just the kind of person who looked closely at things, asked questions, sniffed the air. Not only that, but Cass, with his many faults, had the virtue of honesty. He was a great believer in turning crooks in, and Dee knew that if Cass ever found out about the murder, he'd deliver her to police headquarters himself.

After meeting Bessie and staring at her long enough to be certain she was not some Latin lover in disguise, Cass decided to roam the property while Dee sat with the old lady. Dee thought of asking him not to, then realized that that would just make him suspicious. Instead, she stayed with Bessie a reasonable number of minutes, all the time drumming her fingers on her lap and glancing out the trailer window while the old lady ate.

When Dee came out of the trailer, Cass was waiting. *Has he found anything? Does he know I'm involved in a murder?*

"How long you going to be feeding that old lady?" Cass asked.

"Just until Art gets back," she said.

Cass glanced again at the trailer. Then he pivoted around and took a long, hard look at the property, as if lovers might be hiding in the bushes. Then he smiled at Dee and said, "Okay."

Dee drove the Buick down the driveway and took a right. She was starting to breathe easy again. But Cass, glancing off in the other direction, said something that burned in her ears. What he said was, "Turn around. There's Mike."

"Mike who?" Dee asked, though she had a pretty good idea.

"Irvine," Cass said. Dee turned the car around and there was Mike Irvine waving at them and smiling his country-bumpkin smile. His green Valiant was parked off the road, right next to the Venecia property. The hood was up, and another man, who had his head under the hood, was tinkering . . . or pretending to tinker . . . with the engine. *What in God's name is Mike doing here?* Dee thought. *This is no coincidence. Allen has hired Mike to kill Bessie without telling me, that's it.* But she disposed of that thought quickly. That wasn't Allen's style. Allen would get Dee to make the contact. Allen would always cover his ass.

Cass climbed out of the car and shook hands with Irvine. For several minutes they stood between the cars, talking. Mike said he'd been just jolly-driving, looking to see if there were any old cars around for sale. Now he had a little engine problem but he could fix it okay. He said hello to Dee and threw her a big smile, as if there were nothing the slightest bit odd about his being in front of the house where he had committed a murder that she had contracted for. Dee stared into Mike's eyes, trying mentally to say to him, "Are you out of your mind, coming here again? Are you trying to get us all thrown in jail?" But Mike was oblivious. Then he called over his friend.

"Dee, Cass, this is my friend Bill," he said.

When Dee looked at Bill, she felt suddenly stiff and cold. She would not have been more uneasy if she were being introduced to Charles Manson. Bill was short, muscular, hairy. His eyes were without kindness, and his dirty-blond hair was more dirty than blond. Without speaking a word Bill seemed to scream, "I am evil. Watch out for me." There was no doubt at all in Dee's mind that she was meeting the man who had slashed Art Venecia's throat.

The next day when Dee went to Allen's house and told him about running into the murderers, Allen became unhinged.

"Jesus, that does it," he said. "Bessie has got to be killed."

"What the hell are you talking about?" Dee asked. "What's Bessie got to do with this?"

"Loose ends," Allen said. "Loose ends. It's loose ends, these two lunatics roaming around the property. We need to wrap it up, get rid of the loose ends. That means Bessie."

"No," Dee said.

"Be reasonable," he said. "We kill her and then we won't kill anybody else, I promise."

Dee was tempted. She loved Allen, she wanted to please him. But the idea of killing Bessie was more than she could bear. "No," she said. She knew she had been too obedient to Allen, too anxious to please. Now it was time to stand up to him. "It's out of the question."

"She's Art's mother, not yours, for Christ sake," Allen said. "Don't make such a big deal out of it."

"Allen, murder is a big deal."

"It's not really murder," Allen said. "She's

eighty-four years old, she's going to die pretty soon, anyhow."

"Then there's no reason to kill her. Leave her alone."

"We'd be doing her a favor," Allen said. "If we kill her, she never has to know that her son died."

"Please don't make me fight you all the time on this," Dee said. "Just leave it alone. Bessie's not bothering anybody. I'll just keep bringing her meals."

"You're not thinking, darling. Bessie's the one loose end that can prove we murdered Art."

"I didn't murder anyone," Dee said.

"No? Try telling that to the police."

"We are not going to kill Mrs. Fischer," Dee said. "I will not allow it." But inside she sensed that no matter what she said or felt, they were moving inexorably toward that unspeakable act.

Allen, good salesman that he was, knew better than to pursue his customer with a pitch that wasn't working. He was at times capable of changing his mood as easily as he changed his shirt, and now he seemed to toss aside his concern without a second glance.

"You like her, don't you?" he said coyly, as if realizing for the first time that Dee's blood was a little warmer than his own.

"Yes," Dee said.

"You like her a lot?" He grinned.

"Yes, I like her. What do you think, I'm gay for the old lady or something?" Dee laughed. Allen had shifted gears on her; he had turned on the charm.

"Hey, I don't care. Different strokes for different folks." Now he was playing with her and Dee liked that. She wanted him to touch her. She had begun to want that a lot lately.

"In a way she makes me think of my grandmother, that's all," Dee said softly. "She's just a nice old lady and she's not hurting anybody."

"Maybe you're right," Allen said. "But you'd better keep an eye on her, okay, sweetheart?"

"Okay," Dee said, and things were back to what, at the time, passed for normal.

Things went along that way through most of July. The restaurant, despite all of Allen's pilfering, stayed afloat. When corporate IHOP called to see why they weren't getting their money, Dee was able to put them off. Bessie was getting her IHOP meals every day, and though she asked about her son every day her questions became more and more perfunctory.

Dee never found out what Irvine and Rhodes were doing out by the Venecia property, but she doubts that Mike's car just happened to break down at that spot. More likely, they had come back to the property to see what they could steal.

Despite everything, the fears about Bessie, the drain on the restaurant's money, the pressure from Allen, the murderers loitering near the scene of the crime, it still seemed that the murder had been successful. Allen was rid of Art. Dee had a secure job. Bessie was being taken care of. Rhodes and Irvine had been paid off. Nobody was the wiser and nobody had been hurt except, of course, Art.

Then one morning Dee was taking a break. She sat at her usual back-of-the-room table drinking her usual iced coffee laced with her usual Scotch. She was trying to figure out how much money the franchise really owed the corporate office, and she had decided to ask Allen to cut down on his "profit taking." Better to take a little for a long time, she would reason with him, than take a lot and lose the restaurant in a matter of months.

"Dee," she heard.

She looked up. It was Claire, one of the waitresses on day shift.

"Yes."

"It's none of my business," Claire said, "but I think you should know that there's a rumor going around that you and Allen killed Art and dumped his body in the canal or something."

15

The Decision

When Dee told Allen about the rumor, he was upset, as she'd expected. In fact, he was outraged. But he seemed less concerned about the possibility of the murder's being exposed than about the fact that his friends had said such dreadful things about him. He felt betrayed.

"Rumors? Whose rumors?" he asked. "Who is saying these things?"

"I don't know," Dee said. "Just some of the employees. You know how talk goes around."

"I can't believe my own people would do this to me," Allen said. "I've done everything for them. I've trusted them and now they're talking about me behind my back."

Even though he was guilty of murder, Allen was genuinely hurt that IHOP people would think him capable of such a thing.

The rumor had been planted by Jay Reed, an IHOP cook, who had been troubled by Art's absence. While pouring pancake batter on the grill, Reed was

The pancake house. (Photo by Wayne Fleisher).

Dee as a young woman of 19 or 20.

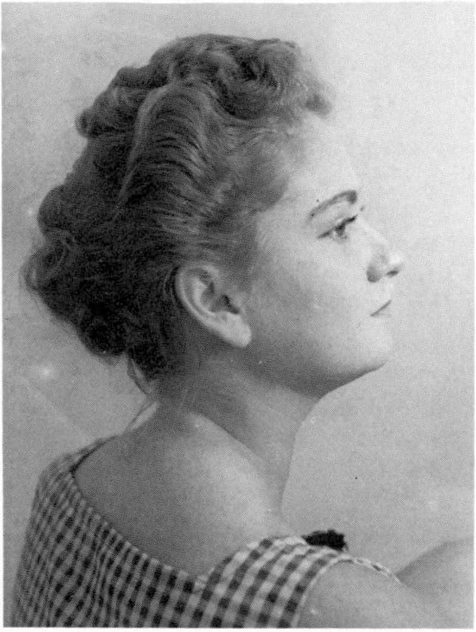

Dee Casteel as a young girl, with her grandmother.

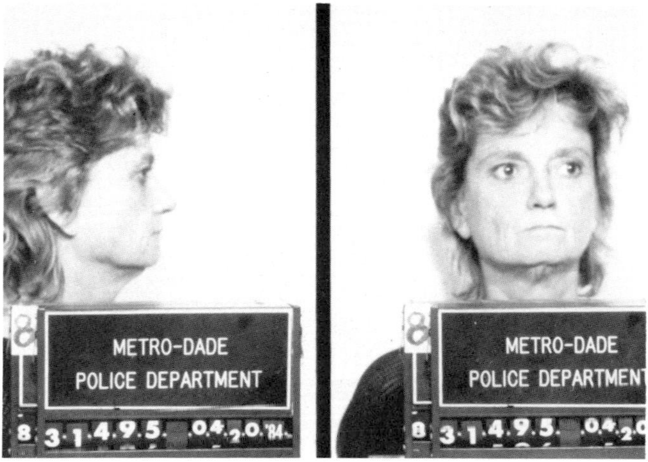

Dee after her arrest.

Dee with her daughter Susan and her grandchild during a recent prison visit.

Michael Irvine. (Photo by Wayne Fleisher).

William Rhodes.
(Photo by
Wayne Fleisher).

James Allen Bryant. (Photo by Wayne Fleisher).

Art Venecia. (*The Miami Herald*/Albert Coya).

Art Venecia's house. (Photo by Wayne Fleisher).

The bedroom where Veneccia was killed.

The trailer where Bessie was murdered.

Police exhuming Venecia's and his mother's bodies.

Some of the evidence exhumed at the gravesite.

inclined to speculate out loud about what Allen might have done with Art's body.

"The Everglades," Reed would ask grimly, "or Biscayne Bay? Take your pick."

Though Reed was the first to whisper the word "murder," he was not the only IHOP employee to think it. Jim Garfield says, "Oh, sure, it had occurred to me that maybe Allen had put an end to Art and ditched his body somewhere. But not with Dee involved. God no, nobody could imagine Dee involved in something like that. She was too fine a lady."

Donna Hobson, who had driven Dee to Bessie's when Dee was too drunk to drive herself, says, "I guess the thing that really got me suspicious was when I saw Carlos, the busboy, driving Art's little red pickup truck. That struck me as strange because that was Art's truck and he never let anybody drive it. I said to Carlos, 'If Art ever saw you driving his truck, he would hit the ceiling.' Carlos just smiled. I think he knew something. I knew something was going on. I guess I never thought it could be murder. The idea of murder was too drastic for my mind to handle. I mean murder is done by other people, not your friends, and not the people you work with. I don't know what I thought exactly, but I knew something was wrong because Art was the kind of guy who would call in often to see how things were going, and it just was not in the man to go away like that and leave the restaurant in Allen's hands and not call in."

So what Jay Reed had begun to say out loud might not have gained the momentum of a rumor, except that it resonated with thoughts already buzzing in the heads of other employees. The buzz was growing louder daily, and Allen knew he had to put a stop to it.

Instead of ducking the issue in his Kendall love nest and having Dee somehow "take care of it," Allen took control of the situation.

"Allen called us all together," Donna Hobson

recalls, "the waitresses, the busboys, the cooks. And we all sat down for a meeting."

They gathered in the employees' break section at the back of the restaurant. Allen stood before them and paced, like a schoolteacher meeting with his most troublesome pupils.

"Some of you don't think Art has gone to North Carolina?" he roared. "That's the same as calling me and Dee liars. Isn't that what you're saying, that we're liars? Who thinks we're liars, huh, who?"

Bristling with indignation, he fired his own accusations. His enemies were gossips, he said. They were ingrates. They were clucking hens. They were gutless little snoops who talked behind his back.

"I'll tell you right now," he shouted, "Art Venecia is in North Carolina and he's left me in charge. I can't be here most of the time, so Dee is in charge. And," he cried, dramatically thrusting a single trembling finger in the direction of the door, "anybody who doesn't like that can get the hell out of here right now. We don't need you."

The employees, embarrassed that they had ever suspected such a wretched thing of Allen, sat transfixed, their heads cast downward.

"And if anybody doesn't want to take my word for it, you can pick up the phone right now and talk to Art."

Allen, his eyes full of fire, stared out over his charges, just daring them to doubt him.

"Go ahead, if you want to make a fool of yourself, call Art up right now in North Carolina and tell him what's been going on here."

Allen let seconds of silence pass, for effect. Nobody took the challenge.

"How about it?" he taunted. "Who here thinks Dee is a liar? Who thinks I'm a liar? Don't be shy now. Just let me know and I'll put you on the phone to Art right this second."

Still, nobody picked up the gauntlet, and the

meeting broke up in tense silence. Dee, sitting in her corner chair smoking her Benson and Hedges, beamed like a proud stage mother.

"Allen was a wonderful actor," she says. "He had them all on the defensive. They were ashamed of themselves. After that performance you could have brought Art's body in on a stretcher and they still would have believed he was alive in North Carolina."

But Dee was wrong. Not all of the pancake house employees were bamboozled by Allen's histrionics. Donna Hobson, for example, remained uncertain.

She says, "Allen raved about how some people didn't believe that Art was gone to North Carolina, and if we didn't want to believe him, we could just call Art there. But Allen never volunteered a phone number, or even the name of a town or anything."

Still, Allen's lecture certainly inhibited loose talk about murder and hidden bodies, especially when he and Dee were at the restaurant. Jay Reed was fired a few days later. But the bacteria of rumor had been spilled, and the only thing that could really stop it from growing would have been a personal appearance by Art Venecia, walking through the front door of IHOP with a bagful of souvenirs from the Tarheel State.

The rumor had been unsettling for Allen, and he was still stinging from it a few days later when he invited Dee to dinner, just the two of them, at Monty Trainer's restaurant on Bayshore Drive in Coconut Grove.

It was not unusual for Allen to take Dee to dinner. He had done it several times, particularly when it seemed that a fine time, a good meal, and plenty of drink might persuade her to his way of thinking on some matter or other. By this time Dee Casteel and Allen Bryant had become very close. The torch, which some people say Dee carried for Allen long before the murder, was certainly flaming by now. Allen treated her, she says, like a queen. He opened car doors for her. He bought her presents. He noticed when she had fixed her hair or bought a new dress. At times he expressed great concern about her drinking and encouraged her to give it up. At other times he showed his affection for Dee by surprising her with a bottle of Scotch he had picked up at Big Daddy's package store. "Because you're such a nice person," he would say, handing over the bottle as if it were a dozen roses.

Dee loved it when Allen took her out to dinner. She'd dress up for it, pamper herself with bubble bath and makeup, and wait for Allen to pick her up in the Lincoln Town Car. At restaurants and nightclubs he would help her with her seat, take her sweater for her if it happened to be a cool night, and smile at her across the table like some smitten beau of old. At his best he was an attentive southern gentleman. In the glow of Allen's youth and charm Dee could pretend that her cheeks had not hollowed out, that her body had not gone as gaunt as a peasant's, that the light had not faded from her eyes. For long moments, especially when she had a few drinks in her, she could be Dee, the Miami Beach playgirl who had broken a few hearts long ago.

When they got to their table at Monty Trainer's that night in late July of 1983, Allen told Dee how lovely she looked and he ordered drinks.

"Dee," he said, "I want to talk to you about your salary." He smiled. "I hate to admit it, but you're right. I've been unfair."

If there was a continuing area of difficulty between them, besides the Bessie problem, it was in the matter of Dee's salary as manager. From the beginning Dee was concerned that as manager she made less money than she did as a waitress. She wanted a check every week and she wanted it to represent at least some sort of a raise. Allen had told her that was silly. "Just take what you need from the register," he had said. That's how he had operated with Art. The arrangement would have suited Dee just fine, except that every time she needed to remove cash from the drawer she was obliged to telephone Allen and get permission. If she needed to get her car repaired, she had to call Allen. If she needed to buy groceries, she had to call Allen. If she just wanted to take the kids out to dinner and blow a hundred bucks, she had to call Allen. Dee was working eighty hours a week and still she felt like a beggar.

Now, at Monty Trainer's, Allen told Dee he'd been thinking it over and he realized that he was being a bit too strict about the money.

"You don't have to call me for every little withdrawal," he said. "Certainly I can trust you. You're my closest friend."

Dee was ecstatic. She yearned so much for Allen's approval and here he was offering his trust and his friendship. They ordered dinner and she ordered another drink. From across the table Allen winked at her. "No limit on drinks," he said.

As usual, they had a great time. They laughed. They gossiped. They joked. And they drank. At some level Dee certainly understood that Allen wanted something, but alcohol had a way of washing away those nagging suspicions. Her friend Scotch always led her, it seemed, to new levels of truth. And the truths that Scotch revealed, as with many alcoholics, were the good ones, the ones that made her life more bearable, the ones that made it possible for Dee to live with herself. It was becoming increasingly clear, as it always did when she drank, that the murder of Art Venecia was not that big a deal, that it was not Dee's fault, that things would get better.

Allen, perhaps waiting for the right amount of alcohol to enter Dee's system, talked about other things.

Allen's favorite subject during these dinners was his intense love for Henry. This was a significant time for Allen in his relationship with Henry because through the practice of Santeria, Allen had cast away his doubts about whether or not Henry really loved him.

Santeria, meaning "worship of saints," is a mixture of ancient African magic and Catholic mysticism. Over the years it has worked its way across the Atlantic to Latin America; and Miami, with its high Latin population, has a good many practitioners, known as santeros. Santeria is neither more rational nor more ridiculous than any other religious view, but in Florida it was known to inspire hysterical headlines locally, and occasionally nationally, mainly because the santeros are inclined from time to time to sacrifice live chickens, though not as often as, say, Colonel Sanders.

One feature of Santeria is the worship of orishas, which are neither saints nor Nigerian gods, but some merging of the two. It is believed that by worshiping a particular orisha, and conducting a magical ritual, a santero can cure illness, attract a lover, destroy a marriage, or exterminate an enemy. This aspect of Santeria had been particularly attractive to a lovesick Allen, who, according to Dee, had been making regular visits to a teacher of Santeria.

A few days before this dinner at Monty Trainer's, Dee had gotten a cryptic telephone call at the IHOP from Allen. He was sending Carlos over, he said, and Dee was to give Carlos one hundred dollars with which to buy two doves.

"Doves?" she had asked.

"I'll explain later," he had said.

Now, drinking cocktails at Monty Trainer's, Allen explained about the doves. A Santeria ritual for lovers required him to take two doves to the ocean at dawn and release them. If the doves stayed together in flight, the dove-releaser and his lover would likewise stay together all through life. If the doves parted, he and his lover would part.

"So," Dee said when Allen was done, "what

happened?" She was hoping perhaps that the doves had parted, that Allen would give up Henry for her.

"The doves," Allen said jubilantly, "stayed together."

"Oh, Allen, I'm so happy for you."

"Isn't it great," Allen said. "Don't tell Henry, though. He thinks all this Santeria stuff is crazy."

Allen, incidentally, says that this conversation never took place. "All that stuff about Santeria is made up," he says. "It's total lies. I was raised as a Christian and I still am one, and I have never done anything with Santeria or Tarot cards or anything like that. It's all lies."

Allen and Dee talked about other things. They talked about Susan. Dee was worried that Susan might turn into an alcoholic or a drug addict. They talked about the restaurant. Dee urged Allen to steal less money. And they talked about the little girl that Allen often baby-sat for. But it was all just filler. Allen ordered more drinks and began to funnel the conversation down to the real reason for his dinner.

Dee, by now, had entered that world not of drunkenness as we normally see it, but of altered personality. Under the influence of moderate amounts of alcohol Dee was neither stupid nor incompetent. In fact, she was quite sharp after a few drinks, certainly sharper than when she had been deprived of booze for a length of time. She was, a Dade County judge would later say, "at her best when she drank." So what followed cannot be understood simply as a product of alcohol in quite the same way that we explain that drunkenness is the reason we danced naked on our neighbor's piano at last night's party. For Dee, drinking meant something more.

It is a difficult thing for the nonalcoholic mind to comprehend, but under the influence of alcohol Dee Casteel was simply not the same person. She was somebody else, with different motives and different values. She walked differently, she talked differently, and everybody who knows her says that if you watched a "before and after" film you would not even be sure you were watching the same person. The allusion that arises in every interview is that of Jekyll and Hyde, a particularly appropriate image because that Robert Louis Stevenson story is about a kind man who took a drug and committed murder.

The way in which Dee was different seems to have depended on whom she was with. With Susan and with Cass, Dee was sometimes mellow, but more often she was a foulmouthed, pugnacious bitch. With Allen the same amount of alcohol produced a laughing, flirtatious, and highly agreeable drinking pal, just as it had with her many lovers during the early stages of romance. After two or three drinks with Allen the significance of their crime was lost, the possible consequences forgotten; judgment was blunted, and Dee became highly suggestible. Allen Bryant, of course, knew this better than anyone.

"When I think of what Dee has done," says Donna Hobson, "I know it had to be the alcohol. Dee was such a sweet, kind person. The alcohol did it, and Allen knew exactly how to work Dee with the alcohol. He knew she was an alcoholic, and he knew she was infatuated with him. He would use alcohol to get her to do whatever he wanted. And that's how it was with Dee back then. Whatever Allen wanted, Allen got."

The voices of all the people in Dee's life repeat the same observation. Long before anybody knew about the murder, it was obvious that Allen was using Dee—obvious to everyone, that is, except Dee.

"I want you to do something for me," Allen said. By now they had eaten an expensive dinner, and Dee had lost count of how many times her empty Scotch glass had been replaced by a full one.

"What?" Dee asked. She smiled coquettishly, licked her lips. "Do you want me, huh, is that it? You've finally decided to swing the other way?"

"That's not it, sweetie."

"Then what? You just name it, sugar. Anything you want, you can have."

"I want you to talk to your friend about Bessie," Allen said.

"Oh."

"Will you do it? It's important, Dee."

"I thought we agreed to just let this thing take its course."

"We did," Allen said. "But frankly, I'm worried about Bessie. Out there all alone."

"I've been worried about her, too," Dee said. In fact, Dee had worried constantly about Mrs. Fischer, and the confusion of images . . . Mrs. Fischer and Mama somehow coming in on the same frequency . . . had continued, perhaps an early warning that Dee was cracking up.

"It's not right, her being out there all alone," Allen said. "I think it would be best for her if we eliminated her."

"Maybe," Dee said. "I don't know. It's so confusing."

"Look," Allen said, "I know it sounds wrong when you say 'murder Bessie.' It sounds awful. But think about it for a minute. She's old and she's going to die soon, anyhow. She lost her son, but she doesn't know it yet. And she doesn't have to know it, that's the beauty of it. She's all alone out there, and if something happened while she was alone, she could suffer for a long time and then die, anyhow. You've said that yourself."

"I know, but . . ."

"It's not really murder," Allen said. "When you think about it, all it is, is a mercy killing."

"I suppose," Dee said.

"Dee, I'm asking you to do this as a favor to me. I'm not asking you to kill anybody. Just talk to Mike. Ask if he'll do the job and find out how much he'll charge us. Will you just do that much for me?"

Allen had shoved his needle into the right vein.

Dee's greatest and most constant fear about Mrs. Fischer was not that the old lady would ask too many questions or that she would find her son's body. The fear, the thing that really ate away at Dee when she worked at the IHOP or when she went home at night, was that Mrs. Fischer would fall down and not be able to get up.

Every day Mrs. Fischer left the trailer once, to fetch her mail from the box at the end of the long driveway. Dee would have brought it to her, but Mrs. Fischer insisted on going out for it as soon as the mailman came. There might be a letter from Arthur, she always said. Dee was haunted by persistent visions of Mrs. Fischer's trudging along the driveway and suddenly turning an ankle and toppling over, perhaps breaking a leg or a hip. In Dee's dark vision Mrs. Fischer would lie helpless along the road, unable to move, unable to have her impotent wailing heard in the isolated area. (And even if somebody did find her, that could be costly, Dee knew. "Where's your son?" a rescuing neighbor might ask, and "What's that awful smell?") Each time Dee drove to the house her fear of seeing a stranger's car was accompanied by her fear of finding poor old Mrs. Fischer's half-dead body sprawled along the road under the pine trees like discarded junk. And in her imagination, when Dee ran to help the distressed old woman, when she turned her face to the sky and checked her pulse for life, the face she saw was sometimes not the face of Mrs. Fischer at all, but that of her own grandmother, Mama.

"So will you do this for me?" Allen said. "Will you talk to Mike?"

"Yes," Dee said.

16

The Calls

Dee Casteel's daughter, Susan, remembers childhood the way soldiers remember war. She remembers having love generously given, then yanked away without warning. She remembers always wondering what she had done wrong. She remembers crying in bed and pretending she had a happy family like the people on television. And the moving, she remembers the constant moving. By the time she was fourteen she had packed up and said good-bye to friends twenty times. She had lived in cheap stucco apartment buildings, boxy little rented houses, and cramped trailers.

Susan remembers being dragged into bars. She remembers the reckless driving, the crushed fenders. She remembers the enormous weight of her secret: my mom drinks. Bullied by her mother, depended on by her little brothers, and questioned by her curious friends, she seemed as if she were always dragging a six-ton block of concrete around with her.

She remembers having to dial the phone to call Dee's employers and tell them, "My mother can't come to work because she's sick today." She remembers her mother being mean sometimes, and she remembers tiptoeing around the house as if it were mined, as if one wrong step would blow the family to kingdom come, and it would be her fault.

She remembers wondering if today would bring good Mommy or mean Mommy. She remembers the feeling of being embarrassed to bring friends home because her mother might be drunk. She remembers growing up too fast, always being the adult, the parent to her brothers, the cook, the housekeeper, the person who kept the family from unraveling. She remembers the fights . . . not just shouting matches, but real punching, screaming, spitting, kicking fights with her mother. She remembers her mother's being beaten time and again. She remembers the wailing. She remembers the fear of talking about her feelings because that would be traitorous. Most of all, she never wanted to betray her mother.

Once, when browsing through an article about the children of alcoholics in *People* magazine, Susan was struck by how accurately the piece described her own childhood. She circled the passage that read:

> Deprived of love and stability, such kids are often taught to hide the problem—and take on aspects of the adult roles abdicated by the parent. Once grown, many suffer from low self-esteem, a need for approval, troubled relationships, and a badly skewed sense of what constitutes normal behavior. Children of alcoholics are also three times more likely than others to become alcoholics themselves.

Though there had been brutal alcoholic men in Dee's life and they had done their share of damage to the kids, there is no question that the person responsible for Susan's miserable childhood was her mother, Dee.

"But I still love my mom," Susan says. "I always have. She's my best friend. It's always been like that. I always loved her even when I hated her. When she was drinking, it was like some devil had entered her body. I didn't understand that alcoholism was a disease then, but I knew that when she was drunk, she wasn't my real mom. She could be cruel and argumentative. Sometimes she was so belligerent with Cass it was like she was looking to get thrashed. But there were times when she went a week or even months without drinking, and she was the best. That was my real mom. When Cass would leave, I would come back and live with her and my brothers. But then Cass would return and I would leave because I couldn't stand by and watch her get beat, and she refused to leave him. But Mom and I would still be friends. When I had a crush on a boy, I'd tell my mom. When I lost my virginity, I told my mom, just like you would tell your friend. When I was worried about something, I would turn to Mom. We used to go to horror movies together. We went to Busch Gardens. We both liked fairs and fast rides. Mom was a real down-to-earth person. She loved gardening, she was good with plants. She could make anything grow. She was a really good cook. We were bargain shoppers, me and Mom; we never had money but we would go to garage sales, things like that.

"My favorite memory from childhood is one summer when the boys went away to visit their father. Cass was gone. We were renting this really nice house in Homestead, and it had a garage that was all bare. We decided it would be our project for the summer. The biggest thing we did was to turn that into the boys' room.

"It was the simple things in life that Mom and I shared. We would go to Neighbor's restaurant and have pie and coffee, or go to McCrory's shopping. Christmas time was always big. Mom never had a fake tree. Not my mom. She was a good mom when she was sober. She was a great mom. My mother is extremely intelligent. She was executive secretary to the mayor of Hialeah when she was eighteen. And she was a good waitress, the best."

If Susan had read a textbook on the children of alcoholics, she could not have played her role more credibly than she was playing it by midsummer of 1983. Her taste in men was like her mother's: she liked them big, she liked them older, and she didn't pursue the ones who handled her with care.

And if a succession of inappropriate boyfriends couldn't give Susan the destruction that she apparently craved, well, she had other weapons. She kept cocaine in the refrigerator. She was drinking. She was, she says, an alcoholic. And just for good measure, she was bulimic.

If Susan at seventeen was on a predictable track toward oblivion, the reason she was not getting to it more quickly was that she'd had the good sense to move out of her mother's house when Dee married Cass, whom she calls "another ex-military, wife-beating lowlife who thinks the country owes him a living." (Susan also notes, "Cass was a very nice guy when he was sober.") Susan had moved in with a woman she frequently baby-sat for. If she had lived those years from eleven to sixteen in the pressure cooker of a two-alcoholic family, Susan might have been emotionally pulverized before she was old enough to drive.

"I should never have let Susan go," Dee has said many times over the years. "I should never have chosen Cass over Susan, but I was so in love with that man. And the way I saw it at the time, the kids would grow up and leave me, and then who would I have? With me and Cass, I thought it was forever."

The years after Susan moved out were less traumatic, but she still had a Jekyll and Hyde for a mom. And she couldn't get it out of her mind that no matter how calm things might be for the moment, there was always a clock ticking, there was always something gaining on her.

What Susan had going for her was intelligence, a willingness to examine herself, to watch for the danger signals. And by summer of 1983 Susan could see plenty of danger signals. She was beginning to realize that she was repeating her mother's life, and she was beginning to think: this is insanity. Things were not great, but she had at least been infected with hope. And then came the phone calls.

"Hi, honey," Dec said.

"Hi, Mom. What's up?"

"Cass is driving me crazy. I need a divorce."

"No kidding? I've only been telling you that for three years."

"Yeah, you're right. I should have listened to you."

"You're drunk, aren't you," Susan said.

"A little bit."

"You're a lot drunk, Mom. Allen's going to fire you if you keep this up."

"He can't fire me."

"What do you mean, he can't fire you. Of course he can fire you."

"No, he can't. Allen and I are into something. My job is safe for life."

"God, you're really stinking tonight," Susan said. "Why don't you go to bed and call me tomorrow when you're sober."

"No, honey, don't hang up. Please. Allen and I are into something and he won't fire me because I know too much."

"What are you into?"

"Oh, nothing. Just a little something."

"What?"

"Now don't be mad at me," Dee said.

"Ma, what is it?"

"He wants to kill Art."

"Oh, is that all?"

"He wants to murder him and take his money."

"Sure he does," Susan said.

"He does. He has a new lover. Henry. A real looker. Allen wants to kill Art so he can be with Henry."

"So? What's that got to do with you?"

"He asked me if I knew someone who would do it. You know, take a contract."

"Great," Susan said. "What did you tell him, Mike Irvine?"

"Yes."

"Ma, that was supposed to be a joke."

"Not to Allen. He wants Mike Irvine to kill Art. Mike and a friend of his will do it."

"Ma, Mike wouldn't hurt a flea, you know that."

"Well, you know how Mike always says he'd kill Cass for me."

"Yes, but he's just kidding," Susan said. "Mike. That would be like hiring Santa Claus to kill somebody."

"No, it's true," Dee said. "Mike really will kill somebody for money. Him and his friend."

"Ma, would you please sober up. I'm afraid you're going to get fired."

That's how the first call went. Neither woman is sure of just how many calls there were, but with each call Dee revealed a little more about the plan to kill Art Venecia. And with each call Susan grew a little more edgy, a little less certain that she was just listening to the crazed ramblings of her drunken mother. One night, when Susan was drinking and beginning to fear that there really was a murder plan, she called her mother at the IHOP.

"Look, Ma, this is stupid," she said. "You don't have to murder people to keep your job. I can help you. We can all be together. You can get rid of Cass. I can get us a place to live, just you and me and Todd and Wyatt." In the morning Susan felt foolish for even thinking the plan could be real.

But the calls kept coming.

And then one night there was a particularly cold and hopeless quality in her mother's voice on the phone.

"They did it," Dee said. "They really did it."

"Who did it? Did what?" Susan asked. She had been more and more troubled by the calls and now her mother's voice frightened her.

"They murdered Art. Mike and his friend."

"Ma, you're talking crazy. I'm worried. You're never sober anymore when you call."

"Allen paid them to do it and they did it."

"Don't be absurd," Susan said.

"I'm involved in a murder," Dee said. "I can't believe it."

"Ma! Will you stop it! You're scaring me."

"They slit his throat." Dee sounded frantic.

"Sure they did," Susan said. "Ma, you have to stop drinking. Can't you see what's happening to your mind?"

"No. Honey, it's true. I talked to Mike and we set it up, and then Mike and his friend went to Art's house and they killed him."

There was a silence. Dee said nothing. Susan was afraid to speak. There was a kitchen counter in front of her. The carton of cream had been left out. Some papers were scattered about. A couple of boxes of cereal needed to be put away. With her free hand she began to neaten up the kitchen, put things in order, make things manageable.

"Please don't hate me for this," Dee pleaded. And Susan knew.

She felt a chill. *No,* she thought. *No, no, no.*

Dee kept talking. She told Susan about the price scribbled on the napkin, the shooting spree on the Keys . . . "No, don't tell me this shit," Susan cried . . . the night in the motel with Allen, the night Mike came to the restaurant to pick up Allen . . . "I don't want to hear this" . . . and the haunted look on Allen's face when he returned.

By the time Dee finished talking, Susan was trembling. She took deep breaths, but air didn't seem to come. Her lungs felt empty. Anxiety was upon her like a heavy, suffocating blanket. "Ma, I can't believe what you're saying to me. My hands are shaking. I think I'm losing my mind."

"It's true," Dee said, "it's true. You don't hate me for this, do you? Say you don't hate me."

"Jesus, Ma." Susan started pounding her fist on the counter in front of her. "Jesus, Jesus, Jesus." Now she was screaming, crying. She yanked open the cabinet doors above the counter and slammed them again and again. "Ma, you're crazy. You're insane. You're a crazy old drunk."

"No, honey, please. I need you. Don't abandon me."

"Do you have any idea of what you've done? You're out of your mind. Oh, my God, my God." Susan fell apart then and started wailing like a child.

"It'll be okay, honey, it'll be okay," her mother said. "I'm so sorry. I shouldn't have told you this."

"How can it be okay?" Susan shrieked. "You've murdered a man. It will never be okay. Never."

"It wasn't me," Dee said. "It wasn't me. It was them. I feel so awful about this, honey. I feel like I've been hit by a wrecking ball."

"A wrecking ball? Ma, you are the wrecking ball. Don't you see it? You wreck people's lives."

"It'll be okay now," Dee said. "I just know it will."

"God, I just can't deal with this," Susan said. "I can't deal with it, I can't."

"Don't hang up on me, baby, don't hang up."

"You're a murderer," Susan said.

"No, honey, I'm not. I'm not."

"Yes, you are," Susan said. "You're a murderer." She hung up.

Recalling the telephone conversation now, Susan says, "I just freaked out. What she was telling me was unbelievable. My mother, the sweetest woman in the world, telling me she had set up a murder."

There is a great deal of confusion about when exactly these calls were made. When Susan talks about the first phone calls, even today, she discusses them as if they happened before the murder. "I should have called the police," she says. "But I didn't really believe it. It was all so crazy. Besides, what was I going to do, turn my own mother in?"

But according to Dee, Susan's got it wrong. Dee says that none of the phone calls really came before Art was murdered.

"It had already happened," Dee says, "but I was so afraid of losing Susan's approval, her love, that I tried to feel her out, tell her about it as if it hadn't happened yet and see how she reacted. I was a mess. I had to tell someone, and Susan was the only person in the world I could turn to."

Both mother and daughter have memories about the timing of the calls that are inconsistent with the other's memories and with their own other memories of this time. Possibly Dee's version was concocted to spare her daughter any guilt over not preventing the crime, and was told so many times that she began to believe it. More likely alcohol, guilt, and the passing of years combined to break these memories into little pieces that can never be put back together.

In any case, Dee had taken her first tentative step into the confessional, and Susan now had the burden of knowledge. Dee had begun to move toward her own oblivion, and Susan had another secret to keep. Dee began to have fewer and fewer sober days, and Susan began to deal with her guilt in the way she had been taught by her mother. With alcohol and work.

"After the calls Mom and I started spending more time together," Susan says. "She needed me near her. I was the only one she could talk to. I started working weekends at the IHOP in Mom's old waitress job. A few times I went with her to feed Mrs. Fischer. One time Mom took me over to the barn and showed me where Art's body was. And she told me that Allen was pressuring her to have Mrs. Fischer killed. But I knew that would never happen."

17

The Roofers

The night after her dinner with Allen at Monty Trainer's restaurant, Dee again drove to Yappell's Amoco station to discuss a second murder with Mike Irvine.

Mike was in a jovial mood. "Hey, Dee, what can I do for you?" he said, offering a tip of his Chicago Bears cap. "You come to have your husband knocked off?"

"No," she said grimly. That joke wasn't so funny anymore. "Allen's decided it would be best to eliminate Mrs. Fischer," she told Mike.

"Who's that?" Mike asked.

"Venecia's mother. She's an old lady."

"An old lady? He wants to kill an old lady?"

"No. He wants you and your friend to kill an old lady."

"Okay," Mike said. "I'll talk to Bill."

"So, it is him," Dee said.

"Huh?"

"Bill. The guy you were with when we ran into you. That's your friend."

"Yeah, sure," Mike said. "He lives right over there." He pointed across the street to the used-car lot. "In a camper. They let him sleep there in return for watching over the lot at night. He's their protection against criminals. Ain't that a hoot?"

"He seems like a great guy," Dee said.

"Hey, Wild Bill's okay," Mike said. "He's a good mechanic."

"I'm sure," Dee said. "Anyhow, you left us with an awful mess last time. We don't want to end up with that kind of mess. This time we want the body buried, too."

"We" this and "we" that, she thought. Allen and she had become a pair in her mind.

"We can take care of that," Mike said.

"How much are you going to charge?"

"I'll have to get back to you," Mike said.

When Mike did get back to Dee, he told her that $2,500 would be the price for Bessie Fischer's murder.

"Does that include burying her?" Dee asked.

"Sure," he said. "Hey, this is a full-service operation here. No extra charge for burying the body."

The payment plan was the same as with the Venecia murder: half the money due up front, half after the work was done.

Allen was pleased when Dee told him that the deal was set. "Good girl," he said. He peeled $1,250 off his roll of IHOP bills and stuffed it into an envelope, which Dee would deliver to Irvine.

By this time Art Venecia's body had been rotting in the barn for six weeks. The stink of it was like something from hell, and the body fluids that had oozed through the seams of the wooden wardrobe had not yet dried up. It was time to find a permanent home for the bodies of Art Venecia and his soon-to-be-dead mother.

In fact, Dee and Allen had begun to make final arrangements for Art Venecia long before they agreed to finish off Bessie. They had hoped that in the silence of some moonlit night they could prowl behind the house with picks and shovels and dig a grave beneath the tall old pine trees. But that plan was as doomed as Bessie. Just beneath the topsoil Art Venecia's property was solid coral, and if you took a shovel to it, your arms would vibrate for a week. Perhaps they could get one of those pneumatic drills, Allen had suggested. But Dee pointed out that the roar of a pneumatic drill pulsating through the still night air in The Redlands would certainly draw unwanted attention.

So Allen had gotten out the Yellow Pages and he put in a call to Wayne's Backhoe Service in Homestead.

Wayne Tidwell, who owns and operates his equipment, recalls his visits to The Redlands house.

"I drove out to the house and met with Dee Casteel in the front yard," he says. "She told me she needed a trash pit dug. It was to be eighteen by eighteen by four feet deep. She had picked out a spot on the southeast corner of the property. I could see she'd need a backhoe. It's the only thing you can dig hard rock with. A bulldozer couldn't do the job. We went into the house to work out a price for the job. The house wasn't very well kept. I guess nobody was living there. I smelled something strong. I didn't know what I was smelling, but I remember how strong the smell was."

Dee and Tidwell agreed to a price of $280. Tidwell drove off and later returned with his backhoe, a small monster of a machine that can gobble up rock like a child eating candy. After five hours of smashing through the coral and dumping the dirt and rock to one side, the hole was dug to Dee's satisfaction and she paid Tidwell the same way she had paid Irvine. In cash.

The intriguing detail in all of this is the date. According to Tidwell's records the hole was dug on June 24, just five days after Art Venecia's throat was slashed. If the stink that permeated the house when Tidwell visited was Art's body decaying in the garage, there lingers the question of why he was later moved from the garage to the barn instead of directly to the hole that had been prepared for him. And with Dee so worried about Art's body's being discovered in the barn, why was the body left there for several weeks after the grave was ready? Certainly these were such delirious times that the memories of the principals have been shuffled like a deck of playing cards, but recorded dates, such as Wayne Tidwell's visit to the property, can be taken as precise.

One possibility, of course, is that Bessie's murder was planned from the start and the hole was being left vacant until both bodies were ready to reside there. But if that's true, then why put off killing Bessie for weeks? Why not just get on with it? Or maybe Dee and Allen figured that Bessie, who had been "sinking fast" for a couple of years by this time, would conveniently drop dead for them. Another possibility is that what Tidwell smelled was merely corpse gas trapped in the garage even after the body had been moved.

All of this could be neatly worked out if this were a novel, but real life is riddled with inconsistencies, and whatever is true, is true whether it makes sense or not. Most likely the body was hauled to the barn as a temporary measure, and because Dee was so busy running the restaurant and Allen was so busy decorating the new house, they simply did not get around to burying Art, the same way that most of us don't get around to fixing the leaky faucet in the bathroom. Moving that dreadful wardrobe with its putrid cargo of death and guilt was, to say the least, an unpleasant task, and those are the kind we all tend to avoid.

So it was the first week of August when Mike Irvine agreed not only to kill Bessie Fischer, but also to bury her body at no extra charge. It wasn't as if he and Bill "Joker" Rhodes would have to do any digging. They would simply toss the body into the hole that Tidwell had unknowingly dug for Art Venecia's body, and they would cover it with something, so as not to alarm the neighbors.

When Dee went to the Amoco station with the envelope containing the first half of the payment, Bill was there working on his Triumph motorcycle. He smiled at her and said hello. Dee shuddered, picturing Rhodes cutting open Art Venecia with his razor. Somehow Mike was never in the mental picture. She still couldn't believe that anyone as nice as Mike could commit murder.

She met Mike in the office, handed him the envelope.

"When?" she said.

"Saturday," Mike said. That would make it the sixth of August, exactly seven weeks after Art's murder. Mike smiled. "We can fit it in then." He seemed to be showing off for Bill, who had come into the office.

They discussed how the murder would be done. Dee explained that Bessie always kept her door locked, so Dee would have to get the men in. It was agreed that Mike and Bill would drive to the property, posing as roof repairmen whom Dee had hired to fix the leaking roof on Bessie's trailer.

"Look, Mike, there's something you've got to do for me, okay?" Dee said before she left. She was shaking. She lit a cigarette. She couldn't believe she was doing this. It's for the best, she had told herself over and over, it's for the best.

"For you, sweetheart, anything."

"I want it to be painless."

"Sure," Mike said.

"I mean it. I don't want that old lady to suffer at all."

"There won't be any problem," Mike promised.

"Are you sure?" Dee said. "I don't want her hurt."

Mike glanced at his friend. "Bill is an expert in

karate,'' he said. ''He knows just where to hit her so she won't feel nothing. It's a spot right on the back of the neck, ain't it, Bill?''

''Yeah,'' Bill said.

''Okay,'' Dee said, ''okay,'' and through that sometimes unfathomable process of denial that is the essence of the alcoholic mind, she drove home pretending that what had just happened had not just happened.

On Saturday at around five o'clock Dee was working at the pancake house. She put in an order for a club sandwich, tea, and peach cobbler for Bessie's supper. She drove to the property. She got out of the car. She looked around. She took a deep breath. She knocked on Bessie's door. Then she lifted the supper tray out of the car and took it into the narrow trailer.

Dee took the food off the tray and set it in front of Bessie on the small table. She tried not to look into the old lady's eyes.

''I've been worried about your roof leaking,'' Dee told her.

''It leaks,'' Bessie said.

''Yes,'' Dee said louder. ''I'm concerned about it. We don't want you getting a cold.''

''No, don't want that,'' Bessie said. She shook her head.

''I've hired some repairmen to fix it.''

''Fix what?''

''Fix the roof,'' Dee said. ''Some repairmen. They'll be here soon, so you let them in, okay?''

''I don't like nobody here,'' Bessie said.

''I know, but the roof has to be patched. They won't take long. You let them in when they come, okay?''

Bessie nodded okay. She thanked Dee for thinking of her. She started eating her supper. Dee, who often sat with Bessie until the old lady was done eating, could not wait. She wanted to get out of there. She didn't want to run into Mike and Bill. Bessie ate her peach cobbler first, and when she had scooped up the last spoonfuls, Dee got up. "I have to go," she said. She took a napkin and wiped a few crumbs from the old lady's lips. Then she gave Bessie an awkward hug, said good-bye, and carried the empty tray out quickly, hoping to get off the property before the "roofers" arrived.

As she drove her old Buick out of the driveway, Mike and Bill were driving in. The two cars stopped aside one another about halfway along the driveway. Dee glanced at Mike, said nothing. He glanced back, gave her a wink. Then Dee drove home and got as drunk as she could.

18

The Second Murder

Your name is Bessie Fischer, and you're worried. Your Arthur has been gone now for, how long is it? Two weeks? Or is it just several days? You can't be sure. You get confused a lot these days. But you feel that something is wrong. Where is he? They say he's in North Carolina, but you're not so sure. Why are the cars gone? Why is the door to the house locked? Why can't somebody fix your phone? Maybe Arthur's had an accident and they're not telling you. It's scary, because Arthur is all you've got in the world. He's a good son and he'll always take care of you. But what if something has happened to him? What will become of you? You don't think you could bear to be in one of those nursing homes. You like it where you are. You've got your little trailer and your television and you've got Cat to keep you company. You wish your phone were working. Then Arthur could call you up.

Thank God for Dee, you think. If it weren't for her, you don't know what you'd do. She's so sweet to bring you your meals every day, and everything is always arranged so attractively on the plate. Sometimes she brings you flowers, and if you need something at the store, she always gets it for you. Dee's a wonderful person and you wish you could help her sometimes because she looks troubled. She seems to have a drinking problem. Such a shame. You like Dee a lot. And you can trust her. You're not so sure about that Allen, but Dee you can trust. She sits with you while you eat, and you like to listen to her when she talks about her boys, and the one daughter—what's her name?—Susan, yes, that's it. Or is it Diane? You forget so much. Dee looks after you. She'll take care of you until Arthur gets back. Like today, she noticed the roof had a leak and she's hired these repairmen to fix it. They're in the trailer now, two men. They seem so big in the small trailer. What are they doing, just looking around like that? You hope they'll fix the roof quickly and leave so you can watch television. You don't feel comfortable having these men around. Something seems wrong about them. They don't seem friendly. Better watch them, so they don't take anything. Now one of them has gone behind you. What is he going to do there? There's no reason for him to be back there. Suddenly you feel a tightness in your throat. Oh, God, something is wrapped around your neck and the man is pulling it tighter. It's so tight you can't breathe. You take big gulps but nothing comes. It's like the time you had your stroke, but it's worse, much worse. Your heart is beating faster. Why are they doing this? Your hands reach up to tug at the thing around your neck . . . what is it? . . . but the man is so strong and you are so weak. You can't even get your fingers between the thing and your throat. You can't get any breath at all now, and you feel as if your body is shrinking. Your mind is screaming. This is horrible, horrible. Where's Arthur, why isn't Arthur here to stop them? Oh, God, the man is killing you. No air will come in. Your body is shrieking give me air, give me air, and you can't get any. You're dying, dying, and you'll never see Arthur again. Please don't kill my cat, you think. And just before you die you realize: Dee did this to me.

19

The Roofers' Stories

As with the Venecia murder, Rhodes's and Irvine's stories are different. Here's how Bill Rhodes tells it:

"Mike Irvine called me over to the station one day and asked me if I was interested in making some money doing a roof job. I said yeah, because I used to do roof work in Kansas. He said he knew about a trailer roof. The people didn't have a lot of money to spend, but they needed it fixed. I said I could probably fix it and I told him we'd need some tar.

"He picked me up around five o'clock one day and we drove to the house. I didn't recognize it right off but it looked familiar. After a while I realized it was the same house where we had gone to rough up the guy. I wanted to go back, but it would have been a long walk to my bike or to town. I didn't bring any tar or tools because we were just going to do an estimate. When we got there, I seen the white Buick I had seen at the station a few times, the one that belonged to Dee Casteel, though I didn't know that was her name at the time. Dee Casteel was in the process of leaving.

She stopped on the way out and she and Michael talked from car to car, without getting out.

"I met Mrs. Fischer at her trailer. She was an older lady. I remember she had on an apron. I said, do you have a ladder, I'd like to see where the holes are in the roof, how bad the damage is so it can be fixed. She pointed to a ladder sitting down alongside the trailer and I set the ladder up to the trailer. Like most elderly people, she is keeping an eye. Somebody is around the place, she watches to make sure you don't mess with nothing, that's the feeling I get. She watches while I go up on the roof and Mike holds the ladder. I found about three or four spots up there that needed some tar mix on because they were dried out, and I was trying to explain to her from up there where they was, but she was talking to Mike about something. I couldn't hear them talk but she wasn't paying attention when I was talking to her. So I came down the ladder and explained to her again she had two holes on one side of the trailer and one right above the back door.

"She mentioned something about the floor in the hallway by the back door of the trailer, can it be fixed? I said probably, how bad is it? She said come in and look at it, so I went in to look at it. We went in the trailer and I let her go first and I held the stairway because the stairwell shifts, it was kind of rickety.

"Me and Mike went in. He was looking at something she was pointing at down in the kitchen. Then she pointed to the hallway towards the back, so I walked back there and she sat back down at the table. So I went down the hallway and was checking the flooring. I looked out the back door of the trailer, tried to look underneath to see if it could be fixed. And I couldn't see underneath it because of the paneling under there. So I closed the door and I come back up the hallways toward the kitchen and I seen Mike behind her with both his hands up behind her head, and I seen the old lady's hands up in front of her like she was trying to get at her throat. She was gasping for breath and struggling. I said, 'Hey, man, you're fucking crazy. I'm getting out of here.' That's when I went out the door.

"I didn't do anything because at the time this happened I weighed exactly one hundred and nineteen pounds. Michael weighed almost two hundred. I'm not proud of my running out of that trailer, but I knew I couldn't handle Mike, he was too big for me. I am not the strongest man in the world nor the most powerful, but I am smart enough to not get myself killed. I am terribly ashamed of myself for what happened to that woman, but I am not the cause of her dying.

"So I ran to the car. I had a bottle of Scotch there. I grabbed my bottle out of the car and I took one healthy drink of it and brought it back down and I seen Mike come out the door, and I took another healthy drink of it and I got in the car and said, 'I don't know what the hell you are doing, but let's get the hell out of here.'

"And Mike says, 'Well, hell, man, we are even,' and I said, 'What do you mean we are even? There ain't no even shit to it.' I said, 'Man, this ain't right. I don't want to hear no shit about this. Get me away from here. It is all yours.'

"He explained about the guy in the house, and I said, 'Hey, man, I didn't kill the guy in the house. I fought with the guy in the house, the guy hurt me. I didn't kill the guy in the house.'

"We went back to the station and there was no more said after that."

Mike Irvine has a slightly different recollection of Bessie Fischer's murder:

"Bill Rhodes came to the gas station and wanted to know if I could help him do some roof work on a trailer out in the country. A couple of days later we went over in his Pacer. I didn't know we were going to the Venecia house. I saw Dee Casteel there but I didn't have any conversation with her. She was leaving and she had told the lady that we was the guys that was there to fix the trailer for her. I saw the old lady standing by the door of the trailer. Bill and I walked over and talked to her. We went inside. The property was starting to look familiar to me.

"I stayed in the kitchen. Bill walked to the back part of the trailer and I was talking to the old lady for a little bit, and when I turned back around, Bill came up behind her with a pair of panty hose and strangled the old lady. I wasn't expecting it, and I kind of froze. Then I got the hell out of there. Bill came out about five minutes later. He said, 'You didn't see anything.' I was afraid. I drove back to the station and then I went up to the station to get my car and I went up to Campbell Square to the restaurant, to the bar, and I went up there and had a couple of drinks."

20

The Money

On Saturday night Mike Irvine called Dee and told her the job had been done. The second half of the $2,500 was due, he said, but he insisted that she not come to the gas station with it. He told her he would pick it up at the pancake house in the morning. On Sunday morning Mike picked up the money, which Allen had put in an envelope.

On Monday morning Dee and Allen drove to the property to make sure that Bessie's body had been well covered in the pit. They pulled onto the property cautiously, as if expecting state troopers to leap out from behind the trees. They parked in the usual spot next to the garage and walked slowly toward the trailer. When they got to it, they peered in the window. Bessie was sitting at her kitchen table. Her head was slumped down onto her chest as if she had fallen asleep.

"Christ Almighty," Allen said. "They ripped us off."

Dee and Allen stared for a moment longer, then

another, watching for the telltale rising and falling of Bessie's stomach. But there seemed to be no movement. They climbed slowly up the creaking stairs, as if they might wake Bessie. They tried the door. It was locked. Allen pulled out his key. They went into the trailer. It was a hot August day and the baked air inside the trailer closed around them.

"Bessie," Allen called softly as though expecting the old woman to wake up and ask for lunch. "Bessie." Bessie didn't move. Allen poked at the old lady's shoulder. Nothing.

"She's dead," he said.

Dee was relieved that there was no sign of brutality on Bessie, but the fact that the body was still in the trailer was extremely upsetting to her. She began shaking, the way she did when she needed a drink.

"This is not right," she said. "This just is not right." Wringing her hands, she swung around in the narrow trailer. "God damn them," she shouted.

"It's for the best," Allen said. "Believe me, it's for the best."

"I can't believe they did this," Dee said, her voice trembling now. "They're a couple of thieves, taking money without doing the work. They told me they would bury the body . . . they promised that we wouldn't see a body here . . . that was part of the deal. They were supposed to bury the body." Dee, stunned and grief-stricken by the realization of what she had done, stood motionless in the trailer. I should have had a drink before I came here, she thought. She pressed her hands to her mouth as if to stop a flow of words. My God, what have I done? she thought. The trailer was like an oven. Dee felt as if she were being fried.

As Allen moved deeper into the trailer, into the bedroom area where he rummaged through Bessie's things, Dee began to rant like some inmate at an asylum. Her words came out in a rush of misdirected emotion. She had helped them murder the old lady, and now standing inches from the evidence, she could feel herself becoming unhinged.

"Well, I'm not going to stand for this," Dee said. "It's their job to bury the body and we're not going to do it for them. It's their job and they're going to do it."

"The jewelry's gone," she heard Allen say.

He stood several feet from her, looking into a large jewelry case that he had just opened.

"What?"

"The jewelry," he said. "Bessie had some very valuable jewelry. She kept it here." He held the case up and tipped it to show Dee that it was empty.

"Bastards!" Dee shouted. "They have no respect for anything. They stole her jewelry."

After they had blocked the window with a pillowcase and locked the trailer, Dee and Allen drove back to the pancake house. They went up to the office and Dee got Mike on the phone. She raised hell with him over the fact that the body had not been buried. Also she railed at him about the missing jewelry; Allen had told her that expensive rings and a watch were missing. Mike swore that he didn't take them.

On Tuesday, August 9, when Dee drove to the property again, the corpse, now grotesquely bloated, was still propped up at the kitchen table in the trailer. Late on Tuesday night Dee, loaded with Scotch and mad as hell, drove to the Amoco station. It was another hot night, and the air was steamy from the afternoon's downpour. Mike was not at the gas station, but Bill Rhodes was.

"I want to talk to Mike," she roared.

"He's not here," Rhodes told her. He came around to the window of her Buick. "You want gas?"

"Well, where the hell is he?" she shouted.

"I haven't seen Mike since Sunday," Rhodes told her. He gave her a cold look. Dee knew she should be afraid of this man, especially after she noticed that he had a pistol tucked into the waist of his trousers. But she wasn't afraid. When she drank heavily, wires got disconnected. All she felt now was, these bastards got paid to do a job and they're going to do it. She told Bill to fill the tank.

"Well, this is one rotten deal," she told Rhodes when he came back. "You were supposed to put Mrs. Fischer in the ground."

Bill glared at her. "I don't ever plant them," he said. "I only kill them."

Even in her sodden state, Dee found these particular words of Bill's chilling, and she would remember them always.

"We paid you twenty-five hundred bucks," Dee said, "and that included burying her."

"Twenty-five hundred?" Bill said.

"Right, twenty-five hundred bucks. Cash."

"Mike only split twelve fifty with me. I didn't know nothing about him raising it to twenty-five."

Dee could see that Bill was upset. But she bore into him recklessly. "And what about the jewelry?" Dee said. "You guys stole Mrs. Fischer's jewelry."

"What jewelry?" Bill snapped. "I don't know nothing about no jewelry."

"You stole it," Dee said. "You guys stole that old woman's watch and her rings."

"Hey, I told you. I don't know about no jewelry," Rhodes said.

What the hell am I doing? Dee thought. This guy is a raving lunatic with a gun in his pants and I'm aggravating the hell out of him.

"Look," Dee told him, softening her tone now, "all I know is somebody's got to finish the job even if you don't know where Mike is. You've been paid for it."

By the time Dee left, Bill, who some people say was capable of charm and even sweetness, had promised to finish the job. Dee drove away, feeling as if she had entered a den of lions and tamed at least one of them.

That night, when Dee left the Amoco station, she was sure she had gotten Mike Irvine into deep shit. Bill had said something to the effect of, "When I get my hands on that son of a bitch, I'll kill him," which, in the case of Bill Rhodes, had to be viewed as more than an idle threat.

The next morning, Wednesday, the tenth of August, when Dee drove out to the Venecia property, the corpse no longer sat at the kitchen table. The body of Bessie Fischer had been thrown into the northwest corner of the pit and covered with dirt.

There is some confusion as to how it got there. Mike Irvine says, "I contacted Rhodes and asked him about putting the box in the pit. He said no. I also felt I was getting too deeply involved."

Rhodes, who had a key to Mrs. Fischer's trailer, apparently changed his mind because he later told police that he had wrapped the body in a sheet, dragged it out to the pit, thrown it in, and covered it with dirt.

A few days before Bessie's body was deposited in the hole, Dee had called the Rental Machinery Company on Southwest Forty-first Street and rented a Bobcat bulldozer and a forklift, which she'd had delivered to Art's property. Now, on the tenth, during a lull in the pancake business, she and Allen went to the property. They drove the forklift into the barn and struggled with the heavy wardrobe. As they rocked it back and forth toward the waiting steel arms of the machine, the body inside thumped against the walls, and to Dee each little thud was as alarming as a knock on the door in the middle of the night. The stink from the body was not as abominable as it had been, but the experience was, nonetheless, nightmarish.

Once they had the wardrobe settled on the forklift, Allen drove it to the gravesite and lowered the huge wooden box and its dreadful contents into the southeast corner of the pit. Then Allen mounted the small bulldozer and tried to plow back the dirt and rocks that Wayne Tidwell had left piled beside the pit. But the bulldozer was ineffectual against the huge slabs of coral rock that stuck up at all angles, and after a few impotent passes Allen threw up his hands in surrender. Instead, he and Dee grabbed an old mattress from the barn and a box spring and tossed that in over the wardrobe. Then they poured whatever trash they could find into the pit until the bodies of Art and his mother were well concealed.

Dee called Wayne's Backhoe Service again. This time she told Wayne Tidwell that she would be renting the house out to a family with kids and that she was concerned about small children tumbling into the debris pit that he had dug. So would he please come back and fill the pit for her?

Tidwell returned to the Venecia property. He went to work, lifting and dropping the big steel blade of his backhoe, pushing the dirt and the tons of coral rock back into the pit, rolling it and packing the surface, and once and for all, it would seem, burying the evidence that Dee Casteel, James Allen Bryant, Michael Irvine, and William "The Joker" Rhodes had committed murder twice.

Because employees at IHOP would notice that Dee was no longer bringing Bessie her meals, Allen told the employees that Bessie had moved to North Carolina to be with her son. Then Allen hitched Bessie's trailer to the back of his Lincoln and drove it to his Kendall love nest.

Things settled down. There was no one left to kill. Except perhaps Mike Irvine, who Dee felt would soon be murdered by Bill Rhodes if he hadn't been already. In any case, those two men were not around. Like so many other men, they were gone from Dee's life, and as far as she was concerned, the farther away those two were the better.

Through the hot days of August Dee continued to work long hours at the restaurant. Allen continued to dote on Henry with a powerful passion. Allen and

Henry often showed up for breakfast at the pancake house, usually accompanied by Allen's entourage of squealing young Cubans. More and more Allen, like some majestic movie star, kept himself surrounded by handsome, dark-skinned Marielitos.

"Marielitos" is the name given to the 125,000 "undesirable" Cubans who sailed from Mariel, Cuba, to Miami in 1980. They were a gift from Fidel Castro, who thought that if America was anxious to give a hero's welcome to those who had escaped from Cuba, he would give the country more of his lawbreakers. Though the shipment included 10,000–20,000 felons and psychos, 90 percent of the Marielitos were only "criminals" because they were prostitutes, drug addicts, homosexuals, drifters, or unruly teenagers.

The Marielitos who followed Allen around were young men who had gotten jobs as IHOP busboys or dishwashers, but as time passed, they spent more time partying with Allen than busing and washing dishes. All of them were gay, or at least gay enough to participate in the all-male orgies that, allegedly, were a highlight of the social life at Allen's house in Kendall. But a few were also devout womanizers when Allen was not around. Like Henry, they could perhaps swing both ways, depending on who was picking up the check. (Henry, incidentally, was not a complete freeloader. All during this period Henry had a job that he liked, at an antique-car dealership, and he went to work every day, leaving Allen in the role of housewife, cleaning, decorating, and cooking big meals for his friends.) Gay or straight, Allen's Marielitos were all interested in getting married, so they could stay in the country. Susan turned down marriage proposals from several of them.

This situation, of Allen's keeping constant company with the IHOP's busboys and dishwashers, played havoc with Dee's management of the restaurant. If Allen's porch needed painting or his screens needed cleaning or if he was just feeling lonely, Dee would have no one to bus dishes that day. In time she solved that problem, along with the problem of not seeing her sons enough, by hiring Todd and Wyatt as occasional busboys at the pancake house. Dee would bring her set of dominoes to work, and when things were quiet, she and the boys could get in a few games. At the IHOP she could keep an eye on them, she thought. In fact, the boys, increasingly worried about Dee's drinking, were keeping an eye on their mother.

Maintaining his entourage was not inexpensive for Allen. While food was free at the Naranja IHOP, it was not at the other fine restaurants where Allen took his Marielitos and Dee for sumptuous dinners and bottomless booze. Money was needed. And money was needed for hefty bets on greyhounds at the Flagler dog track. Money was needed for new furniture for the house in Kendall, a car for Henry, smaller gifts for Henry and Dee and the others, and cocaine.

"Cocaine was always available when Allen was around," says Joanne Rivera, who was sometimes included in the partying.

The money Allen used to finance this extravagant lifestyle came from two sources.

One was Art Venecia's account at the Coral Gables office of E.F. Hutton. At the beginning of June 1983, there was $33,307 in the account, representing Art's ownership of municipal bonds and shares of stock in Exxon and Nabisco. The account was set up so that stocks could be liquidated and money could be withdrawn. If Art needed money from the account, he could call E.F. Hutton and ask that a check be sent.

The E.F. Hutton records show that Allen wasted no time in grabbing Art's money. On June 20, when Art had been dead for about thirty-five hours, Allen Bryant called E.F. Hutton. He told them that he was Art Venecia and asked that a check for $6,000 be sent to him. When the check arrived, Allen forged Art's and Bessie's signatures and cashed it.

On June 27, he got another check, this time for

$9,000. On the same date Allen called E.F. Hutton, posing as Art Venecia, and told them what shares of stock he wanted liquidated. In July, Allen collected a dividend check for some Puerto Rican bonds, then he sold the bonds. On July 15, Allen called and ordered a check for $6,000. On July 25, he called again. This time he wanted $7,000. Again, a check was sent.

By the end of July the account was down to $4,267. Allen apparently knew which people at Hutton would recognize Art's voice, because he varied his routine, sometimes claiming to be Art Venecia's nephew and saying that Art wanted a check sent.

On August 1, Allen called and asked for a check for $2,000. On August 18, he called and ordered another check for $2,000. By September he had wiped out the account. In addition there had been various dividend checks sent directly to the Venecia house. Allen had forged signatures on those also and cashed them.

Allen's other source of income was, of course, the approximately $3,000 a week he was lifting from the pancake-house cash register.

Long before Art Venecia's body was buried in his own backyard, Allen was pillaging the Naranja cash register far more callously than he had when Art was alive. As a result Dee, after meeting the weekly payroll, was being constantly dunned by irate suppliers who hadn't been paid or who had gotten rubber checks. By August, many had revoked credit and put IHOP on a cash-only basis. More significantly, the restaurant had fallen way behind on its payments to the FMS Management Systems, the main office for the International House of Pancakes in Florida.

Under the franchising agreement, Art Venecia had leased the Naranja building and the International House of Pancakes name. His obligation to IHOP was to maintain certain levels of quality in the products and services, buy certain products such as pancake batters and syrups from IHOP or their recommended distributors, and most important, pay IHOP a percentage of the weekly gross that passed through the cash register.

The average weekly gross in Naranja was around $8,500 to $10,000, but with Allen siphoning off thousands from the cash register for his new house and furniture, the IHOP regional office was suddenly getting payments based on a gross of $6,000 or $7,000. The records clearly showed that the franchise was using about the same amount of batter, syrup, and other supplies as before, so you didn't have to be a Harvard business school graduate to figure out that somebody was skimming the profits.

Various IHOP officials called to discuss the discrepancy with Art Venecia. They were told, usually by Dee, that Art was in North Carolina on business and would return the call as soon as he got back to Dade County.

But Dee was concerned. Waiting for Allen Bryant to make good on a debt was as futile as waiting for Art Venecia to come back from North Carolina. She worried constantly about the money for FMS. She knew that they could be stalled for just so long, and then, if they didn't get their checks on a regular basis and for the right amounts, they would take back the franchise. And then where would she be? Right where she was afraid of being in the first place: out of work with no money for booze. Art Venecia would still be decaying under his own property. Bessie Fischer would still be piled like so much rubbish in that same hole. But Dee would have no job. It would all have been for nothing. So she hounded Allen Bryant constantly to come up with the money. But Allen was frustratingly cavalier about it. "We'll get it to them, dear, we'll get it to them. But not yet. I don't have it," he said.

Nonetheless, Allen and Dee drew closer. By this time Dee was openly in love with Allen. She told her daughter. She told her friends. She began to fantasize about making love with him. The relationship took on, for her at least, mystical overtones. They could read each other's mind, she thought. Sometimes she would think something and Allen would say it before she had a chance. Sometimes she would say it, and he had been thinking it. She was convinced that Allen cared about her.

Like an old married couple ignoring their sex problems, Allen and Dee rarely talked about the murders. Sometimes the lack of acknowledgment made the whole horror seem dreamlike to Dee, as if it had never happened. Dee does recall one time driving with Allen along Route 27 in Broward County and passing the women's prison. "That's where you'll end up if you're not careful," Allen said. It gave Dee the chills. Then they joked for a while about how the Cass's and the Henry's might come and go, but they'd always have each other, and how Allen would take care of Dee in her old age.

The killing was done, and the pancake money was coming in. Just as no friends or relatives had called for Art, none called for Bessie. The team had quite successfully gotten away with murder two times, and they had reached that point in their crime where their fate was in their own hands. Only two things could trip them up: greed and guilt.

By the end of August Dee's marriage was gasping its last. Cass was getting ready to pull up stakes and go home to Texas. That was fine with Dee. For some time he had been spending all of his monthly government check on booze, and the shortage of money was working hardships on the family.

Though managing the IHOP was taking much more of Dee's time, it was still not paying her nearly as much money as she'd been making as a waitress. As the summer wore on, it was getting harder and harder for Dee to meet the cost of simply living, even though Susan was chipping in from her IHOP earnings. There wasn't enough money for Dee to raise two teenaged boys, maintain the house in Homestead, and drink three bottles of Scotch a day. By September, she had fallen way behind on the payments for her small house in Homestead. She was on the verge of being thrown out. She complained to Allen and insisted that she had to have more money. Allen told her that she didn't need more cash. What she needed was a place to live for free.

"What are you talking about?" she asked.

"The house," he said. "Why don't you move into it?"

"What house?" she asked.

"Art's house," he said. "There's no sense just letting it sit out there. Somebody could vandalize it."

"You want me to move into Art's house with the boys?"

"Sure," Allen said. "It's perfect. With the woods around it and all that land. It's a great place to raise kids."

21

The Conscience

Your name is Dee Casteel. In your cell on death row, you like yourself. You really do. This is an idea that you could never make palatable for the strangers who heard about you on the six-o'clock news. But you do like yourself. And the people who know you like you, and the God you believe in is a God who likes you. You are convinced that when the state of Florida straps you into the electric chair they will fry a nicer person than the one they let walk freely on the streets five years ago.

But even in your most self-forgiving moments you know that what you did to Bessie Fischer was a horror that stretched the limits of redemption. You know that when you walked out that trailer door, when you delivered Bessie Fischer into the remorseless hands of those two men, your heart had turned to marble and it had pulled you down and stranded you with them in the world of the wicked.

You can concoct a dozen reasons why it was okay to murder Bessie Fischer, just as the state of Florida can devise reasons why it is okay to kill you. But no matter how much you dilute your unconscionable act, it still tastes as vile as piss.

You have given up hope of ever trying to make another person understand. The awfulness of what you did is plain for everyone to see. But still you go over it again and again in your mind, because you want to explain it to yourself. You will never get the forgiveness of others, nor should you. The best you can hope for is the forgiveness of yourself and even that is not coming easily. And so you say to yourself:

"Bessie was an old woman who was doomed to die soon."

"I was an alcoholic, stricken with a disease that scorches the human mind."

"Allen made me do it."

And most important, "I couldn't bear the thought of that poor old woman lying helpless and abandoned by the side of the road."

And to that you add, "I begged them to make it painless for her," and finally, "I was outraged when I saw that they hadn't even buried her."

But the excuses and the explanations and the rationalizations always fade as quickly as the memories of a dream, and in the end you are left with the mournful sound of that trailer door swinging open for the last time, of the crunch of gravel beneath the tires of Mike Irvine's car as "the roofers" drive in. And you think that you don't want to die in the electric chair, that capital punishment is wrong, that "they" don't fully understand what you did and why you did it. But you know, too, that given the facts as they see them, the state's barbaric request that you give up your life in the electric chair is not entirely unreasonable.

22

The House

In September of 1983, Dee moved into Art Venecia's Redlands house with Todd and Wyatt, and her Great Dane, Tasha. She told her sons, as she told everybody else, that Art was concerned about leaving the house empty and had asked her to take care of it. Given that explanation, they must have thought it strange when Allen took all of Art's furniture and Dee hauled in her own, but as far as Dee could tell, the boys suspected nothing. A few days later Susan drove down from Fort Lauderdale and helped Dee turn the Florida room into a bedroom for the boys.

By this time Susan knew about Bessie. She had been shocked at the news. In noisy, violent, bitter arguments she had strafed her mother with every sin from Dee's past, with every cursed moment of their lives. She had proclaimed Dee insane, heartless, hopeless. She had threatened to go to the police. She had wished her mother dead; she had wished herself dead. But in the end, Dee fell completely apart, and Susan, knowing that Dee could not survive long without her, melted. Susan chose to support her mother, reasoning: she's still my mom.

"The second murder tore her up," Susan says. "She was drinking more than ever, and whenever she talked about Bessie, she would break down and cry."

Because her mother needed her, and also because Cass was now gone, Susan moved into The Redlands house, too. Troubled by her knowledge, Susan was soon snorting several lines of cocaine a day, supplied by Allen and his friends, and she was drinking herself silly. Like her mother, she had knowledge that needed to be blotted out. But like her mother, she was able to work. She took a full-time job as a waitress at the pancake house, mostly working the midnight shift with Joanne Rivera.

Soon Susan became friendly with Allen. At the IHOP she had heard tales about his temper, about Allen's stomping his feet, breaking dishes. But she found him charming, helpful, witty. Allen won her over with small gifts and by inviting her to join him and Dee for dinners at Monty Trainer's and several of Miami's other fine dining spots.

For Todd and Wyatt, who had spent their lives penned up in apartments or rented houses with tiny yards, coming to The Redlands was like moving into Walt Disney's Adventureland. Gone were those days of precious sobriety when Cass and Dee would take them to rodeos, carnivals, movies, or to The Moose, where the boys would shoot pool all day. Now Mom always seemed to be working or drinking, but there were new distractions to keep Todd and Wyatt from watching their mother decay. With their friend Danny Lore they roamed the five acres and beyond, climbing trees, exploring avocado orchards, chucking stones at tin cans, and just generally Tom Sawyering their way through life, divinely ignorant of the dreadful things their mother had done.

Dee was thrilled that at least she had provided a good environment for her boys, away from traffic and noise. As long as the kids didn't start asking too many questions about the freshly turned earth on the southeast corner of the property, everything would be fine.

The move to The Redlands also marked the end of Dee's marriage to Cass. Throughout that summer of 1983 she had constantly been afraid that she would get drunk and blurt out her story of murder and deceit. So the need to be separated from Cass had grown more and more urgent. In August when Cass had started talking about going back to Texas, Dee was the supportive wife. "Fine," she said. "Go. I'm filing for divorce, anyhow." Cass headed out and Dee filed for divorce. The state of Florida requires a witness to the incompatibility of the divorcing couple. Dee's witness was James Allen Bryant.

The separation from Cass was not an unmitigated relief. She missed Cass. Despite the beatings, the fights, the abandonments, Dee still loved her husband. In a recent correspondence from death row she wrote:

> God how I loved this man. The first time I saw him, I was beyond saving. I knew I had to have this man at any cost. The first time I slept with him was the most fabulous sexual encounter I have ever had. Too good to be real. Such a wild experience, I didn't go to work the next morning, called in sick, and spent the next two days with Cass. This was the beginning of a wild, crazy, wonderful yet most horrible of relationships. I was his puppet—lost my own self-esteem, sense of self-value—lost Susan. Cass could walk all over me, beat me up, embarrass me, it didn't matter. There were good times, too, lots of them. Cass was generous to a fault, he was honest, and he was good to the kids when he was sober. He was not a bad person. He was an alcoholic. I was an alcoholic. We neither one admitted it, and we were bad for each other. Neither one of us was

strong enough to say no to alcohol for very long. It's crazy but I still really love this guy, even though we're bad for each other and I know if I were free, I could not go back to him without harming myself. I wonder if I could walk away. I would have to, or be lost again.

Allen continued to filch four or five hundred dollars a day from the IHOP cash register. He spent the money generously and quickly. He spent it on jewelry for Henry, dresses and scarves for Dee, dinners for the whole crowd, and cocaine for everybody except Dee, who considered drugs dangerous and refused to take them. Allen also took his friends, including Dee, Susan, and other waitresses, to the Flagler dog track, where he sometimes dropped a thousand bucks wheeling quinellas.

By the middle of September, Allen had wiped out Art Venecia's Hutton account. (Incredibly, in late August Hutton sent a check for twenty-five cents to clear out the old account, and Allen, who risked buying a ticket to the electric chair every time he walked into a bank with one of his forged checks, cashed it.)

There were no more stocks to liquidate, so Allen decided to sell Bessie Fischer's trailer to raise extra cash. Allen and Dee placed an ad in the *Miami Herald* offering the trailer for sale. Their one taker was Russell Philpott, a teacher at Redland Junior High School. Philpott drove down to Allen's Kendall house to look at the trailer, which was parked in the yard. There he met not Allen, but Dee, who again had been cast in the role of front man.

"She was talking about the fact that it wasn't used that much and it was in good shape and so forth," Philpott recalls. "She wanted forty-five hundred dollars for it. I called her later and told her four thousand was the most my wife and I could come up with. Mrs.

Casteel said she had to discuss it with her associates. Later she called back and said that she had talked to her associate James Allen Bryant and they would accept the offer. A few days later I went back to the house and I met with her and a man she introduced as Arthur Venecia. He left right after I was introduced to him. I got the title and Mrs. Casteel notarized it. When I wrote out the check for four thousand dollars, I wasn't sure about how to spell Venecia and I asked Mrs. Casteel. She said that probably the associate, Mr. Bryant, would be handling the check and so just leave it blank."

This was on September 8, a week before Allen's twenty-sixth birthday. Allen cashed the check and gave Dee a few hundred bucks. With it she went out and bought him a poodle for his birthday. Allen had always wanted a house dog, but Art had never allowed it. He named the dog Mimi.

This was the first time the couple—and by now Dee and Bryant were like a couple, talking every day, seeing each other often—had sold any of Venecia's property, and it was also the first time that Allen had posed as Art Venecia. It was not the last. In this transaction and in the ones that followed, there emerges an image of Dee not as a weak and dominated drunkard, but as a cool and competent businesswoman who haggled for the best price and carried off her half of the charade in stunning fashion. Certainly there were times that summer when Dee was drunk beyond functioning, but more often she was loaded with just enough alcohol to stave off panic, just enough to be "at her best."

Still, she was drinking every day, drinking, she says, to "obliterate the terrible facts." On September 11, three days after the sale of the trailer, Dee collapsed and was rushed to the hospital. It was not the first time that alcoholism had caused her to be hospitalized, but it was a signal that life could get worse; there was still a bottom she could fall to.

Even now, with two bodies buried in her yard, with the first of several grand thefts behind her, with her life slipping down into a bottle of Scotch, Dee was a person whom other people loved.

Joanne Rivera, who saw Dee often during this time, says, "Dee was like a mother to me. She would always help me or talk to me if I needed someone. I loved Dee. I still love her. I would do anything for that woman." And Donna Hobson says, "Dee was still great. If you needed something and she had it, she would give it to you."

During the three days that Dee was hospitalized, Susan ran the IHOP. She begged Allen to come in and help but he refused. Though Susan was only seventeen she seemed to catch on to Allen's true nature a lot faster than her mother, and their differing view of Allen became a new source of conflict. In fact, though Susan had rushed to her mother's support in this time of crisis, the relationship between mother and daughter had become more fiery than before. Susan, for all her protectiveness of Dee, was enraged. The knowledge that her mother could do such a thing to herself and her children was almost more than Susan could contain. Only in alcohol and cocaine did Susan find any relief from her own searing anger. She loved her mother, but she also hated her. She became convinced that her mother was salvageable only if the devil could be exorcised from Dee's life. The devil was, of course, James Allen Bryant.

"He's a son of a bitch," Susan said to her mother one afternoon during a visit at the hospital. "He won't even come in and help out." She stood that day by the wide windows of the empty day room, watching a typical Florida rainstorm batter the palm trees on the hospital lawn.

"Well, he's probably busy," Dee said.

"Busy doing what, Ma?" Susan said. She swung around, holding her arms to her body as if to harness the rage she was always afraid would erupt from inside her. "Snorting cocaine? Trying on the latest fashions from Frederick's of Hollywood?"

Dee said nothing.

"He's using you," Susan said.

"No, he's not," Dee said.

Dee, white and tremulous from the lack of alcohol and cigarettes, sat in a simple wooden chair with a shawl across her lap. Like an old lady, Susan thought. God, Ma's going to get old fast now, and I can't help her.

Susan, deeply hurt by her mother's crimes, and bristling with youthful indignation, stared at her mother.

"Of course he is," Susan said. "It's incredible that you can't see it. How can you be so stupid?"

"Watch it," Dee snapped.

"Well, that's what it is, Ma, stupid. This whole . . . crime that he's got you involved in. Can't you see it? He's got it all set up so it looks like you're the mastermind. He made you buy the gun."

"Nobody used the gun," Dee said.

"That's not the point!" Susan shouted. "It's just the way he did it. It's how he works, Ma, he sets people up."

"You're being ridiculous," Dee said.

"Am I? Who actually approached Mike about the murder?"

"I did. You know that."

"Of course you did. And who paid Tidwinks, the backhoe guy?"

"Tidwell," Dee said. "Me."

"Right. And who told Mrs. Fischer about the roofers and who rented the bulldozer and who . . . Jesus, Ma, I don't see how it could be more obvious."

"But I love him," Dee said.

"He's a homosexual, for God's sake," Susan said.

"People change."

"I don't believe this," Susan said. She threw her hands up and turned back to the window. "My own mother's in love with a fag," she announced to the storm outside. "I do not believe it."

When she turned and faced her mother again, Dee was crying.

"He's all I have," Dee said. "He gives me attention."

"All you have? All you have? What are you talking about? How can you even say such a thing? You have me. You have Todd and Wyatt."

"No, I don't," Dee said. "You don't understand. After what I've done, I only have Allen. I don't have you anymore."

"Why?" Susan asked. "Tell me why you say that."

"Because I don't deserve you," Dee said.

By the time Dee got out of the hospital, she and Susan had regrouped. Susan was determined to work hard and save money and someday take Dee away from Miami, to Colorado, where a person could get a fresh start in life.

Meanwhile, back at the Venecia house, Dee had a new terror to contend with: Bessie's big, white, green-eyed cat. The cat had stayed near Bessie's trailer after her death, apparently surviving on field mice.

"That goddamn cat," Dee says. "I had never seen that cat try to get into Art's house. The cat was always around Mrs. Fischer's trailer. It had never hung out in the house. But after Mrs. Fischer was killed, every time I turned around that cat had managed to get in the house. I would go in the kitchen in the morning and the cat would jump at me from on top of the refrigerator. Or it would be on the sink and it would jump. That cat did not like me. Sometimes it would just climb up on a piece of furniture and stare at me. No matter how we locked up the house, the cat always found a way in, and it would always be in places where it shouldn't be, like on the shelf in the closet, hiding, waiting for me. I was scared to death of that cat. I never had problems with my own pets. I've always gotten along very well with animals, but that cat had it in for me. Finally, I called Allen and I said come and get this damn cat. Mrs. Fischer is in this cat and this cat means me bodily harm. Allen drove the cat down to Kendall and let it out in one of the neighborhoods."

Until Allen took the cat away, Dee had fed her every day when Wyatt's cat, Motley, was being fed.

"I couldn't let it starve," Dee says. "I wouldn't dream of not feeding it. And I certainly couldn't kill it. I could never physically hurt anything. But I hated that cat. I think the cat was possessed by Mrs. Fischer. Either that, or the cat was making a last stand on her behalf. I feel that. I never felt that about anything else in my life."

Susan, incidentally, backs up her mother's story about the cat. "That cat always found a way to get into the house," she says, "and it would jump out at Mom from the weirdest places. There was definitely something strange going on with that cat."

As it happened, things would get stranger.

For example, Allen Bryant had continued to study Santeria after his success with the doves at the ocean. On the phone one night he told Dee that he had gotten into Santeria in the first place to protect his relationship with Henry. He told her that he had engaged in a number of rituals that would help him live with Henry in safety. And then, as an afterthought, he said, "Do you still have the gun?"

"The gun?"

"The one we bought in Fort Lauderdale?"

After the murders Allen had given the gun to Dee for her own protection because she was leaving the pancake house so late at night. Dee had carried it always in her purse.

"Yes, I have it," she said.

"I need it," he said. "Bring it to the restaurant tomorrow. I'll have someone pick it up."

Oh, no, Dee thought, not another murder.

"Allen, what do you need a gun for?"

"Felipe has hired a hit man to kill me," he said. Suddenly his voice was full of emotion. He sounded scared, and Dee realized he'd been acting tense for days, but she'd thought it was just the cocaine that did that.

"Felipe? Who the hell is Felipe?"

"Henry's ex-boyfriend. He's hired someone to kill me."

"Oh," Dee said, remembering how Allen had told her about him at the Naranja Lakes Motel. "The guy who was going to castrate you with a switchblade for poaching his lover?"

"It's not funny," Allen said. "He's really hired a hit man."

"How do you know?"

"He called me up and told me."

"He's just trying to spook you," Dee said.

"No. He's not. I know someone's been following me. And someone's been watching the house."

"What's all this got to do with Santeria?"

"I'm doing a special ceremony that will put death on the hit man. It will eliminate him."

"Then why do you need the gun?" Dee asked.

"Dee, it's not funny. Just bring the gun, okay?"

Still somewhat amused, Dee says, "Whether there was somebody really out there to kill him, I don't know. But Allen believed it. He thought by drinking this chicken blood he could protect himself and kill the hit man. All he wanted was for him and Henry to be safe together. Eventually the ex-boyfriend left Miami and that was the end of that. But the whole incident made me realize just how strange Allen could be."

During the autumn of 1983, Dee was being stalked by hit men of a different type: bill collectors. Her main concern was that she was still being pressured by FMS for an accounting of their percentage of the gross. The corporate arm of IHOP seemed closer and closer to reclaiming the franchise, and when Dee was sober, she was terrified of being left without a job. Her only hope was that Allen would come up with the money for FMS, and soon. The money Dee had in mind was to come from the refinancing of the mortgage on Art's house. The annual payment on the current mortgage was coming due soon, and Allen did not have the money, so he had decided that with him posing as Art, they could refinance the mortgage, avoid foreclosure, and end up with some cash.

At ten o'clock one morning, probably in early October, the phone rang in the restaurant. The caller introduced himself as Marty Eagerman of FMS, a regional manager for IHOP.

"I'd like to speak to Art Venecia," he said, his voice as cold as ice cubes.

"Mr. Venecia is not here," Dee told Eagerman. "He's in North Carolina."

"Do you have his phone number there, please?"

"No, I'm afraid I don't. He's very hard to reach."

"Okay. Let me talk to Mr. Allen Bryant."

"He's in North Carolina, too," Dee said. She was wishing she had taken a drink before answering the phone.

"I see," the voice said coolly. "Well, who's managing the restaurant?"

"I am," she said.

"And who, may I ask, are you?"

"Dee Casteel."

There was a long pause. Finally the voice returned. "Mrs. Casteel," he said, "there are a few problems with the Naranja store, things we are very concerned about and—"

"You mean the money," Dee said.

"Yes," he said, "the money. We have been unable to speak to Mr. Venecia for quite a while. Now somebody is going to have to come up here and talk to us about this matter or we might have to take . . . drastic action."

"Okay, I'll come up," she said. What the hell am I saying? she thought. Though she dreaded the idea of having to lie to IHOP corporate right to their faces, Dee took her role as manager seriously. She liked being in charge. "I'll come up and see if we can't get things straightened out."

As always, as soon as the call was over, Dee called Allen and gave him a report. She was proud of the way she had handled things. Allen said it was a good idea for her to go up and talk to them. Like a wise puppy trainer, he gave her the "good girl" 's that she craved.

The regional IHOP office was on Northeast 189th Street in northern Dade County. Allen drove up with Dee as far as the 163rd Street shopping center. He couldn't risk being seen near the IHOP building since he was supposedly in North Carolina. (Actually, Allen had another good reason for avoiding corporate IHOP, though Dee didn't know it at the time. In 1982, after a fight with Art, Allen had gone to work at the International House of Pancakes in Homestead. One weekend he had managed to slip a coat hanger down into the store's drop safe and pull up a bank bag containing $2,200 of IHOP's money. He had never been caught. At Homestead he had been known as James Bryant, and at least so far, nobody in corporate IHOP had ever connected that with the fact that Art Venecia had listed someone named Allen Bryant as the Naranja manager. Still, given the circumstances, Allen would, understandably, not be anxious to have coffee with the fellows at corporate IHOP.)

As they drove up that day, Dee glanced at her watch several times and suggested that they had time to stop for a drink. She was nervous. But Allen, who sometimes urged her to drink and sometimes urged her not to, was against it. Having Dee stagger into the corporate offices of the International House of Pancakes soused and belligerent could be disastrous.

They were both nervous. "Jesus, I can't believe we're doing this," Dee kept saying. "This is insane, Allen, you just don't run a scam on a franchise. They're too sharp. They know about people like us."

"It's not a scam," Allen kept telling her. "We'll give them their money when we have it."

"Okay, okay." Dee took deep breaths, trying to settle her nerves. "I'll try to talk us out of this for a while, but so help me, when we refinance, that money is going straight to IHOP. No buts, no bull, no trinkets for your boyfriends."

"Yes, dear," Allen said, playing the part of the henpecked husband.

"Jesus, I'm scared," Dee said.

"Don't worry about it," Allen said. "You'll do fine. You're good with numbers."

"I am good with numbers, aren't I?"

"You're the best," he said. "Just take charge. You'll be great."

This is when she liked Allen best, when he was encouraging like this, boosting her up, telling her she was good at something. She loved it when Allen made her feel needed.

"Just get them to calm down for a while," Allen said. "We'll get them the money."

At the shopping center Allen got out. Dee leaned across the seat and called to him as he walked toward the stores. "Don't buy anything expensive," Dee said. She blew him a kiss and drove to the FMS office.

She found Marty Eagerman's office. "Come in," he said, "have a seat." His voice was as harsh as it had been on the phone. Dee walked into the office, sat down. Eagerman was a sturdy-looking specimen. Though a little on the short side he looked as if he could be a placekicker for the Dolphins. Dark-skinned and dark-haired, except for two sections of gray that looked as if they had been smeared on his head like paste, he was, all in all, an attractive man. Dee opened her pocketbook, snuck a glance in her compact mirror. She felt pretty today. Allen had bought her a new skirt and shoes for the occasion. She had taken special care with her makeup. She wanted to look sharp for these people.

Eagerman looked up from his paperwork a few times. He was not smiling.

They sat for a moment, he at his desk, she in a rigid metal chair. Under her ruffled white blouse she could feel the beating of her heart, and it occurred to Dee that every time she came in contact with an authority of any kind she was in jeopardy of having her secrets explode. Sometimes she even worried about herself. There were moments when the urge for confession was as powerful as the urge to drink, and she never knew when she might just purge herself of everything she knew. Now, while Marty Eagerman sized her up, she pushed these thoughts from her mind. He doesn't care about Art, she told herself, he just wants his money.

"Mrs. Casteel," he said, "we have a problem, and I've asked you here so that we can find ways to solve it."

"That's what I'm here for," she said somewhat flippantly. Does it show that I'm nervous? she wondered.

"Now we at IHOP have always dealt with Mr. Venecia in good faith," Eagerman went on. "And we've always gotten the same in return. Until recently. You know what I'm talking about?"

"The money."

"Yes, the money. We don't like to take tough measures, but it looks like that's what it's coming to. I don't mind telling you the word 'foreclosure' has come up in this office recently with regard to the Naranja store. The way we are being dealt with now is just not fair."

He sounded bitter, as if his own money were at

stake. Perhaps the company holds him responsible for collecting, Dee thought. Maybe he even has to make good on it, the way waitresses have to make it good if one of their parties walks a check. God, she thought, even a strong-looking man like this, wearing an expensive suit and a nice watch, has people whose boots he must lick. It seemed as if everybody was trying to please somebody else.

Staring at Eagerman while he stared at papers on his desk, it occurred to Dee that the IHOP executive looked like a gangster she had once dated back in the days of Henry Milander and the nights of partying and dancing, when sex was plentiful and alcohol never seemed to be a problem. And she was pretty. Jesus, I was, she thought, I was really pretty. Around her little finger she had wound plenty of tough guys then, guys a lot tougher than this IHOP character. Back then, she thought, I could have charmed this guy right out of his socks.

Dee shifted in her seat, pushed at her hair, fussed with her skirt, and said, "You're right."

"Huh?" Eagerman looked up, surprised.

"You're right. It's just not fair what he's done." And then she added, "To us."

"Who?"

"Art," she said.

"Mr. Venecia?"

"Yes." Now she stretched her legs out in front of her, leaned forward, and lowered her voice as if the conversation had suddenly become intimate.

"Look," she said, "I like Art, but he's put you and me in a real spot here, going off to North Carolina like that."

"Yes, he has," Eagerman said. "Where exactly has he gone?"

"Well, that's the thing," Dee said. She pouted. "That's what's so annoying. I never know exactly where he's going to be. He's on the road up there, talking to contractors, looking at other properties, that sort of thing. I don't know exactly what's going on with Art. I've been putting the money in the bank account, just the way he told me, and sending him the deposit slips. All I've got is a post office box number. He should be sending checks to me for the right amounts, but he's not doing that."

"Exactly," Eagerman said. He laid his hands on his desk. He seemed a little less rigid.

"So it's making you look bad and it's making me look bad," Dee said.

"Yes," Eagerman said, smiling now, as if to say, "Now we're getting somewhere."

"But there's a solution to every problem," Dee said.

"That's what they say," Eagerman replied. "Would you like some coffee?"

"Sure," Dee said. "Black, please." And with an ounce of Scotch added, she thought. "May I smoke in here?"

"Go right ahead," Eagerman urged.

He doesn't care about Art, he just wants his money, Dee told herself again as she rummaged around in her pocketbook for her Benson and Hedges. She lit a cigarette and blew out a long trail of smoke. Back then the men would jump to light her cigarette, she thought. Oh, well, things change.

Eagerman left the office. He came back a few minutes later carrying two styrofoam cups filled with coffee. "So," he said, placing the cups on his desk. "What can we do?"

Dee thought about it while she inhaled her cigarette again and carefully blew the smoke away from Eagerman.

"I'll tell you what I'll do," she said. "Let me simplify this for you. I will make it my responsibility to see that you, personally, get your check. Just give me two weeks. I'm refinancing my house and I'll have some cash then. I will personally deliver the check. You shouldn't have to worry about Art Venecia. If he's up in North Carolina being a little careless about business, that shouldn't be your problem. It should be mine. You'll get your money. I will guarantee it."

"Well, that's very generous of you," Eagerman said. "It certainly makes my job easier."

God, Dee thought, it's working. He's lapping it up. How on earth are we getting away with all this?

She smiled her prettiest smile. "It shouldn't take two weeks," she said, "but let's just call it two weeks to be on the safe side."

"Fine," he said. "That will be fine. As long as we can get this cleared up, that's all I ask."

Later, when he led her to the door, Eagerman laid a hand on Dee's shoulder. "I can't tell you how pleased I am that this is working out," he said. "It's been a pleasure dealing with you."

The success of this little performance was a great triumph for Dee and she crowed about it for days to Allen and Susan, the only people she could tell.

"It felt like graduation," she said to Allen that same day over celebratory drinks at lunch. "It was fantastic. I went in scared, and by the time I left, I had that guy eating out of my hand."

When the money from the refinancing of the house came through, Dee insisted that corporate IHOP be paid. She wrote out an IHOP check and drove up to North Dade where, as promised, she placed the check directly into Marty Eagerman's hands. Eagerman was delighted. The following week he called to tell her a few IHOP executives were coming down to meet her and look at the restaurant. "Nothing to worry about," he assured her. Nonetheless, Dee prepared herself. Allen went out and bought her a new suit. She got her hair done, put on heels, and made herself as lovely and ladylike and competent-looking as she could. By the time the IHOP bigwigs showed up, Dee had gotten the restaurant spotlessly clean. Not a fork was out of place.

Whatever she did, it worked. The vice president

of something or other, and the head of finance, and some other man whose title she missed were thoroughly charmed. They told her the roof would need to be painted, and that was about the only thing they could find wrong with the operation of IHOP Naranja. When they left, they each shook her hand in turn and said that they had heard great things about her from Marty Eagerman. Dee was ecstatic. As long as they got their money and she managed things well, they wouldn't care if Art Venecia never returned. It was incredible the things you could get away with, she thought. These people were dealing with a total nobody. She hadn't signed anything. She wasn't legally responsible for a dime of their money. They knew nothing about her. And yet, she was practically a franchise owner, and if Allen would just keep his fingers out of the till, he and she could run the restaurant forever.

One particularly satisfying aspect of this newfound respect was that she was figuratively able to cut Charlie Jannsen's balls off. Jannsen was an inspector for IHOP. It was his job to come around and give each store the white gloves treatment. Jannsen, everybody agreed, was a prick. To Dee he always seemed like the whining schoolboy who was just itching to get something on you. "How come you've got a can of Heinz ketchup in the kitchen instead of the IHOP recommended brand?" "Why doesn't that waitress have her apron tied in the prescribed manner?"

Jannsen was a pain in the ass, and he seemed to have a special dislike for Dee. One major fight with Jannsen had erupted over waitress uniforms. The standard IHOP uniform then, the one sold by IHOP to the franchise holders, was a dark-blue dress gathered at the waist, with a tan apron, or a tan dress with dark-blue apron. Allen had not liked the uniforms and so had bought new uniforms for the women from another supplier. When Jannsen saw them he had flipped out.

"What the hell is going on here," he had

screamed at Dee. "You can't just put these girls in any damn thing you want. I'm going to report this."

It did no good for Dee to explain that she didn't pick out the uniforms.

"There's going to be hell to pay," Jannsen had warned. "I'm going to close the doors on this place if you don't smarten up. You have one hell of a nerve, changing uniforms. You'll buy your uniforms from IHOP and no place else, is that clear?"

Dee had despised Jannsen and it pleased her no end when, after her visit from the IHOP executives, Jannsen came in, routinely went through his inspections, and meekly left with never another word spoken in anger. Clearly, it burned his ass that she had gotten friendly with Eagerman, and that he could not come in and bully her anymore. It made her think that there was some justice in this world, after all.

The honeymoon with corporate IHOP, however, would be short-lived. After Dee cleared accounts with FMS, Allen began shortchanging them again immediately. With his name being bandied about so much at FMS, it was inevitable that someone would say, "Bryant? Bryant? Wasn't that the name of the fellow who ripped us off for twenty-two hundred bucks down in Homestead a few years ago?"

One morning shortly before Christmas of 1983, Dee was in the upstairs office at the restaurant when one of the waitresses came up.

"Dee, there are two detectives downstairs to see you."

Dee was shocked. "Detectives? What do they want?"

"I don't know. They said they want to talk to you."

"I'll be right down," Dee said.

Dee was sober at the time, which made it harder for her to deal with this sort of thing. By the time she got downstairs to greet the detectives, she was shaking.

"Dee Casteel?" one of the cops said.

"Yes."

"We're from the Homestead police department."

The cops introduced themselves. Dee reached into her apron and pulled a cigarette from her pack of Benson and Hedges. When she tried to put her lighter to the cigarette, her hands were shaking so much that she couldn't light it. Oh, my God, she thought, they'll see my hand shaking, and they'll know, they'll know. She put the cigarette down as if she had changed her mind.

"Would you like some coffee?" she said.

"No thanks," one of the detectives said. "We'd like to know the whereabouts of James Allen Bryant."

"Allen?"

"Yes, do you know where he is?"

"No."

"We heard he was working here."

"Well, he was," she said. "But he's in North Carolina. He's working up there. Perhaps I can help you?" How much do they know? she wondered.

"We'd like to know if you can give us any information on Mr. Bryant, concerning a theft in Homestead."

"Homestead?"

"Did Allen Bryant ever work at an International House of Pancakes in Homestead?"

"I think so," Dee said.

The detectives told Dee that they wanted to talk to Allen about the mysterious disappearance of $2,200 from the IHOP drop safe on the same day that he disappeared from IHOP. At last it had occurred to someone at FMS that there could be a connection between the James Bryant who worked at the company-owned restaurant in Homestead and the Allen Bryant who was listed on the franchising agreement as the manager of the Naranja IHOP. They had asked the police to investigate to see if James and Allen were the same person. This was the first Dee had heard about the $2,200 robbery, and she was, understandably, relieved that the police were only asking about that.

After the police left, Dee went upstairs and called Allen.

"Allen, the police are looking for you," she said. "Something about money you stole from IHOP Homestead."

Allen told Dee it was a misunderstanding, but still, he wanted her to contact Marty Eagerman and say that he wanted to make good on the money, if IHOP would drop the charges.

"Ask him if he'll take your personal check for the money," Allen said.

"My check?" Dee said. "What are you talking about, my check? Allen, don't play any more games with me."

"Don't worry, darling. I'll cover it for you."

"When?"

"In a couple of days. For God's sake, don't worry about it. Just call Eagerman, will you, before they put me in jail."

Dee called Eagerman. He agreed to accept her check for the $2,200 and drop charges. Dee sent the check, wiping out her bank account. Allen never paid Dee back.

By now it was clear to FMS that the Naranja store was in crisis. One morning in January 1984, Dee woke up to the ringing of the phone in Allen's Kendall house, where she had spent the night. It was an IHOP waitress.

"Dee, you'd better get over here right away."

"What's wrong?"

"There's a man here from IHOP. He says they're taking over the restaurant."

The man from IHOP got on the phone and told Dee that the company was taking over the restaurant. "You have a good crowd here," he said, "so I don't want to close the doors. I'd like you to come down here and surrender your keys."

Dee took her time. She stayed at Allen's house for another hour and had, she says, "five or six drinks." Then she drove to the International House of Pancakes in Naranja for the last time. From the upstairs office she got her sweater, her "office bottle" of Scotch, and a few pictures of the boys that she had taped to the walls. She turned over her keys to some man from IHOP, and without ceremony, she left. She was out of work. Her nightmare had come true.

23

The Selling

In October 1983, three months before they lost the pancake house, Allen and Dee's decision to refinance Art's house so that they could pay FMS led to an unnerving and inexplicable incident, which probably helped push Dee closer to the edge. In the *Miami News,* Allen found an ad for a broker who would connect people facing foreclosure with moneylenders willing to take on a second or third mortgage. The broker was a woman named Ramona Feldman, who had a small office on Flagler Street in downtown Miami. Dee telephoned Ramona. "I'm interested in securing a second mortgage on a house belonging to my boss, Arthur Venecia," Dee said. She made an appointment to meet with the broker.

In Ramona's office a few days later Dee explained that Mr. Venecia was away on business in North Carolina, and that she, Dee, would be handling financial matters for him. Mr. Venecia, she said, would be available for the closing.

Dee was well qualified to do this sort of thing.

Her understanding of mortgages, loans, and interest rates is quite thorough, and even today on death row she can easily rattle off the exact numbers associated with the various transactions she made during this period.

Ramona listened carefully while Dee explained the situation with the house. The broker was a large woman, well-tanned, and dressed for success. But there was about her a certain flamboyance. Several gold chains dangled from her ample neck. Six rings decorated her thick, fleshy fingers, and her silky, black hair was long enough to hang down behind the back of her wooden swivel chair. Ramona seemed to stare at Dee as if she could see right through her.

The two women went over the numbers and Ramona seemed to think she would have no trouble finding a lender, or an "angel," as she put it. Then she leaned back in her swivel chair, gave Dee a good solid look, and said, "You know, Dee, I'm not just a broker. I'm also a seer."

"A seer?"

"A psychic," she explained. "I see things that others don't."

Dee's heart jumped. She had never given much thought to whether psychics were legitimate or not, but now the idea of somebody's being able to read her mind was disturbing, very disturbing.

"Oh," Dee said.

"Yes. And, well, it's none of my business, but what I'm getting as I sit here listening to you is that you know too much about Art Venecia's business."

"I do?"

"You are not just his secretary," Ramona said.

"I'm not?" Dee forced a smile.

"No. I think you're in love with him."

Dee was relieved. Some psychic, she thought, she's got me in love with a man who's dead and buried.

"I'm sorry," Ramona said. "I'm imposing."

"That's perfectly okay," Dee said.

"Anyhow, it's not important," Ramona said. "It's just that when I get these feelings, I like to share them."

"I understand," Dee said.

After that the two women seemed to hit it off. Ramona talked about her daughter. Dee talked about Todd and Wyatt. When Dee left, Ramona gave her a warm handshake and suggested that they might get together for drinks sometime.

A few days later Dee telephoned Ramona to see about the second mortgage. The call was set up so that Allen could listen in from his home in Kendall.

The conversation began with business. Ramona had found a man by the name of William Sussman, a lawyer on Biscayne Boulevard, who would take on the second mortgage. After Dee and Ramona discussed the details of the closing, Ramona changed the subject.

"Tell me to mind my own business if you want to, dear," she said, "but I've been getting feelings about you and Art Venecia and I want to tell you about them."

"Oh, really?"

"Yes. I've been getting very strong feelings that this man you're in love with is a homosexual." Then she paused, perhaps waiting for Dee to object. "And he's a pathological liar," she added.

My God, Dee thought, she's describing Allen. Dee took a deep breath. Her hands were shaking. Either this woman had made some lucky guesses or she was picking up psychic material of some sort on James Allen Bryant. It was frightening to think that Ramona could get inside her mind, especially when her secrets were so horrendous. It was one of those moments that came to Dee now and then, moments when she was driven by the urge to just confess the murders to somebody, wrench from herself the dreadful secrets that seemed to be growing like a tumor in her chest. She wanted to say to Ramona, *Listen to me,*

I've done something terrible, I've murdered my grandmother. But she didn't. And with Allen on the other phone listening to this, Dee had to suppress another, very different urge: the urge to laugh out loud.

"I appreciate your saying these things to me," Dee said. "I'll give them some thought."

There was one more troubling conversation with Ramona, and it came about two weeks after the closing on the second mortgage, at a time when Allen was going full tilt with his Marielito friends, and at a time when the murders were still known to no one except the murderers. Ramona called out of the blue. "Dee," she said, "I just had to call. I'm getting very strong feelings about Art. I see him surrounded by dark-skinned men, and I see him behind prison walls."

As bizarre and interesting as these psychic revelations were, there was nothing Dee could do with them. Things had gotten very weird before Ramona came on the scene, and all Dee could do was wonder what, if anything, it all meant.

Whatever Ramona's psychic talents, they were apparently not sufficiently developed for her to divine, when she finally met "Art Venecia," that he was not Art Venecia at all, but James Allen Bryant posing as Art. Ironically, it was Ramona's lack of cognizance that would lead to financial troubles for others later on concerning the Venecia house. According to Dee, Ramona not only didn't sense that something was amiss at the closing, held in William Sussman's office, with Allen in the role of Art Venecia, but she accepted Allen as Art without even asking for proper identification.

The closing on the refinancing took place on November 8. The first payment on the new mortgage was due on December 8. It was not made. By Christmas William Sussman had joined FMS in the rattling of foreclosure sabers.

Allen, still recklessly spending four hundred dollars a day out of the cash register (access to which would soon be taken away from him by IHOP), looked around to see what salable items his lover had left behind. His eye settled on Art Venecia's boat, *Osprey*. The yacht, a 1971, thirty-five-foot fiberglass Bertram equipped for fishing expeditions, was docked at a marina in Homestead. Even before Art died, a broker by the name of Wayne McWilliams had inquired about the possibility of selling the boat. Art had always declined. In August when McWilliams heard that Art had gone to North Carolina, he called again and asked Allen Bryant if Mr. Venecia was now interested in selling his yacht. Allen, thinking the yacht would make a fine party boat for him and his friends, had said no.

But in January of 1984, with a lifestyle that burned through money like a laser beam, Allen changed his mind. He asked Dee to call McWilliams and find out just how many bucks the boat was worth.

Dee, who knew nothing about boats, drove to the marina with McWilliams to inspect *Osprey*. It was in pitiful condition. Albert Riccio, who eventually bought the boat, describes it this way:

"It was in a state of disrepair, almost abandonment. The boat wouldn't run. Engine parts were scattered in it. There was a broken window. The teakwood deck had turned black. The cord that plugs the boat into the dock to get power was lying in the water so long that barnacles had started to encrust it. The batteries were dead and the water in the bilge was coming up almost to over the batteries. Had it continued, the boat would have just sunk because the batteries didn't have enough power to power the bilge pumps to keep it up."

As Dee showed McWilliams around *Osprey* that day, she felt as if she'd been brought down to police headquarters to discuss the mysterious disappearance of Arthur Venecia, local businessman. McWilliams was asking about the boat, but Dee, ridden with guilt and intimidated by her own ignorance of things nautical, felt as if she were being interrogated. McWilliams asked her about the bilge pumps, but it felt as if he were saying, "Where is Art Venecia?" He talked about the dry rot, but it felt as if he were asking, "And what about Mrs. Fischer, where is she?" He asked about dockage fees, but it felt as if he were hammering away with, "What did you do to those people? Where are the bodies? Why did you do this awful thing?"

When they finally finished inspecting the boat, Dee was wrung out, but McWilliams was not alarmed. He guessed that for the boat he could get $38,000, which, after the mortgage and back taxes were paid, would leave Allen with enough profit for about three weeks' worth of cocaine, dog races, fine dining, and gas for the Lincoln. Dee authorized McWilliams to look for a buyer.

While McWilliams searched for a buyer, Allen and Dee made several trips to Fort Lauderdale to negotiate a price and schedule for repair of the boat's two engines, which had been sitting in a marine supply store for six months, waiting for a part. "I didn't know anything about boats," Dee says, "but somebody had to hold Allen's hand." When the engines were ready, Dee and Allen drove up in Art's pickup truck and hauled them back to the marina.

But getting the engines was not the only problem. There was another. Wayne McWilliams knew Art Venecia on sight. Allen could not present himself as Art.

It was decided that Allen would become a notary public so that he could notarize documents giving Dee Casteel the power of attorney for Arthur Venecia. Allen filled out the appropriate forms and sent them off to Tallahassee. A few weeks later he was a notary public. Next, Allen and Dee went to a stationery store and picked up power of attorney forms. They filled in one form, authorizing Dee Casteel to sell Art Venecia's yacht. Then Allen forged Art's signature on the power of attorney and notarized that it was authentic.

Wayne McWilliams, in the meantime, had advertised the boat in a boating magazine and had gotten a call from Riccio, a businessman from New Britain, Connecticut, whose hobby was buying and restoring old boats.

Riccio offered $36,400 and Dee agreed on behalf of Art Venecia. The closing was held in February at the Community Bank of Homestead and Allen was there, this time presenting himself as James Bryant, a representative of Mr. Venecia. Dee signed the certificate of title and Riccio paid for the boat.

After paying off their debts, Allen ended up with a check for $9,545, which was made out to Dee Casteel. Allen was still pouring money into his house, his friends, and his nose, so the nine thousand dollars didn't last long.

By this time, of course, they had also lost the goose that laid the golden eggs, the pancake house. So, the next item to go up for bids on the Art Venecia clearance sale was Art's beloved organ. Allen and Dee started with an asking price of $14,000.

The buyer, Dale Haskins of Portland, Oregon, describes how that deal went down:

"I collect theater pipe organs. It's a hobby. Ridiculous hobby. In September 1983, I listed an ad in a magazine called *Theatre Organ*, looking for a theater pipe organ. One of the responses I got was from Dee Casteel in Miami. She sent me a letter saying she had inherited a theater organ and wanted to sell it. I wrote back and asked for a full description of the organ. She sent that, along with some pictures, but by then I had bought four more pipe organs out of California and I was up to my neck in the hobby and I didn't want any more of the things.

"Then in February I got a call from a gentleman who said he was Mr. Casteel. Allen Casteel, he said. He wanted to know if I would like to buy the organ at a greatly reduced price. He said he had to sell it. I told him I still was not interested. But then I wrote him a letter and said that if the price was ridiculously low, so that I could afford bringing it to Oregon, I would consider buying it.

"I got another phone call from Allen Casteel. He asked me if I would like to buy the organ for two thousand dollars. He said he desperately had to get the organ moved, and I thought about it a little bit and for the fun of it, I threw back a question at him, not really being interested. I said, 'Would you like a thousand dollars for it?' He thought about it a little bit. There was a pause, and he said, 'Yes, I would take a thousand dollars,' and this was still subject to me looking at it.

"I got off the phone and shook my head. I didn't really want to pursue it because I already had too damn many of them. But I went down and put in a reservation for a rental truck to haul the thing back in if I bought it. I got a baby-sitter for my daughter and plane tickets for me and my little boy and flew down to Miami. That was during March of 1984. Mr. Casteel met me at the airport. At least I assumed he was Mr. Casteel. He took me to one motel and they wouldn't accept small children, then he took me to another. We made an appointment for ten o'clock the following day to go see the organ. The next day he was late. I remember because they evicted me out of my room because it was eleven, so I waited for him to show up. I called his wife, Dee Casteel, and said he was late. Finally he showed up around noon. That was the last time I saw him. He left a station wagon with me and directions for me to meet his wife, Dee Casteel, at a hamburger place in Homestead. I met her and from there we went to see the organ.

"The organ was in a big, kind of beautiful, new giant steel building, concrete floor, and the organ was a disaster. It was scattered from one end of the building to the other, and it was in extremely poor condition. I was very, very disappointed with what I saw. I had assumed it was in much better shape.

"I wasn't going to pay a thousand dollars for it.

Mrs. Casteel mentioned something about selling a car and I was toying with the idea of spending five hundred dollars and buying the car and driving back to Oregon, instead of flying, and forget the whole thing.

"But finally we agreed that I would buy the organ for six hundred dollars. She called somebody on the phone to make sure that was okay. While we were finishing up the negotiations, I tried to find out how she came to own the organ. She said she had inherited it from a close relative, and he had died at a young age. I don't remember how. I tried to find out more, but she didn't want to talk about it. I paid her six hundred dollars cash and I spent a week loading the organ. I didn't see Mrs. Casteel again, not on the property, anyhow. She never arrived there once. There was no power at the place where the organ was . . . it was very desolate . . . so I did the work from early in the morning, packing the parts in the rented truck until it was dark."

Hal Henry, a Venecia acquaintance from the organ society, had also looked at the organ some weeks before, and his recollection gives some insight into Allen and Dee's desperation for cash during this period after the IHOP had been reclaimed.

"I knew that Art had this authentic Wurlitzer organ that came from a Baptist church in upstate Florida," Henry says. "I went down to look at it. I met Dee Casteel. She seemed very nice. She had like three kids and they just really loved her. She said that Art was in North Carolina, drying out. She was asking thirteen thousand dollars for the organ. But when I looked at it, I saw that it had been so badly treated it was only worth like scrap. There were parts missing and nothing was complete, so I offered five hundred dollars, and she accepted it. But somehow it never worked out, I don't remember why. Anyhow, the house was being foreclosed on and she tried to sell me the furniture and the house."

Dee and Allen also sold a camper of Art's for

$4,000, and they would no doubt have sold the Lincoln if it hadn't been repossessed. During this warm Florida winter of 1984, they also started looking for a buyer for the biggest item: Art's house and five acres of property, complete with two buried bodies at no extra charge. Allen's plan, at first, was simply to get out from under the loan. William Sussman, the lawyer who had financed the second mortgage, was foreclosing on the property, so Allen had Dee prepare a warranty deed and send it to Sussman. Then Allen called Dee one night and said, "This is crazy. Why should we just break even? We ought to work it so we can make some money on the deal." Allen called Sussman and told him that Dee had sent the warranty deed without permission. "She was not authorized to do that," Allen said.

By this time Dee had been the front woman for several sales and had never gotten more than a few hundred dollars for her work. Susan's refrain of "He's using you" was becoming more and more difficult to ignore. When Dee found out about the call to Sussman, she was furious with Allen. But Allen, as usual, was able to charm her into compliance, and before long she was trying to find a buyer for the house.

Dee's friend Lynn Lore knew a woman by the name of Cynthia Kaiser, who managed the Callusa Country Club in Kendall. Kaiser had a friend by the name of Richard Higgins, a landscaper who was looking to buy a parcel of distressed property. Higgins was a good-looking young man, a former circus acrobat who counted among his friends rock stars Rod Stewart and David Bowie. Still in his mid-twenties at the time, Higgins had already been in the landscaping business for six years. He designed and installed landscaping for residential clients as well as big commercial clients like McDonald's and Burger King, and he was in the market for a large piece of land at a good price so that he could grow plants that would be incorporated into his landscaping.

After Cynthia Kaiser told Higgins about the Venecia property, he and Cynthia drove over to take a look at it, probably sometime in February. There they met Dee. They spoke briefly, then Higgins inspected the property. The inside of the house, according to Higgins, was a terrible mess. Apparently Dee, who had never left dirty dishes in the sink, who always made the beds before leaving for work, by now was either too busy or too apathetic to bother with housework.

Higgins looked at the shade houses, the greenhouses, and the large metal barn where Art's body had been kept. He concluded that they were all structurally sound even though, like the house itself, they were all a mess. The land, too, was a tangle of weeds, encroaching trees, and junk. Higgins knew it would take weeks just to clear the land and get it ready for his business.

On his next visit Higgins was introduced to a slim, somewhat effeminate young man who Dee Casteel said was the owner, Art Venecia.

There followed several meetings between Higgins and Allen Bryant, posing as Venecia. The price for the house and the five acres of property was extremely low, $150,000, a fact that for Higgins was both an attraction and a warning flag. Why was it so low? he wondered. When he asked about it, Allen told him that his grandmother was gravely ill in another state and that he was anxious to be with her.

For weeks the deal was as close to death as Allen's poor grandma. It was on-again, off-again. Every time Higgins would get close, some inner voice would whisper "back away" and he would stall. For one thing, Allen and Dee seemed to be in a big rush to close. For another, Allen had asked that his money be delivered in cash.

Higgins had a couple of peculiar meetings with Allen at the Callusa Country Club.

"We met for lunch, me and Cynthia Kaiser, and

Allen," Higgins recalls. "Of course I knew him as Art Venecia. He was well dressed, he looked all right. But when we started negotiating, he got real strange. I was asking questions about the house, locations of the wells, that sort of thing, and all of a sudden he freaked out on us. I don't remember exactly what he did. He didn't shout or lose his cool or anything, but he got real weird, then got up and left. I remember thinking, this guy is a real asshole.

"Then we met a second time and the same thing happened. We're talking and all of a sudden this guy gets weird and says, 'I don't feel well. I'm leaving.' A friend of mine was there, a big guy who was annoyed at Allen because here we had taken the time off to come down and talk to him about the house and he was acting like a jerk. So my friend went after Allen and brought him back. By this time I'm thinking this guy is too strange and I was backing away from the deal, and they had to bring me back to getting involved again."

Cynthia Kaiser recalls the meetings, too, and remembers thinking that something was wrong.

"I remember feeling funny vibes. Venecia [Allen] talked in fragments and his answers were short. I couldn't get friendly with the guy. I said to Rich when we left, 'God, that guy's weird.' Certain things just smelled funny, like Richard had to come up with fifteen thousand dollars in cash and bring it to the lawyer's office. We both thought this was weird. But I think Richard was blinded by the deal. He was getting a fabulous deal, a nursery which he wanted, in the beautiful Redlands, at a great price."

At some point early in the negotiations Dee, knowing the house would be sold, had moved out. She borrowed $3,500 from Allen and used it as a down payment on a small house in Homestead.

On the morning of the closing, March 28, 1984, Higgins kept a previously scheduled appointment for minor surgery. Then he had to run all over town gathering $15,000 in cash from various sources. He was still dopey from medication by the time he and his girlfriend, Sandra Lochard, along with Cynthia Kaiser, drove to the office of attorney William Sussman at 100 Biscayne Boulevard for the closing. Dee and Allen followed them in Art's pickup truck. Allen drove.

Higgins, whose regular lawyer was out of town, wanted an attorney present for the closing because he knew that the Venecia land was distressed property and several bills were unpaid. He wanted to make sure that he wasn't going to get stuck with the bills. Cynthia called Sam Danziger, a lawyer whose firm often held functions at the country club. Danziger's office was just around the corner from Sussman's. Higgins hired Danziger to come to Sussman's office and witness the closing.

"Everything seems to be in order," Danziger told Higgins after various papers were passed around. "I'll just need to see some identification."

Dee and Allen perhaps stiffened slightly (getting caught at one crime could lead to discovery of the others), but if they did, nobody noticed.

"Identification?" Allen said.

"Yes, Mr. Venecia. Just a precaution. I'll just need something to verify that you are Mr. Venecia, the owner of the property."

"Oh. Sure," Allen said. He reached into the pocket of his slacks, which were so tight they looked as if they had been painted on. He made a face. Then he reached into another pocket. Then he stood and patted his back pockets.

"Oh, damn," he said.

"What seems to be the problem?"

"I don't have my driver's license."

"You don't."

"No. The pants are so tight, I never carry my wallet when I wear them. I didn't drive today, so I didn't think I'd need it."

Another warning flag. Allen had driven the pickup truck to 100 Biscayne, right behind Higgins and his friends.

Why Richard Higgins didn't just run for the hills then and there is hard to say. Danziger, to his credit, did not want his client to buy a house from someone without identification. But Higgins was dazzled by the bargain price. Higgins believes his thinking was also skewed by the medication he'd been given for his surgery. "I should have killed the deal right then, but I wasn't thinking clearly enough."

Instead of throwing in his hand, Higgins asked for William Sussman to be brought in. Higgins had serious doubts about this Venecia character, but Sussman was a prominent Miami attorney and his word would settle the matter.

Sussman came in and Danziger explained to him that Mr. Venecia had forgotten his wallet, and identification was necessary.

"Can you identify Mr. Venecia for us?" Danziger asked.

"Oh, certainly," said Sussman, who had been introduced to Allen in the role of Venecia back in November at the original refinancing. "He's Art Venecia, all right, I've dealt with him before."

That seemed to satisfy everyone except Danziger. Allen signed all the papers and Higgins received a deed signed "Arthur Venecia" by Allen.

When the old mortgage and all the debts were subtracted from the $150,000, Allen and Dee were left with the $15,000 that Higgins had brought in cash to the closing. According to Higgins, the money was stacked on the table and it was Dee Casteel who seemed to be in charge. "She grabbed the money and started counting it, and putting it into some kind of satchel," he says. Higgins was left with an image of Dee as the aggressive, even dominant, partner in this scam. Cynthia Kaiser does not remember who took the money, but she does remember Dee Casteel as the person who was "calm, in control."

Dee says Higgins is wrong. "Allen took the money," she says. "By this time I was a wreck. I don't think I even touched the money."

In any case, it would be the last money that either Dee or Allen would receive from the estate of Art Venecia. The seeds of their downfall had been planted eight days earlier.

24

The Bottom

"It's just for a couple of days," Dee said to Allen one morning in mid-March. She had spent the night at Allen's home in Kendall. So had Todd and Wyatt. And now, getting ready to leave in the morning, she had told Allen that she wanted to visit Cass in Texas.

"No," Allen said. "You can't."

"Please," she said.

"No," Allen said. "You're crazy. The man beats you. You finally get rid of him and now you want to go visit him."

"I know," Dee said. "But. It's hard to explain. I just want to see him down there and know that he's okay."

"No," Allen said again. There was finality in his tone. His eyes frightened her. "Dee," he said. He looked around to be sure the boys were out of earshot. "We can't risk being separated like that. Do you know what I'm talking about? You drink. You might say the wrong thing."

He's going to kill me, Dee thought. Allen's going

to murder me. When the time is right, when he can get away with it, he'll hire somebody, they'll come in the night, they'll put a razor to my throat. It was a nutty thought, not based on much of anything, but it was real to her.

She drove home that morning, still convinced that Allen wanted to do away with her. The boys sat beside her, good-humoredly complaining and making fag jokes. They hated it when she dragged them to Allen's and they all ended up sleeping there. Allen's gay friends made the boys uncomfortable.

"Well, you were safe last night, Ma," Todd joked. "I'm not so sure about Wyatt. I think that Freddie guy kind of likes Wyatt." He jabbed his brother with an elbow. "If you know what I mean."

The joking continued, and Dee tried to smile for the kids, but she really wasn't with them. She was with Allen in her mind, trying to figure out how she could have loved so despicable a person.

During the selling period Dee had gradually come to understand that Allen did not love her, that for a thousand bucks, or even five hundred, he would probably sell her, too. And now she believed that Allen was planning to kill her. It wasn't anything he said. There were no real threats. It was all a creation of her mind, and she knew it. Maybe he's not planning to kill me, she thought, maybe I'm just getting paranoid. But he doesn't care about me. Of this she was sure.

For Dee there were many moments like this, when she was with the boys or Susan, or her friend Lynn Lore, but wasn't really with them at all. She was in some private world making sad discoveries about herself, like, *Allen never really cared about me, he just used me*.

This knowledge, when it came to Dee, seemed to free her and doom her simultaneously. It was as if, one by one, she had been cutting the cords on a parachute. The last two cords holding her up were her job and the belief that she and Allen had a special relationship. Her job, of course, was gone, and now she had cut her emotional connection to Allen. She was falling deliriously toward what experts on alcoholism call the bottom.

"The bottom" is that point at which the alcoholic finally chooses sobriety. For each person it is different, and some bottoms are deeper than others. For a man who beats his wife while drunk, the bottom might arrive when he finally sees her packing a suitcase. For someone else the bottom might come when the car is repossessed. One alcoholic doctor might reach the bottom when his license is revoked, another might keep his license and not reach the bottom until he accidentally kills a patient during surgery while drunk. "There is," writes Arnold Ludwig in *Understanding the Alcoholic's Mind*, "almost no limit to how bad the situation could potentially get as long as individuals are still alive." Ludwig also notes that many alcoholics are not aware that they are experiencing a personal bottom at the time that it is happening. "Quitting drinking," he says, "may sometimes not start out as a matter of choice."

Just as the nondrinking alcoholic tosses out banana skins to make drinking inevitable, the heavy-drinking alcoholic may toss out a few skins to make sobriety unavoidable when the demon inside knows that survival is threatened. Among Ludwig's examples: "An individual develops an allergy to alcohol, becoming deathly sick whenever he drinks it. A judge issues a court order for hospitalization or sends the individual to jail. Or an individual joins the navy and then ships out to sea."

During the early months of 1984, Dee Casteel consciously understood that her choice was (a) stop drinking, or (b) die. She also knew that she wasn't the only one who might die. Susan was coming home drunk; Susan was making jokes about suicide. Probably at some other level Dee also knew that she would never stop drinking unless something big and impenetrable were put between her and her friend Scotch.

In any case, whether she understood it or not, whether it was she or the demon who was running things, it is clear that Dee was getting ready to toss out the biggest banana skin of all. She needed to reach the bottom, and she would do whatever she had to in order to get there.

There were, of course, the terrifying incidents with the haunted cat. Maybe the soul of Bessie Fischer did inhabit that mysterious white beast; maybe some demonic force did compel that animal to leap on Dee from strange places and hide in closets. But more likely the cat's craving for revenge was a creation of Dee's mind. Sure, Susan verifies the bizarre behavior of the cat, but Dee's daughter was lugging around her own heavy yoke of guilt.

But even after Allen took the crazed cat away, Dee was not free from terror.

"One night I was at the Venecia house alone," Dee says. "Susan was working, and Todd and Wyatt were out. It was about nine o'clock and Tasha, my Dane, was outside. All of a sudden Tasha started barking something awful. It was startling because Tasha was not the type of dog to bark at every leaf that fell off a tree. She didn't even bark at cats or squirrels or other dogs. There was only one time when Tasha would bark, and that was when there was somebody on the property.

"I looked out the window and Tasha was in the garden area right below the window where I had planted some croton shrubs. She had taken a stance there. She was upset. The hairs on the back of her neck bristled. It was a protective posture, as if to say, 'There's something out here. Come here, human, and see what's going on.' I looked but I couldn't see anything. No car. Nothing. My skin tingled. I was afraid that it might be an intruder. I told Tasha to quiet down, but she kept on barking and barking and staring right at one spot away from the house. I looked over there and I thought I saw like a ghostly figure standing out among the palmettos. I was scared out of my wits. I called the dog in the house. 'Tasha, come baby,' I called. She growled.

"When she came in, she went right to the window and looked out at that same spot. This dog that never barks growled at that spot for an hour and a half nonstop. I was a wreck. I thought somebody or something was out there. I wasn't drinking when it first happened, but I stood by the window, pouring one drink after the other, and looking at that figure. It was the eerie outline of a man. He had on a raincoat and a soft-brimmed hat that was pulled down. It was strange. I could define what he was wearing; it was beige. But at the same time I could see through him. There was no depth. I stared at it and stared at it. He just stood there out past the cleared area, right on the fringe of the woods, a few feet beyond the graves.

"I know something was out there. I don't know what it was. Maybe it was just a shadow or something, but it was something that made my dog growl. It's hard to believe that a ghost would just stand there for an hour and a half. And what the hell was he doing wearing a raincoat and a hat in southern Florida when it wasn't even raining? I don't know what I saw, but I know Tasha would never go near that spot again.

"It was a onetime thing. I never actually saw anything else. But there were times when I was in bed and was awakened by something that sounded like someone trying to open my window. My bed was on one side of the bedroom and Susan's was on the other. Sometimes it would wake us both and it would sound like someone trying my window, and then running around to the other side of the house and trying Susan's window. It was frightening. We could never see anything. It was so black out there and we had no outside lights."

There is an interesting sequel to this ghost story,

though it has nothing to do with Dee. It comes from Richard Higgins's girlfriend, Sandra Lochard, who moved into the Venecia house after Higgins bought it.

"I have two cats," Sandra Lochard says. "Blake and Nika. They had always been house cats and they had always been extremely affectionate. But they absolutely refused to stay in that house from the day I moved in. If I brought them in, they would seem frightened and they would dart out. Even when I tried to be affectionate with them, they would squirm out of my arms and bolt for the door. Blake was particularly attached to me. In other places where I lived, he would sleep with me all the time. But he would not stay in the Venecia house, he wanted nothing to do with it. I would bribe the cats into the house with food, and they would eat it quickly, then run for the door. It was very strange.

"I'm not a superstitious person, and I was never afraid about the murders, but I never felt comfortable in that house. I always felt as if there were some kind of presence. One night I bolted up suddenly out of a dead sleep. There was a light shining on the mirror in the bedroom. I looked at the clock. It was two twenty-five in the morning. I looked into the mirror. I thought, Why am I awake? I was frightened. I started to walk into the living room. I saw that the light was on in the kitchen, and it had been reflecting off the television in the living room and onto our bedroom mirror. I froze. I knew I had turned off all the lights. Richard grabbed his gun and we looked around. Nobody there. I checked all the doors and made sure they were locked. I shut off the lights and went back to bed.

"In the morning when I got up, I went into the kitchen and started to make coffee. I saw that the door into the garage was open. I stopped in my tracks. The door was not just unlocked, but wide open. This was not the kind of door that can blow open from a draft, and the other garage door, the one leading to the yard, was still closed. Oh, my God, I thought, this is freaky.

I had locked it the night before, and I had checked it in the middle of the night and now it was wide open.

"Things like this kept happening, so finally we had Richard's aunt and uncle come to the house. They are very religious and they did a ceremony, like an exorcism. Richard's aunt brought holy water and she prayed and drew little oil crosses over the doorways. They spent a lot of time denouncing the devil and they sprinkled holy water all over the house. After they did that it did quiet down, and my cats would stay in the house. It was unbelievable. Sometimes I wish I had actually seen something, so I could be sure."

Incidentally, the garage door that Sandra says was open was the one that Art and Allen always used to enter and leave the house. They never used the front door. One final note of interest to those who put stock in ghost stories: the last three digits of the phone number at Venecia's house were 666.

Whether ghosts are real or not, it is not surprising that a woman as stressed out as Dee was at that time would be seeing them. The fact that Dee was falling apart had been obvious for weeks, not just to herself, but to others. Donna Hobson recalls an earlier visit to the Venecia house.

"Dee was living in the bottom of a bottle," Donna says. "I was at her house one night when she was totally out of it, so drunk she couldn't keep her eyes open, and I'm sitting on the couch talking, saying, 'Why don't you go to bed,' and she said, 'Oh, no, I can't go to bed.' I said, 'You are so tired, why don't you just lie down and go to sleep and I'll stay here until you're asleep,' and she said, 'No, I can't go to sleep.' And I said, 'Why?' and she said, 'If I go to sleep, they'll kill me like they did the others.' I said, 'They'll what?' and she said, 'Kill me like the others,' and I said, 'What others?' and she just mumbled, 'They'll kill me.' So I let it drop and then she started crying. It was so sad. Nobody was home and she was sobbing because she was afraid to sleep by herself that night because somebody would come and get her. I didn't know what she was talking about, but then I started putting it together with other things I had thought about, like Art being missing, and how odd it was that he was letting Dee stay in his house with three kids. And I thought maybe Dee and Allen killed Art."

Susan remembers a lot of crying during this time. "Ma would have a few drinks and she'd start talking about Mrs. Fischer. She couldn't talk about Mrs. Fischer without crying. It was tearing her apart."

The early-1984 image of Dee Casteel that emerges from the memories of people like Donna Hobson is quite different from the Dee Casteel observed by Russell Philpott, Albert Riccio, Cynthia Kaiser, Richard Higgins, and others duped into buying property from a bogus Art Venecia during the same period. Those people remember a competent woman, somewhat charming, but nonetheless hardheaded about business, an intelligent woman with an excellent mind for figures. During the mortgage negotiations, for example, it was Dee who could compute interest rates in an instant, and who recited the language of the business as if she were a banker. It is interesting to note that the closing on the house, with Dee "calm" and "in control" according to Cynthia Kaiser, was held on March 28, even though Dee had tossed out the final banana skin on March 20. Apparently, Dee's "Jekyll" personality was available for special appearances all through the flight to the bottom. And as in the Stevenson classic, the two personalities would fight for control until the very end.

There were times during this period when Dee would think she had stopped breathing and she would be struck with panic until minutes had gone by and she'd realize that her body must be taking breath even if she couldn't feel it. It seemed as if she had to concentrate just to remain stable. She had to say to herself "I am here. It is now" in order not to become unglued. Dee's greatest fear was that she would lose her mind.

Kenny Baldwin, the rescue-squad driver who had gone to the Venecia house the night Allen tried to strangle Art, remembers a later visit to the same house.

"We got a call that a woman was having difficulty breathing," Baldwin says. "We went out there, same house where the two guys had fought, and here was this Dee Casteel living there with her kids. I asked her where the owner was and she said he was up north. The trailer that had been there was gone. She looked real stressed out. Whenever I asked her about the owner of the house, she looked shocked, real nervous. I think something was really bothering her."

By the third week in March 1984, a lot of things were bothering Dee. Allen didn't love her. Cass was gone. She could live with those things. But she could not live with the fact that she had murdered Bessie, a woman who, in Dee's muddled mind, was also Mama. And she could not live with the fact that Susan was drinking more, staying out late, and slowly giving up on life. Dee could not bear to watch her daughter fall apart.

"He's the lowest form of life imaginable," Susan said to her mother on the morning of March 20, 1984. "He's a user and he's got you involved in murder."

The subject, of course, was Allen.

By this time they had moved out of The Redlands and into the house on Southwest 300th Street in Homestead. It was a typical Dee Casteel home, a squat, cramped bungalow.

"I know," Dee said. "I know." Dee sat on the small couch in the living room. She smoked a cigarette and stared off into space. She looked like an amnesiac who was trying to remember who she was, where she came from.

Todd and Wyatt were at school. When Todd and Wyatt were home, Susan always had to swallow her comments about Allen. The boys knew nothing about the crimes. But now, in the middle of getting ready for work, Susan had erupted again. She stared angrily at her mother, wondering, why do I do this, why do I yell at my mom about things that can't be fixed?

"Allen is a devil," Susan said. "He's ruined your life." Then she added, "And mine."

"Well, why don't you just leave then," Dee said. "Just get out. It's not your problem. You don't have to live with it the way I do."

"Oh, sure. And what will you and the boys live on, huh? You think Allen's going to buy groceries and pay the mortgage?"

"I'll get by," Dee said. "I don't need you or anybody else."

"Sure you will, Mom. Look at you, you're in great shape."

The fire of Susan's anger had further been fueled by the fact that Dee was out of work, and Susan, with a new waitressing job at Wag's restaurant in Homestead, was the only breadwinner in the family. She was used to being mother to the boys, but now she was mother to the mother, and it was infuriating. Money was extremely tight, and Dee's spending it on Scotch didn't help. In addition, Susan was resentful that every dime she made had to go for the family, while Allen was buying gifts for his boyfriends with money that should have gone to Dee.

Like her mother, Susan was hung over. Though the cocaine supply was drying up, the alcohol was not, and during this period Susan was no more immune to its ability to soothe emotional pain than her mother was.

The one bright spot in Susan's life at this time was David Keeter, her new boyfriend whom she had met at Wag's. But even David was a frightening reminder of what could happen to Dee. David was a Florida State trooper.

"He should be giving you half the money," Susan said.

"Huh?"

"Half the money," Susan said.

It had been bad enough that Allen had persuaded Dee into setting up murders, she thought. But now Dee was letting him use her to sell off Art's property and he wasn't even splitting the money with her.

"One-half, Mom, you've earned it," Susan said. "What's he giving you?" Susan knew the answer.

"Zilch," Dee mumbled. She crushed out her cigarette and lit another. What she really wanted was a drink, but she knew that if she poured a glass of Scotch, Susan would hit the roof.

"You're damn right, zilch," Susan said. "A few hundred here, a few hundred there. It's ridiculous. Ma, you're the biggest sucker going, do you know that? Always doing things for people. And what has anybody done for you? What has Allen done for you?"

"He lent us the money for this house," Dee said. Though Dee had turned against Allen by this time, she still felt the need to defend him.

"Yes," Susan said, "and you can bet he won't let you forget it. Every time he wants somcthing from now on, he'll remind you of that."

Dee smiled. It had already happened many times.

"God, I don't know how you could have gotten yourself into such a mess," Susan said.

Dee was exasperated. How many times were they going to go through this? "Look," she said, "what's done is done. It's over and it can't be undone. What do you want me to do, slit my throat?"

They stared at each other.

"Poor choice of words, Mom."

"I guess," Dee said. "But what I'm trying to say is, honey, I just don't know what you want from me. Do you want me to call the police, turn myself in? What is it?"

"I don't know," Susan said. "But you should demand more."

"More what?"

"More money."

"Is that what you're so angry about? Money?" Dee asked. "Is that what all this means to you?"

"I'm not saying that," Susan said. "All I'm saying is you're in this mess anyhow, you might as well get something out of it."

"Wonderful," Dee said. "Maybe you think I should have yanked out a couple of Mrs. Fischer's gold fillings before we buried her, huh?"

Susan didn't answer. She left the room. There was nothing else to say.

Dee closed her eyes, leaned back on the couch, pressed her hands to her temples. Her mind felt gray and leaden and suffocating. The awareness of what she had done to Mrs. Fischer never left her, not for a minute, not even during sleep. Sometimes her friend Scotch could dilute its grayness, lighten its weight, but lately even Scotch had been unable to make the feelings bearable.

"What do you want for supper?" Dee shouted to Susan, who was in the bathroom. At least Dee could go to the grocery store and think about prices, and she could cook and think about what vegetables to make. That was the key to everything, just keep thinking about little things.

Susan didn't answer. Dee lay on the couch, smoking and wondering what would become of them all, while Susan finished dressing. It seemed that the anger between mother and daughter was always in the house now, like a huge piece of furniture that couldn't be ignored. The boys, perhaps thinking that a hell of a lot of anger was being generated over something so trivial as Mom's unemployment, had begun to act up. Dee felt that things were getting out of control. More and more she just wanted to give up. Sometimes Susan talked about taking them all to Colorado. It was a great dream, but Dee didn't believe in dreams anymore.

"I'm going to work," Susan said. She stood stiffly in the doorway of the living room, dressed in her Wag's waitress uniform. A waitress, just like me, Dee thought.

"Supper?" Dee said.

"Chicken," Susan said. "Spaghetti. Anything." Then she softened, walked across the room to her mother, leaned down, and hugged her good-bye. "I love you," she said. "I'm sorry I yelled at you."

Then Susan, looking as if she'd forgotten something, went back to the bedroom. From her position on the couch Dee could see that Susan was slipping something into the pocket of her apron.

"What have you got?" she said when Susan came out.

"What?"

"In the pocket of your apron. What did you just put in there?"

"Nothing," Susan said. The two women stared silently at each other. More silence. "Just a couple of nips," Susan said finally, pulling the miniature bottles of alcohol from her pocket and waving them at Dee. "No big deal."

"Oh, Susan," Dee said.

"Ma, don't give me that 'oh, Susan' crap, okay? I need something to get me through the day. This hasn't been easy on me, you know."

"I know," Dee said sadly. "I know." I'm taking her down with me, Dee thought. I'm still the wrecking ball.

After Susan had gone to work, Dee called her friend Genvieve "Jackie" Ragan. Dee and Jackie had known each other since 1981 when Dee was a waitress at Sambo's and Jackie was a customer. They had gotten close. They would talk on the phone a lot. Later, when Dee worked at IHOP, Jackie would sometimes sit at the back of the restaurant and the two women would do crossword puzzles together. Jackie was a particularly bright woman with a great vocabulary. Dee liked that.

"When Dee called that morning, she wanted to get out of the house," Jackie says. "She wanted to go and have some drinks. She said she had to get drunk. I didn't want her to drink, but I went. I drove because I knew that Dee would drive if I didn't drive for her."

The two women spent the day at three Homestead bars. They went first to the Leisure Lounge. There Dee started drinking heavily. She talked about how much she missed her job at the pancake house, but when Jackie tried to understand how Art could have let the payments slip so badly, Dee changed the subject.

Later at the Golden Lady, Dee got maudlin about the kids. Do you think my boys are good kids? she asked. Of course they are, Jackie told her. Do you think they'll turn out all right? Dee asked. Do you think they could make it on their own? Then she told Jackie how worried she was about Susan and how something had to be done to stop her daughter's slide, but she couldn't tell Jackie what was troubling Susan so much.

Oddly, the last bar they went to was a place called The Last Chance, and by the time they got there, Dee was teary and barely coherent. She talked about her whole life, and how it had come to nothing. Jackie felt there was something that Dee was trying to tell her, but she didn't press it. Her instincts told her that whatever it was, she didn't really want to know.

"She drank until about three that afternoon," Jackie says. "When she was done drinking, she couldn't even walk."

Jackie drove Dee home and Dee went to bed. Jackie stayed in the house so somebody would be there for the boys when they got home from school. At seven o'clock Dee got up. The boys were out, but

Susan and Jackie were in the kitchen drinking coffee. Dee came into the kitchen. She was sober.

"Susan, would you get some paper and a pen," she said.

There was a look on Dee's face. Susan understood what was going on.

But Jackie didn't, and she looked at them both.

"I have to say something because I can't live with this any longer," Dee said. And then, "This is just insurance, honey, that's all. You keep this. If anything happens to me, you go to the police with it."

Dee asked Susan to take down what she said. They all went into the dining room and sat at the table. Dee talked. Susan wrote.

Jackie sat there in shock as Dee revealed detail after detail about the plan to kill Art Venecia, the murder, the moving of the body, the cleaning up, the murder of Bessie Fischer. Jackie's heart was pumping furiously. I don't want to hear this, she thought, I don't want to hear this. She got up from the table and walked into the living room while Dee was talking. But it was all one big, open room, and as she stood by the window staring out at the night, she could still hear every word.

"Art's mother was becoming increasingly difficult to convince that Art was merely on vacation," Dee dictated. "This left us in the position of having to dispose of Mrs. Fischer, also." Jackie put her hands to her ears. She could still hear Dee talking and Susan writing down every word. "Mrs. Fischer was karate-chopped in the back of the neck," Dee said. (This is what Dee believed at the time.) Jackie started crying.

"Why?" Jackie said. "Why are you writing all this? Why are you saying it?"

"Life insurance," Dee said. "I'm doing it so Allen won't murder me."

When the confession was finished, Susan dated it. Then Susan and Dee signed it. Jackie Ragan, thoroughly shaken, went home.

For the first time a record had been made of a crime that was now nine months old. Was Dee writing an insurance policy to protect herself from Allen Bryant? Or was she arranging to be caught, to be put away, separated once and for all from alcohol? No one can say for sure. But the banana-skin theorists would ask simply, why didn't she write her confession when she and Susan were alone? Why did she do it in front of Jackie Ragan?

25

The Whistle-Blower

The rumors that Allen had so dramatically tried to drown in the summer of 1983 had quickly resurfaced and gained strength as weeks and then months went by without a word from Art Venecia. Throughout that hot, wet summer and the warm, dry Florida winter that followed, a sense of uneasiness moved like a flu virus through the population of those close to the mystery. The feeling seemed to be not necessarily that Art had been murdered, but the more general and less frightening feeling, as several of them put it, that "something was wrong."

Donna Hobson, who had watched Allen's performance at the employees' meeting, later spoke to a friend in the park service about it. She asked her friend how to file a missing persons report in another state. She was told that she couldn't file if there was no evidence that a crime had been committed.

The apprehension about Art's absence also infected people unconnected to the pancake house.

Reid Welch, who knew Art from the organ society, recalls an August phone call from another of Art's casual friends.

"He was worried about Art," Welch says. "We talked about it and we thought the way Art had left town so suddenly was extremely strange, not like Art at all. But that was all."

George Freitas, Art's accountant, who had called IHOP during the first week after Art's disappearance, called several more times that summer and fall.

"I thought it was odd," Freitas says, "because a week before Art disappeared he and I were supposed to have a meeting about his taxes. But he canceled it. He called up and said he'd had a terrific fight. Allen was in the hospital and Art was in no condition to meet with anybody. Art said that Allen's mother was going to have Art arrested for beating up her wonderful child. I called several times after that, always spoke to Dee. I was told that Art was looking at property for a motel and restaurant in North Carolina."

In October, two other friends from the organ society were driving through The Redlands one day when they decided to drop in on Art, whom they hadn't seen around for a while. They met Dee, who explained that she was taking care of the house while Art was away, but they found the shabby condition of the greenhouses and the grounds disturbing.

The condition of the plants was particularly shocking to Hal Henry, the man who had come by to look at the organ. Henry is an expert on orchids.

"In that huge shade house, which must have been about forty by a hundred or so, there had been many valuable plants, orchids from some of the best hybridizers in the country. To me it looked like somebody had gone through with a defoliant and just maliciously killed everything. It didn't look like simple neglect to me. I think somebody had to deliberately do something."

Still, despite the suspicions of several people, the crimes went on undetected and unpunished.

On Valentine's Day, 1984, five weeks before Dee's confession, the rumors got a pretty good going over at a dinner party in South Dade. The party was held to celebrate the return of Jackie Ragan from North Carolina, where she had been living since April with her sister.

While living in North Carolina, Jackie had tried, unsuccessfully, to locate Art Venecia, with whom she had established a friendship, first as her customer and then as her boss, during her three years as an IHOP waitress. Over dinner Jackie told the guests that she had returned to Florida because Allen Bryant, with whom she was also friendly, had called and said he'd bought a house for her to live in. Dee Casteel, he had said, was living in it temporarily. (This would be the house in Homestead, which Dee had bought with a loan from Allen. In fact, Allen had insisted that the house be in both their names, but at the last minute, when Allen was not around, Dee arranged for the deed to be in her name only.) But when Jackie got back, Allen avoided her. All of this might have meant nothing, but it led to speculation that Allen just wanted to get Jackie out of North Carolina, where her snooping around might not have been in his best interest.

Over roast beef and potatoes various theories about the disappearance of Art Venecia were put forth, and by the time the party broke up, everybody was feeling anxious. Jackie decided to call the North Carolina motel and restaurant association. Allen had recently told people that Art had bought a restaurant in Boone, North Carolina. Jackie was certain that the association would know about it. Her concern deepened when she was told that nobody at the association had ever heard the name Art Venecia.

The Valentine's Day dinner was held at the home of Anne Chepsiuk, the pseudonym for a woman who had until this time not really been on the stage of this drama, or even in the front rows. But Anne was about to become a crucial player. She would be the one who would make these private and perfect crimes finally public and imperfect.

Anne was afraid then and is still afraid that her involvement in the case could jeopardize the lives of her children and her grandchildren, so she will sleep more comfortably at night knowing her real name has not been used. Her fears, while perhaps unrealistic at this point, are not uncommon. With any murder there are tense people not just near the center, but also out on the fringes, people who fear they will be stabbed, shot, or bludgeoned by the criminal or friends of the criminal. Of course, they are sometimes right. But more often the unfounded fear is a way of casting themselves into the drama. One man, whose only job was to identify a photo and say "Yes, that is a picture of Art Venecia," now proudly asserts, "I'm the one who put those people in the electric chair. I have to be careful, they could come in the night and get me." Another man, who never met any of the principals in the case, but who was dating an IHOP waitress at the time, worries that the killers might get him. He reasons that they murdered other people, why not him?

So, even though the offenders are safely behind bars, Anne Chepsiuk worries from time to time, and she has better reason than most. After all, she's the one who blew the whistle.

Anne had gone to work as a waitress at the pancake house four years before Dee was hired. Anne's last day at the pancake house was about a year before Dee Casteel's first day, and the two women have never met. But they were both part of that South Dixie Highway network of waitresses and cooks, so they knew of each other, and they talked on the phone often, though briefly, when Dee would call for Jackie Ragan, Anne's housemate.

During her three years at the pancake house Anne worked on and off, because of Allen Bryant. Though Anne had always gotten along well with Art, whom she calls "a very fine man," her relationship with

Allen was less than cordial. That was because during Anne's first IHOP stint Allen had moved out of Art's Redlands house and into a house that Anne managed, next door to her own. Anne says that after the initial payment Allen, and the three friends who lived with him, never paid the rent.

"I would come for the rent," she says, "and Allen would always say, 'I'll have it for you next week, I'll have it for you next week.' " Relationships were frayed even further, Anne says, by the fact that Allen ran up monstrous phone bills, including several calls to Cuba.

When the overdue rent rose to $1,200, Anne threw Allen and his friends out. When she called the company from which he had rented a stereo and furniture, she was told that he hadn't paid for those, either.

After that, Anne was permanently on Allen's shit list, and when he visited IHOP, he would always stop and peer through the door first, and if Anne was working, Allen would not come in.

In time Allen and Art Venecia had the inevitable reconciliation, and a sad-faced Art arrived at Anne Chepsiuk's door one morning to tell her she had been terminated. Art liked Anne, he said, but Allen had been reinstated as manager of the pancake house, so Anne was out. When Allen and Art had their next big fight, Allen moved out again, and Art rehired Anne. When Allen came back, Anne was out. And so it went.

Not surprisingly, Anne Chepsiuk thinks Allen Bryant is scum. He is, she says, "a two-faced liar," and it was Anne who said, "If everybody in Miami got a piece of rug every time Allen told a lie, nobody would need to buy any rugs."

So a few days after the Valentine's Day dinner, a curious Anne Chepsiuk, perhaps anxious to get something on Allen, drove out to the Venecia property where she had visited Art from time to time. By now Dee and the kids had moved out, but the property had not yet been sold.

Anne walked around the empty acres that late February day, sniffing the air, staring at the ground, searching like a detective for some evidence of tragedy. When she saw the greenhouses all tumbled down in such terrible condition and the house such a mess, she knew for sure that something was wrong. Art, she thought, would never, ever, let his property go like that.

As she stood out on the graveled driveway looking at the house, something else troubled her, but she couldn't quite pin it down in her mind. A breeze rushed by, tossing bits of trash that had been left behind by Dee's family. Anne turned and walked gingerly along the driveway to the barn, where the body had been. She stepped inside and shouted, "Hello," just to listen for the echo. The place seemed so lonely.

Walking back up the driveway, Anne stopped at one point. She crouched down and picked up a crumpled white piece of paper. Pressing it against herself, she smoothed it out and read it. It was an electric bill. The bill had a large overdue balance. It had not been paid for months. Art would never leave his bills unpaid, she thought. It was a small thing, but disturbing. It was as if a voice were whispering in her ear, "Can't you see what's happened here, Anne, can't you see that it's true? They really did murder him, they really did. It's not just dinner conversation. It's murder." She looked up then and realized what had been bothering her all along from the moment she'd gotten on the property. The trailer. Art's mother's trailer was gone. She stared at the spot where it had been and she felt a chill.

At the local police department Anne had a friend, Ronald Patano, an officer who more than once had helped her jettison troublesome tenants. She called Patano and told him her suspicions. He told her that nothing legal could be done about hunches and rumors; there was still no evidence that a crime had been committed. Anne understood. But murders had been committed; she was sure of it. And the thought of lives lost without mourning, and bodies buried without ceremony, grated on her moral sensibilities.

And so on the night of March 20, when Anne's housemate, Jackie Ragan, came home, shaken and wretched, and related to Anne the tale of deceit and treachery that she had just heard, Anne knew what she had to do.

"I wrote it all down," she says. "Everything Jackie told me. I even made a diagram of the house and marked where the bodies would be."

The next day Anne called Patano and told him everything. He said he'd get back to her.

After several days Anne had heard nothing from the police. She called Patano to see what was going on. He said nobody had gotten back to him. Another couple of days passed. Anne began to get edgy. She had reported a murder and the murderers were still on the street. What if they found out she had told on them? She called Officer Patano again and was told that he was on vacation. Anne, reluctant to give her name to anyone else, waited in silence. The nights, especially, were tense.

"I had called and called," Anne says. "When he came back from vacation, I called again and he said he was going to send somebody out. Nobody came. I called again."

Patano, apparently skeptical about a story so bizarre, had not reported it. When he finally called Anne back, he told her he wanted more information before reporting the crime.

Anne and Patano drove out to the Venecia property. Again she told him about the rumors, the uncharacteristic neglect of the house, and Jackie's story about Dee's confession. She told Patano that the body had been stored in the barn. He went there and found stains from fluids that could well be the drippings from a dead body. Before Patano left Anne, he told her that he was going to send a detective from homicide to talk to her. This time he did report it.

It is a satisfying thought that James Allen Bryant might have sealed his own fate when he said just once too often, "I'll have the rent for you next week." But Anne says her motivation for blowing the whistle was not to get even with Allen, whose guts she hated.

"I just wanted a decent burial for Art and his mother," she says. "Everybody is entitled to a decent burial."

26

The Investigation

Here is how Officer John Parmenter, one of the investigators of the Venecia-Fischer murders, explains the workings of the homicide division of the Metro-Dade police, Miami, Florida.

"We're set up in teams of four guys, squads. Each guy on the squad is the lead detective on some homicides, and a helper on all the others that are assigned to his squad. The lead detective for each homicide is chosen on a rotating basis. If it's your turn and a murder comes in, it's your murder, you're the lead detective.

"Okay, so a murder comes in today at such and such address. The whole team will go to the scene, and everybody on the squad knows who's going to be the lead. We get down there and the lead guys looks it over to see what he's got. Maybe we've got a body and another victim is in the hospital. Four witnesses are on the scene, and we have the name of a subject. That's a suspect, we call them subjects. Someone says the subject was supposed to be going over to his mother's house after he left here.

"Okay, so the lead detective says to one guy, 'You go to the hospital and find out about the victim.' To a second guy he says, 'You take these witnesses downtown and get statements from them.' To the third guy he says, 'You stay here and document the scene work.' That's whatever the lab guys do—prints, photos, whatever is done on the scene. Then he says, 'I'm going to take a uniformed guy and go to the mother's house, see if the subject is there, and see if he'll come to the station with us.'

"Then late that night the four guys on the squad will get together and talk about what they've done, who they talked to, what they found out.

"Maybe at seven o'clock the next morning they'll have another meeting and the lead detective will have a 'lead list' of things that still need to be done on the homicide. 'Okay,' he says to one guy, 'I want you to go to the morgue for the autopsy.' To another guy he says, 'I want you to go to houses around the area and see if anybody saw the subject run out of the house. Me, I'm going to the state attorney's office to talk about the charges I placed.' Maybe one guy says, 'Let me out of doing your canvas because I've got things on my case I need to do.' Fine. At this point the lead detective starts to wean the rest of the squad off and work mostly with just a partner. The lead is going to end up doing most of the bullshit work. That's the way I work it. I don't want the guys on my squad mad at me for making them do the piddling stuff."

Parmenter applied for assignment to the homicide division after seven years in uniform because in homicide there is less boredom and more overtime. Although he is a detective by occupation, it is not his title. He is simply a police officer working a plainclothes assignment, and his pay scale is the same as that of the uniformed man on the streets. The homicide division handles all sudden deaths: pedestrians hit by cars, babies drowning, people falling from trees. That is the troubling part of Parmenter's job. Murders are generally less distressing, he says, because "eighty percent of the murder victims deserved it. They were involved in something they shouldn't have been involved in, and it led to their deaths."

Parmenter likes his job, but it's not quite as exciting as "Miami Vice." He's only fired his gun once in the line of duty, and even then only because he happened to be in a shopping center where a subject was fleeing from a uniformed cop.

"We don't see that kind of action," he says. "We're not in any danger. By the time we get called, a homicide has occurred and the subject is long gone. It's the uniformed cop who's really on the line. He's the first one on the scene."

Though murder is a growth industry in Miami, and bizarre crimes are as common as trade shows, Parmenter says the most interesting case he's been on was the Venecia-Fischer murders.

"I've never handled anything else like that," he says. "I don't think anybody has. Those people had committed the perfect crime. If Casteel hadn't written that statement, they never would have been caught. It was perfect. I've had a lot more brutal cases, ones that made for lively conversation at parties, but this one was fun to work. It was a fun case. Things fell in place. We got good leads. They panned out."

The first lead, of course, came when Anne Chepsiuk's message finally got through to homicide. The case was turned over to Detective Ken Meier. Meier, who has since dropped out of police work and moved to Kentucky, had never been a lead before.

"Meier was a junior man," Parmenter says, "and the case was handed off to him. Nobody really believed there was anything to it. Bodies in the front yard! People liquidating everything! It just wasn't believable."

Parmenter, with eight years of homicide experience, was put on the squad to watch over Meier, make sure he didn't make mistakes.

On Tuesday, April 17, Ken Meier, along with Detective Jerry Todd, met Anne Chepsiuk at a doughnut shop in Homestead. There, over coffee and jelly doughnuts, she told them about the confession that Dee had given in front of Jackie Ragan. Anne also gave the detectives two pictures of Art Venecia and one of Allen. She told them Art's address and said that the bodies were buried there.

Later that day the detectives and Anne picked up Jackie Ragan. Ragan led them to Dee Casteel's house in Homestead. The detectives drove by, noting the registration number on the red pickup truck that was parked in the driveway. Later they ran a check on the number and found that the vehicle was registered to Art Venecia.

Next, the detectives drove to Kendall Drive, where Anne pointed out Allen's house.

Meier and Todd then went to Wayne Tidwell's backhoe service and asked him if he remembered doing any digging at the Venecia address. "You bet I do," Tidwell said. "Broke a piece of equipment, digging in that coral rock."

Two days later on April 19, Richard Higgins was cutting trees on The Redlands property he had bought in March. Already he had people working for his landscaping business, but the property had been a mess when he bought it and most of his time so far had been spent clearing away debris and just getting things into some kind of order for business.

Around noon he heard the sound of men running across the property. He looked up and saw five of his Mexican employees hightailing it into the woods on the north side of the property.

He shouted to them in Spanish, saying more or less the equivalent of, "Hey, where the hell are you guys going?" The men ignored him, running deeper into the woods.

Two men wearing suits and ties came around from the front of the house. Immigration officers, Higgins thought. You didn't have to be a hardened criminal to see that the men were some sort of policemen. No wonder his workers had left so hurriedly.

"You can tell your boys they can come back," one of the cops said. "We're not INS." The men flashed badges and identified themselves as Meier and Parmenter. "We're from homicide."

"Homicide?"

"Metro-Dade," Parmenter explained. "Are you Richard Higgins?"

"Yes."

"You're the owner of this property?"

"That's right."

"Who did you buy the property from?"

"Arthur Venecia," Higgins said. "The owner." This line of questioning was making Higgins nervous. He had put his last dime into the property.

Parmenter reached into his suit pocket and pulled out an envelope. From it he removed a black-and-white glossy photo of a handsome, dark-skinned man who looked to be about forty-five years old. It was one of the Venecia photos from Anne Chepsiuk.

"Who's that?" Higgins asked.

"Arthur Venecia," Parmenter said. "Is that the man you bought the house from?"

Higgins felt suddenly very weak. "Shit," he said. "Let me find someplace to sit down." He backed away from the policemen until he found a tree trunk to sit on. "The Arthur Venecia I know is about fifteen years younger than that guy," he told the police.

"You've been working around here?" Meier asked.

"Yes."

"Have you noticed any areas that look as if they've been recently dug up and filled in?"

Higgins had. There was an area on the southeast corner of the front yard that Higgins had taken small note of where dirt had obviously been brought up and put back. It had not been a particularly significant find on five acres that had been left so neglected. He told Parmenter and Meier about it and led them to the spot.

"We'd like permission to dig," Parmenter said.

"What are you looking for?"

"Bodies."

Higgins gave the detectives permission to dig, so they called Tidwell. Tidwell showed up around three o'clock with his backhoe.

"This was very weird," Higgins said. "I called up my friends and said, guess what, the police are down here digging for bodies in my yard. My girlfriend came over to take a look. After a while more cops came, and more cops, even the police chief showed up in his helicopter. It was like some military operation."

At five o'clock Tidwell unearthed the wooden wardrobe. The door on one side had broken from its hinges and fallen in. Staring down into the pit, Meier could see several articles of clothing, bath towels, bedsheets, and a human skeleton. Meier had seen enough. He called Detective Marc Richter and asked him to pick up Bryant and Casteel. Parmenter and Meier put in calls to Dade County Medical Examiner Valerie Rao, and Assistant State Attorney Dave Gilbert.

"Then the press came," Higgins said. "They wanted to come on my property, but I wouldn't let them. I guess I sensed already that my business was in trouble. I didn't want the exposure. I had clients like McDonald's and Burger King. If there was a lot of publicity and those companies thought I was going out of business, I knew what would happen. They'd say, you're a great guy, Rich, see you later, and I wouldn't have them for clients anymore. So I told the reporters they couldn't come on the property. Next thing I know there's all these choppers hovering over my yard, shooting film of the digging. Channel Seven. Channel Four. Channel Ten."

Detective Richter, along with Detective Alejandro Alvarez, went to the Holiday Inn in Coral Gables, where Allen had gotten a job as a waiter. They were told that Allen usually worked the earlier shift and was not there.

At seven o'clock Richter and Alvarez went to Dee's house.

Dee describes the scene.

"Jackie Ragan was there with her son. And these two detectives come to the door. They asked me to step outside for a minute so we could talk. They said they wanted to ask me a few questions about Art Venecia and did I know him. I started to shake. I was sober. I was trying to quit drinking again and this was the first day off the booze. They asked me if I would come downtown with them. I said yes. They allowed me to go inside to get my purse and cigarettes. They followed me in and said they were investigating a missing persons report and would bring me back after questioning. Jackie Ragan was out of there in a flash, and I thought that was strange. Now I realize she must have known what was going on. She must have just about had a heart attack when the cops showed up while she was there. I told the boys not to worry, I'd be back. I thought I was just going to the Cutler Ridge station. I started to get edgy when I realized the detectives were taking me into Miami, to homicide."

Though Dee was nervous, it did not occur to her that she would be accused of murder. In her mind, even if the police knew all the facts, they couldn't charge her with murder. To this day she does not think of herself as a murderer.

"They took me downtown and gave me coffee and started questioning me. On the first go-round I didn't admit to anything other than having known Art."

Dee told the Art-is-in-North-Carolina story to Marc Richter. She said there had even been a rumor once that Art had been killed, but that several employees said that Art had told them he was going to North Carolina. She also explained that she had lived in Art's house only because she had bought a house and the previous owners hadn't moved out right away.

"After a while they excused themselves, and the door was open and I could hear the police radio," Dee says. "I knew all the codes from my days as a police dispatcher, and I heard a call for service from Art's address, two one nine oh oh Southwest One Hundred Thirty-fourth Avenue, two 'forty-fives,' which I knew were DOAs. By this time it was eight-thirty. I knew it was over."

At this time the police, the assistant state attorney, and police photographers and other scene specialists were still at Higgins's place, where lights had been set up, and Dade County Medical Examiner Valerie Rao was supervising the removal of the bodies.

When Richter came back into the room, he told Dee that Art's body had been found earlier in the day, and now a second body had been found.

"Art's mother," Dee said. She felt as if the weight of the world had been dropped from her shoulders. She was ready to talk.

Dee told Richter everything. She told him she had expected to be caught. She told him she was relieved. She gave Richter the address of the Amoco station. She told Richter that she went through with all the selling because Allen had promised her a lifetime job at the restaurant. In the parlance of the cops who questioned her, Dee "talked out."

"I didn't even think about prison at the time," Dee says. "I figured they'll probably charge me with grand theft, I'll post bond and go to trial. I'm not sure I even thought that far ahead. Being in withdrawal from alcohol, I had the shakes real bad."

At eight-thirty that night Meier and Parmenter went to Wag's looking for Susan, but she was not there. They were told that Susan dated David Keeter, the state trooper. When they found Keeter, he told them he didn't know where Susan was but that he would find her and bring her to homicide.

At nine-thirty they went to Dee's house and impounded the Buick Skylark.

At ten-thirty that night, Detective Jerry Todd picked up Allen at a house on Southwest Eighty-eighth Street. They brought Allen in, and Meier and Parmenter, still on the job at eleven P.M., questioned him.

"My first impression of him was that he was a devious little punk," Parmenter says. "The woman's story matches what we know, but Bryant's resisting. He goes into this bullshit story about being forced to go to the house at knifepoint. What he told us wasn't enough for an arrest, so we let him go."

The questioning of Dee went on for several hours. At midnight she signed a formal statement.

"Can I go now?"

"No," Parmenter said. "We have to hold you until we know what the grand jury is going to do with you."

At ten o'clock the following morning Parmenter took Dee into his office. He got her a cup of coffee, came back, sat behind his desk, and offered her a cigarette.

"Well," he said, "we know what the grand jury's going to do with you."

"Do you mind telling me?" Dee said. Still, it was grand theft in her mind.

"They're going to indict you for two counts of murder one."

Dee nearly fell off her seat. Her mouth flew open. She felt numb. She was struck with horror. This can't be happening, she thought. What will happen to the kids, who will take care of them?

"Can I get bond?" she asked Parmenter. It sounded to her as if someone else were speaking the words.

"There is no bond in the state of Florida for murder one."

"My God, what about my kids? How can they do this? I didn't kill anyone."

"That's not the way we see it," Parmenter said.

"What about an attorney? I don't have any money."

"The state will appoint an attorney."

Now Dee says, "I never realized how much trouble I was in until that man opened his mouth and said I would be indicted for murder. It was like he had dropped a building on me. My stomach fell out. I got goose bumps."

Parmenter stepped out of the office. Dee, still in shock, sat alone for several minutes. She figured out the household bills in her mind. The bills were paid for a month, she realized. The kids would be okay until then.

A few minutes later Detective Jerry Todd came in. Dee knew him. He had been a customer when she worked at Denny's. Todd said he was sorry about what had happened to her and he asked if she could help them find Mike Irvine.

Dee said she didn't know Mike's address, but she could point out the house. It would be her last look at the world outside.

"Richter and I took her out for a ride to show us the house," Parmenter says. "We were all tired. We'd all been up all night. We started talking about her life; she was telling us about being an alcoholic. The bottom line was she had finally given up. She said, 'I don't care what happens to me, I'm tired of it all.' "

The next day Todd interviewed Susan. She told them everything she knew. Todd impounded Dee's handwritten confession.

Ken Meier and Jerry Todd spent the next several days trying to track down Mike Irvine and Bill. Neither Dee, nor anybody else they spoke to, knew Bill's last name.

At Mike Irvine's house in Leisure City they talked to Dan Burns, who rented the place from Irvine. Irvine hadn't been around since July, but Burns gave them the address in Marion, North Carolina, where he sent his rent checks. At the Amoco station the detectives learned that Mike had gone on vacation in July and had never returned.

At Webster's used-car lot, Bernard Murphy told them that Bill was gone. Murphy also told them that Bill was normally armed with a straight razor. Bill's nicknames were Joker and Cowboy, he told them, but he never knew Bill's last name, thought it might be Rives or Reid.

Parmenter and Meier went to see Richard Higgins again. They asked him about the closing on the house and showed him a photo lineup. Higgins identified Bryant as the impostor who sold him the house. Now they had enough for an arrest.

On May 2 the detectives got a warrant for James Allen Bryant for two counts of first-degree murder. They went back to the Holiday Inn and got a new address for Bryant.

"It turns out Bryant is staying in this flophouse in town, just the other side of the bridge, real run-down place," Parmenter says. "He had come down in the world, evidently. We knock on the door and there's four guys in there, naked, all sleeping in one bed. We took Bryant in."

Bryant told the police that he and Art Venecia had been lovers. He repeated his story about two guys forcing him at knifepoint to go watch while they killed Art. Dee was behind the whole thing, he explained. He said that he and Dee regularly took food to Art's mother, Bessie, but that Dee told him that Bessie was asking too many questions and Dee was going to have her killed. He said Dee made him participate in the liquidation of Art's assets and that the money was split fifty-fifty.

By this time the press had run its stories about the bodies found in a Redlands yard and had moved on. The story was fascinating, but it didn't get as much coverage in Miami as it might have in another city because in Dade County murders are as ubiquitous as palm trees, and each day's murder must leave column inches open for the next day's murder. But of the stories that did run, the item that seemed to register most vividly in the public's mind was an anecdote that Pulitzer Prize–winning reporter Edna Buchanan tagged on the end of a long story about the case, which appeared in the *Miami Herald*.

"The victims' deaths were not a total secret," Ms. Buchanan wrote, winding up her story. "A scruffy little white dog, a toy poodle owned by one of them, emerged regularly from the woods during the past year to lie whimpering at the grave site, nursery workers said."

There are two interesting things about the story. One is the response it got from the public.

After the story appeared, Richard Higgins got hundreds of phone calls. Each day's mail brought letters from people inquiring about the dog. People showed up at his door, asking about the dog. One fourth-grade teacher called up because several of her students, concerned about the dog, had brought copies of the story to class. Everybody was worried about this "faithful shaggy survivor," as the dog was described in another *Herald* story, and dozens of people offered to adopt the brave little creature. The dog was a hero, and people who didn't read the stories carefully told other people that the dog had solved the case.

The other interesting thing about the story is that it's not true.

Dee Casteel, sitting in her cell at the women's annex, reading about the shaggy "innocent victim of violence and greed," the "eyewitness to murder" that "fled into the wilds of South Dade a year ago after her owners were killed and buried in their own front yard," was amused. She had always suspected that newspapers made up stories and here was proof. There wasn't any dog. She had lived in the house and she had never seen the dog. Susan had never seen the dog. Todd and Wyatt had never seen the dog. Art Venecia had never even owned a poodle during the time she knew him. Art did have the Doberman, Shadow, but Shadow had disappeared a few weeks after the murder and had never returned.

Dee and everybody else close to the case assumed that Buchanan, well-known for her love of neglected animals, had made up the story. But she hadn't. Higgins had.

"I made up the story," Higgins says. "After the story about the bodies being dug up hit the papers, there were a lot of 'poor Richard' stories in the newspapers, stories about how I had invested all my money in the house and would probably lose everything. These were terrible for business. Big clients won't come near you if they think you're in trouble. Who the hell was going to contract with me if I might not be around to finish the work? So, in order to get the 'poor Richard' stories out of the paper, I made up the dog story. There really was a dog hanging around but he'd only been around for a couple of days. And he wasn't whimpering at any grave site. I made that part up. I told Edna the story and she printed it. I had no idea it would be such a big deal. I hadn't gotten one call from anybody concerned about 'poor Richard,' but everybody called about the dog. It turned out the dog only lived a few houses away. Two weeks after the story came out a woman and her little girl came to the house. It was the girl's dog and she had been looking all over for it."

Early in May, Parmenter called the Marion, North Carolina, police department and spoke to Sergeant Eddie Smith.

"Sure, I know Mike Irvine," Smith told him. "I gave him a ticket just last week. I know his wife." (This was a new wife, Mike's fourth. Between murders he had once dropped in at the pancake house and proudly shown off his new girlfriend. He told Dee then that he was going to get married.)

Smith told the Miami cops that Irvine was working at a gas station and also at a box factory.

On May 4, Parmenter and Ken Meier flew to Marion, a city of about thirty-six hundred people northeast of Asheville. Sergeant Smith took the two detectives to the gas station where Irvine worked, but Mike wasn't there. Next they went to Irvine's home.

"So Irvine came to the door," John Parmenter says. "He looked like your basic country bumpkin. Smith said, 'Hi, Mike, how you doing? These fellows are policemen from Miami and they'd like to talk to you.'

"So we tell him who we are, and he doesn't even question what it is we want to talk to him about. We take him down to the police station. We tell him we're on a murder investigation and his name has come up. 'I don't know what you're talking about,' he says. So we show him a picture of Dee Casteel. 'Do you know this lady?' He says yes. We tell him, 'Well, she's confessed, and James Allen Bryant has confessed.' So then Irvine got into a story. He shaved the story to favor himself, but still he hung himself. In his story he just takes Rhodes out there, but Rhodes is the killer all the time. He says he's afraid of Rhodes and that's why he left Miami. So we tell him, 'We're going to call Miami and we're going to try to get an arrest warrant and have it teletyped up here and you will be arrested.' So he says, 'Well, I guess I might as well stay around here.' Legally, he could have walked out the door at that point. If we were in Dade County, we could have PC'd [probable cause] him, but outside of Dade County we're nothing. So he could have walked, but maybe he didn't know that. He probably thought he had to stay, and it wasn't like we said, 'Hey, Mike, it's okay if you want to leave.'

"So Richter got a warrant and teletyped it up to Marion and they arrested him. The legal process of getting him back to Miami would take about a week. So now we had the name Bill Rhodes and we came back to Miami to start looking for him."

From various sources the police by this time had also accumulated three more of Rhodes's nicknames: Wild Bill, Crazy Bill, and Greasy Bill. But Rhodes had left the Sunshine State. He had seen television news reports about the grisly discovery in The Redlands area and had decided it would be best to move on.

In late May, Meier interviewed a young woman who had known Bill for two years. She said that around the middle of the month Bill had dropped by at her apartment. He had told her that he was in trouble, and "if the police come around asking questions, you tell them you don't know where I'm staying." He told her he had opened an automobile repair shop in Homestead. (In fact, Rhodes had been working at an auto repair shop in Homestead.) Before Bill left, he gave the young woman a jackknife for her birthday.

Meier also talked to Bill's girlfriend, Migdalia Ramos. "Mickey," as she was known, said that Bill had given her a yellow AMC Pacer, but about a month ago he had shown up with a tow truck and taken the car back, saying he was going to use it to drive to Texas, where he had a sick relative.

Mickey said that Bill seemed to come into money the previous summer. He had given her a lady's ring, white gold with three diamonds, and a lady's wristwatch, which he said were gifts to him from a friend. Mickey had sold the ring, but she still had the watch, so the police took it into custody. Later they showed it to a nephew of Bessie Fischer's, who identified it as hers.

On May 28, one day short of a year since Allen had found Dee's oregano bottle, Joker made a collect call from the little town of Pine Apple in south-central Alabama to his sister Paula in Illinois. He told her he had "messed up." When Paula asked him what he meant by that, he told her he had killed a guy, had beaten him to death. He asked Paula for money. He also wanted her to put him in touch with their mother and brother to see if they could come up with some cash.

He must have been concerned about a possible wiretap on his sister's phone because he told her, "If you get hold of Ma, tell her to meet me in the last place where we were together." He said he would be driving the same blue Mustang he had driven when he left Illinois.

Paula, alarmed and distressed by the call, telephoned Frank Natale at the Springfield police department and told him that her brother had called and claimed to have committed a murder. Natale checked with Florida for warrants on Rhodes, but none had been issued yet. He called Paula and told her that if Rhodes called back to pump him for more information.

Bill called Paula again two days later. This time he was in Tennessee. He bragged to her that there had been another car with Illinois plates in a parking lot and he had switched plates with it. He asked her about the money.

Paula told Bill she hadn't gotten hold of her brother or any money yet. Then she cautiously asked Bill why he had killed a guy.

"The guy owed me money," Bill said.

"How much?"

"A lot of money," he told her.

"Well, who was this guy? What was his name?"

"I don't know," Bill said. "We went by nicknames."

"Bill, I don't understand. How can you kill a man if you don't even know his name. Who was he?"

"He was just a guy," Bill said.

"What do you mean, 'just a guy'? What kind of guy?"

"He was a guy who owned a business."

"Where?"

"In Florida, Dade County. He owed me a lot of money, that's all. This happened a year ago."

"A year ago?"

"Yeah, but they just found the body. They dug it up. His partner had buried it."

Paula didn't push her luck with any more questions. She told Bill she would try to get some money.

Paula called Frank Natale again at the police station and told him what she had found out. Natale called Metro-Dade homicide and asked them if they were looking for a Bill Rhodes. They were, of course, having gotten the name from Mike Irvine. Ken Meier flew to Illinois.

By the time Bill called again on Friday, Paula was a wreck. She had gotten a migraine headache and gone through bouts of vomiting brought on by the tension of knowing her brother the murderer was on the loose. Bill told her he was in Memphis, Tennessee, and he wanted her to wire sixty bucks to an old air force buddy who lived there.

Possibly Rhodes had already borrowed the money from the friend and was now arranging to pay the debt. Possibly he wasn't even in Memphis anymore. In any case Paula visited her sister's trailer park the next day and saw a car just like Bill's parked near the trailer. That same day an anonymous telephone caller told the Springfield police department that Rhodes was at the trailer park.

The trailer park, beyond the city limits, was outside of Natale's jurisdiction, so Natale and Meier, along with several men from the Sangamon County sheriff's office, went to call on Bill. Prepared for the possibility of a shoot-out with an armed murderer, they got instead an exhausted little man sitting on a toilet seat.

"He looked undernourished," Natale says. "He was frail and weak looking. He went along without any problems."

At the sheriff's office Rhodes stonewalled it at

first. But when Meier told him some of what the police knew, he began to fidget.

"Look," he said, "I know everything that you want to know. I just need some time to think about it. I want to talk to my mother. Come back tomorrow and I'll tell you everything."

The statement that Rhodes gave to Meier the next day at the Sangamon County jail was his story about going to the house to rough a guy up, and then returning several weeks later to repair a roof. He also explained that he only used his razor for scraping gaskets from auto parts. And he told Meier that he had gotten the ring and watch as payment for mechanical work he had done for a black guy named Mike. Rhodes was extradited to Miami and put in jail.

Throughout the summer of 1984, detectives gathered information and evidence. They talked to Philpott, Riccio, Sussman, and all the other people who had been duped by the fake Venecia. They gathered bills of sale, canceled checks, bank statements. From these they got handwriting samples and fingerprints that would be used as evidence. They had solved two more of Dade County's murders. There were, by the way, 468 other murders in the county that year.

27

The Witness

On her second day in jail Dee got a visit from Art Koch, a Dade County assistant public defender who had been assigned to defend her.

By this time she had been transferred to the Women's Annex in the northwest section of downtown Miami, a pleasant enough lockup that might have passed for a college dormitory if it had no steel bars and guards.

"My first impression of her was that she was very distressed and an alcoholic," Koch says. "She was thin and haggard. But what came through to me after I'd been with her awhile was her humanity and her intelligence. When you have drug abusers or alcohol abusers in the structured setting of a jail away from their substances, that's what usually comes through, their humanity. Dee struck me as typically middle class, not like my usual clients. She was the kind of person you could sit down with and actually have a pleasant conversation with."

Koch's goal on this first visit was just to make

Dee trust him. "Defendants usually don't trust public defenders at first," he says. "They see us as part of the establishment that's out to get them."

Dee, sitting on the other side of a small cubicle, smoking her Benson and Hedges, neither liked nor disliked Koch. He was in his late thirties, dark, muscular, good-looking, a friendly enough guy. He seemed very sharp, but at this point she was beyond caring about such things. She only cared that someone was there to listen to her.

Art Koch and Dee talked mostly about her kids. Dee was worried. Where would they live? What would they eat? As much as she worried about their physical survival, she worried more about the emotional damage that might be wrought by the shock and disgrace of having a mother hauled off to prison for murder.

"Will they still love me?" she said to Koch, to herself, to the walls. "I wish I could see them."

"You will," Art assured her, "you will."

"I'm mostly worried about Wyatt," she said. "Todd will be okay, and Susan? Hell, Susan's a lot more grown-up than I am. But Wyatt?"

Dee could feel the heaviness in her chest from just thinking about poor, vulnerable Wyatt. "You know, Mr. Koch, Susan and Cass always said I babied Wyatt. Maybe I did. But he's the one who feels the most. He's the sensitive one. Such a daydreamer." She felt tightness in her throat, pressure behind her eyes. Smiling sadly, she said, "Wyatt could always amuse himself for hours with nobody but himself for company. Wyatt's so special. If there's a little scrap of paper on the ground, and it's the only thing Wyatt can take to school with him, he'll take it and find a way to make it his center of attention."

Dee pushed her face down into her hands and sobbed. After a minute she looked up. Her face was wet with tears. "Mr. Koch," she said, "I know my little boy has great dreams for his life and I . . . I just don't know if I've ruined them for him."

For several minutes she talked about other small things, things the kids had once said, places they had gone.

Koch listened patiently. There would be plenty of time for the questions he would have to ask, the facts he would need, the strategy he would plan for the trial.

Finally Dee took a deep breath. "So, that's the past, I guess. Now, the future." She tried to swab her tears away with her shaking fingers. Koch handed her some tissues he'd brought with him.

"You come prepared," Dee said, managing a smile through her tears.

"I've been through this enough times," he said.

Dee wiped her eyes, pulled herself erect, lit another cigarette. "I must look a mess," she said.

"You look fine," Koch lied. Then, "I've read your arrest affidavit," he said. He looked at her to be sure she was okay. "I'm sure the state attorney's office will be seeking the death penalty."

"The death penalty?" Dee was stunned.

"The electric chair," Koch said.

"I don't understand." Her heart was pounding.

"Well, you'll probably be charged with two counts of murder and—"

"Murder?" Dee shouted. There was that word again. "I didn't murder anyone."

"Well, that's what the state's going to have to prove," Art said. "It's our job to see that they don't prove it beyond a reasonable doubt."

"But how can they even say I murdered someone?" Dee said. "I was just the go-between. I could never murder anyone."

"Your statement to the police is the biggest thing they've got," Koch said, but Dee was hardly listening. Murder, she thought. It had sounded preposterous when Parmenter had said it, and it still sounded crazy. She just didn't understand how anybody could call her a murderer. If she were a murderer, she would feel like a murderer, wouldn't she?

"You'll be arraigned," Koch told her. "I'll be filing motions. I'll try to get that confession squashed. I'll try to have you severed from the others, and so forth. It's a long process. We've got a lot to talk about, but there will be plenty of time for that."

"The death penalty," Dee said. She shook her head. "The death penalty." The whole idea was too absurd to be taken seriously.

Koch stayed another twenty minutes, more to give Dee the company than to gather information. He asked her about her marriage, her jobs, even her childhood. He asked her about the arrest. Whom did she talk to, what did she say, and was she informed of her rights?

"You realize," Koch said before he left, "that a big part of my job will be to try to discredit the state's star witness."

"Who's that?" Dee said.

"Your daughter, Susan," he said.

"Oh," Dee said. "Of course. Do whatever you have to do."

After Dee was arraigned, along with the others, her first visit from the boys was scheduled. Susan would bring them. Dee had seen Susan on the night of the arrest. Susan had come to the police station and had put her arms around Dee and told her that everything would be all right. The two women had cried together, and then Dee had taken off her jewelry and handed it to Susan. She had told Susan what bills had been paid, and she told her to apply for state aid. Within days of Dee's arrest, Susan had gotten legal custody of the boys and had filled out the various applications for welfare money from the state.

By the time the visit was scheduled, for a Sunday in May, Dee had become more concerned than ever about Wyatt. Susan had told her that Wyatt was getting in fights every day.

"One of the kids says something and Wyatt doesn't ask questions, he just jumps," Susan had said. "He's always defending you."

What the kids at school were saying was, "Hey, Wyatt, your mother's in jail for murder, I saw it on television."

On the morning of the scheduled visit Dee woke up early, her heart pumping furiously. She couldn't eat her breakfast. She was edgy. She wanted to cancel the visit. She could just hide. After all, what on earth could she say to her children?

"I'll probably be in prison for the rest of my life, have a nice day"?

"I might even fry in the electric chair, and you can watch"?

The whole idea of speaking to her children, and knowing she might never play with them again, might never go to their graduations, their weddings, might never hold their babies, sometimes made her want to die.

That morning Dee wrestled back her apprehensions. She groomed herself carefully, like a girl getting ready for a date. In front of the boys she didn't want to look old or anguished or beaten, though she felt as if she were all of these things. She didn't want them to worry about her.

By this time Dee, whether she liked it or not, had kicked alcohol. From the moment of her arrest she had been cut off from Scotch. No weaning, no counseling, no Antabuse. Alcohol, her lifelong friend and demon, was not going to jail with her. There had been many sleepless nights. A rash had broken out all over her body. She had itched miserably from head to foot, and even the inside of her head for a while seemed constantly to itch, as if a swarm of insects had nested in her brain. She craved liquids all the time and she smoked, but for several days the idea of food had been repulsive. Still, for all her symptoms, Dee, compared to other alcoholics going through withdrawal, had gotten off easy and she knew it.

The kids arrived at ten o'clock. They were led into the day room where prisoners met their visitors.

It was an odd tableau, the two boys and Susan staring at their mother for a frozen moment, sizing things up. It made Dee think of those Keane posters where all the kids have eyes as big as silver dollars.

While Susan filled Dee in on the latest—the state aid, her job, the boys' grades—Dee glanced at Wyatt. He was quiet, still, wide-eyed. He looked scared. What on earth does he think of all this? she wondered. He glanced around the day room, perhaps looking for dangerous criminals, or perhaps, she thought, avoiding looking at me. Oh, God, I don't think I would want to live if my children stopped loving me.

Then Todd spoke. He asked Dee about the conditions at the "prison," as he called it. "Is it like on TV?" he asked. "Any of the women try to rape you? Do people threaten to slit your throat?" Dee assured him that she was safe and Todd began to relax. Todd was in the middle of telling her about new things in his life when Wyatt spoke up suddenly.

"What about your coffee?" Wyatt asked.

"Huh?"

"Do you get your coffee?"

"Sure," Dee said. "I have coffee in the morning, and there are coffee machines."

"Can you get it black, the way you like it?"

"Of course, honey."

"Oh," Wyatt said. And then, "Can you smoke? Do they let you have cigarettes?"

"Yes," Dee assured him. "I get cigarettes at the canteen."

"Benson and Hedges?"

"Yes."

"That's good," Wyatt said.

For many years Dee had had a frequent craving for chocolate, and her answer for the craving had always been a Snickers bar. Now Wyatt stared at her long and hard, as if he were about to ask the most important question of all.

"Do they have Snickers at the canteen?" he asked.

"They have Snickers bars, Wyatt."

"Oh, great," he said. "How much do they charge you? Can you get me some cheap? I've got to pay forty cents out on the street."

"I'll see what I can do," Dee said.

"So you're all right, Ma, huh, you can get Snickers and everything you need."

In Wyatt's eyes Dee saw the relief. She realized that in Wyatt's mind things would be all right now . . . if she could get her coffee and her cigarettes and her Snickers bar, then everything was going to be okay. The fact that she might be gone from him for the rest of her life, and that her life might even be cooked into oblivion by Sparky, was light-years from reality. Snickers bars and cigarettes, now, they were real.

When Susan and Wyatt went off to get Dee a Snickers bar and coffee from the machine, she moved closer to Todd.

"Honey, do you remember that time when you were twelve and you came home all upset because some kid had offered you a joint?"

Todd smiled. "Mom, I was so innocent then."

"Yes, you were," she said. "And you were real nervous and confused and you asked me what you should do if he kept asking you to try marijuana and you didn't want to?"

"Yes."

"And I said, 'Gee, Todd, I don't know. What do you think?' "

"Yeah, I remember that," Todd said. "Steve Laverne, that was the kid's name. He was a real pothead."

"And you said you thought you shouldn't play with the kid anymore, because if you were around him, he would always ask you and sooner or later you might go along with it, and you didn't want to do that."

"Yeah," Todd said. He stared at his mother. "So?"

"So," Dee said, "you came to me for advice, but I didn't really give you any. I knew you had common sense of your own. I knew if you thought about it, you'd do the smart thing."

"Oh."

"And that's the way it's going to be for a while, okay, honey? You can't depend on Susan for everything. You have to think, use that brain of yours, do the smart thing. It's the same as it always was, only you won't have me to say, 'Gee, Todd, I don't know. What do you think?' "

"I get you," Todd said. There were tears in his eyes. Dee couldn't remember the last time she had seen him cry.

In the months that followed, it was Susan who did a Jekyll and Hyde routine. On visits to her mother, Susan was the supportive and naively hopeful daughter. They scrapped sometimes, but for the most part their time together reflected the loving side of their complex relationship. The hate Susan felt for her mother, no less valid and no less painful, emerged in the context of Susan's role as chief witness.

"I knew from the beginning that Susan was going to be a difficult witness for us to deal with," says Art Koch. "It was clear right away that Susan harbored considerable hostility towards her mother for what had happened. Susan was not only a cooperative witness for the state but an enthusiastic one."

Koch has vivid memories of Susan at her deposition, given on the eighth floor of the Metro-Dade criminal justice building.

"Along with the hostility, it was clear that Susan liked the attention she'd gotten from the police and the state attorney's office," he says. "All the lawyers for the four defendants were there in a big conference room and Susan's demeanor seemed to say, This is my big day. Though she was mature for her age, she was still a kid. When Sally Weintraub (a state prosecutor, who would prosecute the case along with Jay Novick) got there, she wanted to take a break so that Susan could reread the statement she had given to the police, to kind of refresh her memory. But Susan didn't need to. It was clear that she had prepped herself, not just emotionally, but in terms of her testimony. You could ask her about some relatively obscure date and she'd have it written down. The animosity toward her mother was obvious to everyone in the room. It was as if she were saying, Here's the payback for all those miserable years.

"Susan was extremely hostile to her mother, even to the point of exaggerating things that it turned out later she didn't know. Much of her deposition was based on assumptions. Of course, she would have ended up being a state's witness in any case, but at this point she was giving them a lot more than she had to.

"As it turned out later, Susan's attitude began to change. She met with me a number of times and said, 'Well, this was not true, and I was assuming this was the case,' and so forth. Her problem was she had testified under oath and she was in a kind of legal bind. Susan, of course, could have been charged, concerning the crimes, but she never was. She was never given a specific grant of immunity in any formal way, it was more a case of prosecutorial discretion. What's the point in charging a daughter who's a witness against her mother, and hurting her as a witness? As time went by, it turned into an odd situation. Susan was the state's top witness against my client, but she would also call me, as a concerned daughter. The Susan–Dee relationship was extremely volatile, and how I related to Susan pretty much depended on how the mother and daughter were getting along. I had to handle her carefully; I didn't want to antagonize her."

Susan's life at this time was, to say the least, turbulent. Her mother was in jail for murder. She had two teenaged boys to worry about. She was still trying to hold down her job. In the aftermath of this family tragedy she had vowed that she would not let alcohol destroy her life. She would fight. But with pressure coming at her from all directions, it was not an easy fight.

Fortunately, she had help.

Susan had come under the influence of David Keeter, possibly the first good man she had ever been close to. It was Keeter, the Florida State trooper, who had broken the news to her about the arrests. He had found her and said, "Your mother's been arrested for murder. What's going on?" Then he had driven her to the police station.

Keeter, like the other men Susan had gone with, was big, and at twenty-five, he was eight years older than she was. But the similarity between him and the thugs who preceded him ended there. Keeter was a deeply religious man, a vegetarian who touched neither alcohol nor tobacco. For Susan he was a revelation. About all she had known in the adult world were drunks and lowlifes, and now here was this guy who didn't even swear and he was telling her that she was precious.

David had an incredible patience with Susan, for she did not easily turn away from alcohol and cocaine. He talked to her. He understood her insecurities even better than she did, and sometimes it seemed as if he could stare straight into her soul. He talked to her about self-esteem, self-love, God, philosophy, hope, and aspirations. Keeter awakened in Susan what had been a passive Christianity and turned her into a churchgoer, a Bible reader. He helped her to see how destructive the drugs and booze were. Susan began reading books about psychology, trying to learn about herself. Later she would say that he had saved her life.

A year after they broke up, David Keeter developed cancer. Six months later he was dead. "It took me four years to get over it," Susan says.

The spiritual and emotional growth that Susan was experiencing wrought great changes in her attitude toward her mother. What had been a love-hate relationship became, simply, a love relationship. The girl who was anxious to testify turned into a woman who was horrified at the idea of taking the stand against her mother.

"I can't do it," she said to her mother during one visit. "I feel so awful. I don't want to get up there and say bad things about you. I'll run away."

"You have to testify," Dee had said. "There's nowhere for you to run."

David Keeter was not the only influence on Susan during this period. Thelma Lofton, a corrections officer who had befriended the family, sometimes spent time with Susan, telling her about the corrections officer job and the training required. More subtly, Susan also came under the influence of Sally Weintraub at this time. From time to time Susan had to meet with the state's prosecutors, Novick and Weintraub. By all accounts the two prosecutors handled Susan with the delicacy required of a situation in which a daughter was testifying against her own mother on trial for murder. But Sally, because she was female, particularly impressed Susan. Sally was always well dressed. Sally was sophisticated. She was competent. She had an important job. She was, Susan often thought, the kind of woman she'd like to be. Susan began to think that maybe she could make something of herself, just like Sally. Maybe she could be a state prosecutor someday.

Sally Weintraub, incidentally, is another of those people whose comments on Dee would be comic if they were not so common.

"What Dee did is the most cold-blooded thing I have heard of in this office," Weintraub once said in an interview that happened to take place the day after she had finished the trial of an ex-cop who had murdered nine people. "It was horrendous what she did to Bessie Fischer." And yet, before the interview had ended, Weintraub, who along with Novick had pushed for the death penalty even though her colleagues said she'd never get it for a woman, had added, "I liked Dee. She seemed like a nice person."

In the matter of Dee Casteel, Sally Weintraub was just doing her job. Her job, and Novick's, was to get first-degree murder convictions against Casteel, Bryant, Irvine, and Rhodes.

During that first year after the arrests, when Susan was being reshaped by the good influences in her life, Dee was being reshaped herself, by coming out from under the influence of alcohol.

As the months passed and Susan's hostility receded, mother and daughter spent long hours together talking about their relationship, their love, their difficult past. It excited Dee when Susan talked about Sally or David, or a book she had read. It was a thrill to see her daughter smile, laugh, dream. It was as if Dee had been thrown back in time to the days when Susan was a little girl. When Susan said, "I'm not drinking anymore," it was as if she had spoken her first words. When Susan talked about taking courses at Miami-Dade Community College, it was as if Susan had taken her first steps. Those exquisite moments of discovery had returned. Dee remembered how she used to dream her dreams for Susan, and she wondered what went wrong along the way.

With alcohol now gone from her life and her body, Dee was, perhaps, becoming the person she always should have been. At the annex she was a favorite of both the staff and the inmates. From her maximum security area on the fourth floor of the detention center, she was often brought downstairs to do typing jobs for the social services department. She was given other office jobs and she ran things efficiently. A stranger in the annex would have been hard put to guess whether Dee was an employee or an inmate. At the annex everybody called her "Miss Dee" as a signature of respect, and the other inmates came to her with their problems. They nominated her to be cell counselor. They loved her, they respected her. They felt, as Calie Maitland had felt, that Dee Casteel was "the nicest person you could ever want to meet."

As Dee grew more and more to like this new, sober self, she renewed her Christian faith, just as her daughter had. However, where Susan became very vocal about her Christianity, Dee has kept it largely to herself. Jailhouse Christians make her sick, and she has a horror of being mistaken for one.

At first Dee thought often about Bryant. In time he began to fade in memory, like the other men in her life. At certain hours there were phone privileges, and she was able to talk often to Susan and to Lynn Lore and Jackie Ragan. Dee's conversations with Jackie, ironically, were often preceded by a few minutes of chitchat with the housemate who answered the phone: Anne Chepsiuk. Dee also had slight contact with Mike Irvine.

"Hi, Dee, it's Mike," he said when he called her one day, exercising his own phone privileges at the men's detention center just a few blocks away.

"Mike. How you doing?" Dee said. Dee was struck immediately by the absurdity of the situation, the two conspirators talking to each other from their respective jails.

"Not so good," Mike said. "Look, I've got a plan."

"A plan?" Oh, God, Dee thought, Mike has flipped out.

"Yeah. You got to change your story, see, say I had nothing to do with it, it was all a mistake when you said I was involved."

"Mike?"

"You've got to, Dee, I want to get out of this place."

"Mike, I don't know."

"You do this for me, Dee, and then I'll get a crew of guys together and we'll bust you out of there."

Dee almost laughed. Poor Mike. Maybe he had seen too many gangster movies as a kid.

"We'll see," she said. "We'll see." But she was thinking there was no point in trying to reason with him.

One guy who lived in a cell with Irvine at the county jail says Mike was always talking about how he would get out, and he bragged about the big scores he would make. "He let on like he was a big-time dealer," the ex-inmate says.

At one point during his stay in the county jail, Irvine tried to bribe an undercover police officer to make his file "disappear," as he put it. He offered the cop $50,000, an amount that would hardly seem accessible to a guy who was willing to murder for half of $5,000.

Dee didn't object to the pressure from Mike. From her point of view he was only doing his job, just like Sally Weintraub and Jay Novick. Mike's job was to try to get out of prison.

Everybody was doing their job. Lawyers for Bryant, Irvine, and Rhodes were doing their jobs, each trying to get his guy off the hook. Bryant had his own private lawyer. Rhodes and Irvine had private lawyers, appointed by the state, to avoid conflict of interest within the public defender's office, where Art Koch, representing Casteel, was doing his job. Koch's job was to save his client's life, and to a large extent, that meant discrediting the state's star witness.

Dee's job was to go along with her attorney's advice, to do whatever was necessary to improve her already slim chances of being acquitted. She was being asked to do no less than to try to save her own life. But as she came closer and closer to being at peace with herself, Dee wasn't so sure she liked her job.

"Tell me again about the cocaine," Art said to her on one visit. "Susan kept it in the refrigerator?"

"Why?"

"You know why," Art said. "We need to discredit Susan as much as possible. If we can make her look like a cokehead, then maybe the jury won't believe her."

"No," Dee said.

"Huh?"

"No, I don't want to do this to Susan. I don't want to embarrass her."

"What are you talking about? We've been through this a dozen times."

"I know, but it doesn't feel right anymore."

Art was exasperated. "Don't you understand, we're talking about the death penalty here."

"I know."

"This is Florida," Koch went on. "We're not talking make-believe. They kill people here. And Susan is the one who can put you in that chair."

"They're going to find me guilty anyhow. My own statement is damning enough."

"There's a lot of things Susan could say that aren't in that statement," Koch reminded her.

"But this could hurt her," Dee said. "She's hoping to have a career. Saying she took drugs and everything, it's just not right. I want you to go easy on her. I've put her through enough."

"Susan knows about this," Art said. "You've told her. She understands. It's okay with her."

"But it's not okay with me," Dee said. "I don't want her hurt by this."

And, Dee thought, I don't want her always to feel bad about this, either.

Perhaps it was becoming clear to Dee that a sacrifice would have to be made. A small sacrifice, really, because the state had the goods on her; they had her confession, and Dee was not inclined to change her story. The small chance of her getting off was not worth the burden of guilt that would be placed on Susan. Or perhaps there was nothing at all sophisticated about Dee's thinking at this time. All that is clear is that Dee's instinct for survival gave way to her instinct for motherhood.

Susan had been talking about running away to avoid testifying. Dee could not let that happen. There was too much good in Susan's life to be thrown away.

On one of Susan's weekly visits to the annex, the two women sat at a long wooden table, where Susan laid out snapshots she had taken at the beach. It was Susan's way of bringing her mother to the world out there. The beach, Dee thought; she loves the beach just like her mother.

They caught up on everything—the boys, the job, the people they both knew there at the annex—and then Dee took her daughter's hand.

"There's something I want to talk to you about. I want you to promise me that you will not run away to avoid testifying."

"Ma, I can't do that."

"You have to. Tell me you won't run away."

"But Ma, it's the electric chair. They're saying you could get the electric chair."

"I won't get any electric chair," Dee said. "They've never given it to a woman, and they're certainly not going to start with someone like me who didn't even actually do the murders. I'll probably get life in prison."

"Oh, great," Susan said. "Is that all?"

"Hey, it's not so bad," Dee said. "Think about it. It will be a better life than I had outside. The truth is, if I hadn't gotten arrested, I'd be dead by now."

Susan thought about this. She knew it was true. Still, to testify against her mother?

"Promise?" Dee said.

"Okay. I promise." And then, "I'll lie. Or I'll just refuse to testify. What can they do to me?"

"Honey," Dee said, "from all this I've learned that it's not what they do to you, it's what you do to yourself." She took Susan's face in her hands. "Look at me. Is this how you want to end up? This is what happens when you don't do the right thing. I should have told Allen to go to hell when he asked me about Mike. That would have been the right thing. I should have done a lot of right things in my life, but I didn't, and that can't be helped now. But Susan, honey, I want you to do the right thing. I want you to testify. I want you to tell the truth. And for the rest of your life I don't want you ever, ever, to feel bad about doing it."

There were other moments like this. Probably a lot of them during a three-year period. That's how long it took for the case to come to trial. And during the period of delays the attorneys on both sides were aware that Dee was encouraging the state's top witness to tell the truth, no matter how damning it might be to her.

"I believe," says Sally Weintraub, "that there was a nobility of purpose in Dee, trying not to hurt Susan any more than she had. My sense is that she was trying to shield her daughter, letting her know that it was okay to be a witness. This was Dee's finest hour."

28

The Trial

Dee Casteel and her partners in crime had entered a legal system that operates mainly according to appointment books. Lawyers have other clients. Judges go on vacation. Courtrooms are unavailable. Things get backed up.

There were many reasons why it took three years for Dee to get from arrest to trial. Pretrial motions, continuances, and the like. But the most significant delay, more than a year, resulted from Art Koch's concern over the issue of proportionality, an issue that was well publicized in Florida when Koch brought it up.

"Our position was that the death penalty should not be applied to Dee because of her relatively passive role in the crimes," Koch says. "In the legal sense that is called proportionality. It's a myth, but theoretically at least, in all capital case convictions, defendants should be treated the same in proportion to their crimes. The appeals court is supposed to review to see that imposition of the death penalty is proportionately fair to what someone else gets. This is difficult, particularly when the courts also say that the prosecutor's office has almost unlimited discretion in seeking or not seeking the death penalty.

"I had a case where a person had kidnapped two people and stolen ten thousand dollars. He transported these people to a secluded area in Dade County and shot them both in the back of the head with a shotgun. And the state waived the death penalty! Prosecutorial discretion. So my argument was, how can this woman be subject to the death penalty when they don't even seek the death penalty in this other case?

"What I was trying to do was to say that the judge should have the opportunity to make this proportionality review before the case comes to trial. I did it at this point because you don't want to have to go in and pick a death-penalty-qualified jury, you try to avoid that.

"At this stage of capital litigation all the broad issues have been litigated and decided. You can't argue the constitutionality of the death penalty. What you can do is say, fine, we'll accept the constitutionality of the death penalty, but as applied in these circumstances with this particular defendant it is not valid.

"So Judge Person ruled, not that my position was well taken on the merits, but that there should be an evidentiary hearing to find out how come the state waives the death penalty here and doesn't waive it there. The state appealed on the grounds that the judge didn't have the right to conduct such a hearing. The issue went to the Florida supreme court, took a lot of time, and got a lot of press because of the allegations of discrimination in the use of the death penalty.

"The supreme court came down with the worst possible decision for the defense. They said, in essence, that the judge had no authority to conduct such an evidentiary hearing."

By the time Dee Casteel and the three men went to trial, a lot had happened.

Todd and Wyatt were living with their father in Starke, home of Sparky.

Susan, influenced by Sally Weintraub and Thelma Lofton, had become an officer with the Florida Department of Corrections. She was also working toward a college degree in criminal law and a master's degree in psychology.

The trial was held in June of 1987. Susan testified. She told what she knew about the murders. Art Koch went easy on her. When Dee testified, she made no attempt to deny her role. She told the jury about the murders. Mike Irvine and Bill Rhodes told their stories. Of the four defendants, only Allen Bryant, on advice from his lawyer, chose not to testify.

Jackie Ragan was a witness, too. She talked about the writing of the confession. Richard Higgins testified; so did Albert Riccio and Dale Haskins and the other people who had bought Art Venecia's property. Some people came from E.F. Hutton to explain about the forged checks. The medical examiner came and talked about the bodies she had found. Bill Rhodes's sister Paula talked about the phone calls.

During the trial the four murderers bonded, even though they were saying things that could get each other cooked.

"The trial brought us closer together," Dee says. "It was strange. In court we were all accusing each other, but it was okay, we were each doing what we had to do. There was a sense of shared experience, and it drew us to each other. We had been through something together. And the men, Allen, Mike, and Bill, were more concerned about me than they were about themselves. They would put their arms around me and say, 'Don't worry, Dee, everything will be okay, we'll beat this thing.' "

During the early part of the trial Dee lived in constant fear of Bill Rhodes.

"I was frightened to death of him," she says. "I mean, it was my confession that had put us all in jail, and Mike had told me that Bill could kill a person with one karate chop. He was already up for two murders, what was to stop him from doing another? Sometimes when we walked along the corridors between court sessions, they wanted me to walk in front of him. I said no thanks. There were even times when we were cuffed together. It was terrifying. Kind of funny when you look back on it now, though.

"Anyhow, Bill was always a gentleman. He was sweet and sensitive and he showed genuine concern about me. During the trial I began to see him in a whole different way. He always treated me like a lady."

On July 17, the jury agreed. All four defendants were guilty of two counts of first-degree murder. Casteel and Bryant were also guilty of grand theft.

In Florida, capital cases are conducted in two phases. Phase one is the trial, guilt or innocence. In phase two, the penalty phase, the jury considers what sentence it will recommend. During this phase defendants are allowed to bring in character witnesses, people who will come in and speak well of them.

Mike Irvine had Irma Sorrell, one of his ex-wives, and Natalie Stewart, a friend. They talked about him being gentle, being a teddy bear. They talked about how good he was with the kids.

Bill Rhodes had Dr. Jethro Toomer to say that he was a troubled person, implying the tragic consequences of an abused childhood. Rhodes also had Harlem Mussard, his minister, who described Bill as "a fine individual" and "a fine believer." Eve Merino also spoke for Bill, and so did Eve's retarded daughter, Sandra.

"Bill and me, we used to watch *Knight Rider,*" Sandra said. "He'd play Sorry with me and we used to play 'Noply, and we'd go out walking around and we'd just do a lot of stuff, and he helped me one time put a bike together and that's about it."

"Do you love Bill?" Rhodes's lawyer, Joe Lang Kerhshaw, asked.

"Huh?"

"Do you love Bill?"

"Yeah. I want to take him home with me."

Several members of the jury were in tears when Sandra left the witness stand.

James Allen Bryant had three corrections officers from the Dade County jail. They all spoke well of him. They said he was polite, a good worker, and not a troublemaker.

Dee had Shirley Blando, assistant chaplain at the women's annex. She also had Thelma Lofton and Edwina Talley, corrections officers. They all praised Dee for her kindness, her ability to counsel the other inmates. Also called to the stand for Dee was Dr. Syvil Marquit, a psychologist who had evaluated Dee. He told the court that Dee would be a model prisoner.

"In addition to that," he said, "I think she would be a person who could contribute materially in some fashion to the needs of the prison. Much of her life and her ability to think was deadened by her addiction to alcohol. It is my assumption that she will not be getting alcohol in prison, and I think that under those circumstances she will be a cooperative, willing person, able to make a distinct contribution."

When asked if he could see her ever being any kind of danger in prison, Dr. Marquit said, "I don't think so. She is not a fighter. She is not one who enters into conflicts. She is not one looking for trouble. As a matter of fact, she likes to avoid confrontations, although she has in her makeup a competitive spirit. She is well aware that she can overstep her bounds."

Dee also had her daughter.

Susan, who had not been allowed as a spectator at the first phase of the trial because she was a witness, came to the second phase both as a witness and a spectator. Though the verdict had already been rendered, Susan, apparently, had not accepted it. Stunned, she operated on two levels. She knew that her mother had been found guilty, and yet she sometimes spoke as if that were not true.

"I don't think Susan ever really understood the seriousness of what was happening until the day of the sentencing," Art Koch says. "Right up until the end she was saying things like, 'When Ma gets out, I'm going to take her away someplace.' Dee was a woman who, at best, was facing two life sentences."

From the witness stand Susan talked about her mother. She told the jury she loved her mom.

"What kind of a mother was she when she was not drinking?" Koch asked her when she was on the stand.

"The best," Susan said.

"Why do you say that? Can you give some illustrations?"

"She is my best friend," Susan said. "She always has been. She is the closest person to me. I love her more than anybody in the whole world. We were the best of friends." Her voice started cracking. "We worked together. We shared the same room together. We wore the same clothes. We had no secrets from each other. We had the same goals, you know."

"In light of what's happened, do you still feel that way now?"

"Very much so," Susan said. "We plan on going to Colorado together."

In the penalty phase of a trial the jury listens to witnesses and then makes a recommendation to the judge for or against the death penalty. The jury can vote anything from 12–0 in favor of the death penalty for one defendant, to 12–0 against the death penalty for another defendant. The judge makes the final decision.

In this case the jury voted for the death penalty

on each murder count, for each defendant. As a result, there were some interesting differences in the votes. For the murder of Art Venecia, the jury voted 11–1 that Mike Irvine should get the death penalty. For the murder of Bessie Fischer, the jury voted 12–0 that Mike Irvine should get the death penalty. In other words, somebody on the jury felt that Irvine had a greater degree of responsibility in Bessie's death than in Art's. Dee Casteel is of the same opinion.

"I've always felt that Mike is the one who actually strangled Mrs. Fischer," Dee says. "I just think it was a case of 'Bill, you did a murder, well, I'll prove I'm a man, too, and I'll do one.' "

With Bill Rhodes the jury voted 11–1 that he should die for the murder of Art Venecia, but only 10–2 that he should die for the murder of Bessie Fischer.

For the murder of Art Venecia, the jury voted 12–0 to recommend the death penalty for James Allen Bryant. For the murder of Bessie Fischer, they voted 11–1 that Allen should be executed.

Dee Casteel fared no better than the others. For the murder of Art Venecia, the jury voted death, 10–2. For the murder of Bessie Fischer, they voted 12–0.

On September 15, 1987, Judge Person, who had never given a death sentence, condemned William Rhodes to death for the murder of Arthur Venecia, and Mike Irvine to death for the murder of Bessie Fischer. Each man was given a life sentence for the other murder.

On September 16, Judge Person sentenced Allen Bryant to life in prison for the murder of Bessie Fischer. And for the murder of Art Venecia, Bryant was sentenced to death.

Rhodes, Irvine, and Bryant are all on death row at the Florida State Prison in Starke. Unlike Dee, they all claim to be innocent.

On the same day, Dee was the last to be sentenced. For the murder of Art Venecia, Dee was given life in prison. And then, in the same formal language he had used for the others, Judge Person pronounced Dee's other sentence:

"It is, therefore, the judgment and sentence of the Court as to the first-degree murder of Bessie Fischer, Dee Casteel be adjudicated guilty of murder in the first degree and that she be sentenced to death.

"It is further ordered that Dee Casteel be taken by the proper authorities to the Florida State Prison and there be kept under close confinement and supervision until her execution."

Susan, hysterical, ran from the courtroom when the sentence was announced.

Judge Person ended the session by saying: "The Court takes the position in these cases that it will be unconscionable for the Court to sentence to death the two executioners in this case and not, likewise, sentence those whose conduct led to those executions by paying, hiring, and securing the deaths of the individuals involved."

Now, on death row, Dee knits a little mint-colored outfit for her granddaughter. Life moves forward for others; Susan has gotten married, and her baby, Savannah, was born in September of 1988.

"I've got some pictures of the baby," Dee says. She hands me the photos. "Isn't she about the most adorable little girl you ever saw?"

Dee has been waiting for some word about her appeals, but the wheels of justice move as slowly as ever. Dee has lots of time to remember and to wonder. Perhaps she is getting closer to answers about her life, about everybody's life, but they are coming slowly.

"I don't know," she says. "I suppose I'll never understand why I did what I did. But as I think over my life, more and more I remember the day that I had that terrible fight with my father and he said, 'You're as cheap as piss.' God, that hurt me so. I don't know why, but that one moment pained me so deeply. It seemed to send me off in some bad direction."

She goes silent for a minute, staring at the yarn as her hands, now expert, work it into a shape.

"Don't know when I'll get my next yarn shipment," she says. "Things move slowly here."

And then, "And I think a lot about Mama and I can remember just how much I felt as if I was a burden to her. I always had that feeling of not being wanted. My real mother didn't want me. And when I was taken away from Mama, maybe I felt it was because she really didn't want me. I guess I felt that nobody loved me.

"And I think about Cass and how I always pushed him and pushed him until he beat me."

She looks up, stares at some distant memory, perhaps one of the good ones with Cass. "I know that if I had just left him alone when he got belligerent, he would have gone someplace and brooded and cooled off. But I never did that. I always had to edge him on until he beat me. I mean, I knew he would beat me and I went ahead and did it anyhow. It's almost as if I wanted to be beaten. It doesn't make any sense. Because if I wanted to get beaten, then I must have wanted to be punished for something, and I don't know what it is. Then there was the alcohol, of course.

"It's all so crazy, isn't it?" she says. "The way we think." She laughs. "Or don't think. I mean, does all this have something to do with the terrible things I did?" She glances one last time at the sweater she has made for the baby. "Could love have made the difference? Who knows."

Epilogue

Since the original hardcover publication of *Without Mercy* by Pocket Books in January of 1989, Dee Casteel's state-appointed appeals lawyer, Lee Weissenborn, and lawyers for the other defendants, have appealed on a number of grounds. Their most compelling argument, it seems, was the one which said that Casteel, Bryant, Irvine and Rhodes should have had their cases severed. That is, they should have been tried separately.

While working on the book, I would from time to time ask Dee Casteel about the appeals and what would happen if the Florida Supreme Court reversed her conviction and she were faced with the prospect of a new trial.

"I wouldn't risk another death sentence," she told me. "I would plead guilty and plea bargain for a life sentence."

She had told me many times that her greatest

dream was to have her sentence reduced to life in prison.

"No one who hasn't been through it can imagine what it is like to have a sentence of death in the electric chair hanging over you every day," she said. "You can't imagine what it is like being alone twenty-four hours a day."

With a life sentence Dee would have more privileges. She could walk in the yard without handcuffs. The little things would come easier—getting visitors, receiving packages, canteen purchases. But most important, by far, she would have the company of other women. To her, a life sentence would be a life renewed.

On March 29, 1990, Dee's dream came true. The Florida Supreme Court reversed the convictions of Dee Casteel, Allen Bryant, Mike Irvine, and Bill Rhodes, and ordered that they be tried again.

The supreme court's ruling was based on two points.

During the jury selection phase of the original trial the state had used five of its first seven peremptory challenges to excuse jurors who were black. This, from a pool of 68 white and 12 black jurors. With each exclusion, Bill Rhodes' lawyer, Joseph Kershaw, a black man, requested a Neil inquiry. That is an inquiry by the trial judge to determine whether or not the exclusion of these black people was racially motivated, which would, of course, have been illegal. At the time the state argued that since all four jurors were white they had no standing to protest the systematic exclusion of blacks. The Neil inquiry was not granted.

In its March 1990 ruling the supreme court noted that "the objecting party does not have to be a member of the race being challenged to have standing," and that "the objecting party does not have to be a member of the race being challenged to have standing," and that the defendants did not get the inquiry to which they were entitled. The court was not saying that the prosecutor was racially motivated in his exclusions, only that the inquiry should have been made.

The second reason for the reversal was the one on which Dee had pinned her hopes: severance. The supreme court said that tying the defendants together in one trial worked against the defendants because Allen Bryant was never put on the stand and, consequently, was not available for cross examination by the lawyers for Casteel, Irvine, and Rhodes. The court also noted that the jury might have been confused by the use of redacted statements, that is, defendant's statements in which the word "someone" or pronouns were substituted for names of codefendants.

All four defendants will be retried separately.

G.P.